Bicycle Road Racing

Bicycle Road Racing

COMPLETE PROGRAM FOR TRAINING AND COMPETITION

by Edward Borysewicz

1980-84 Olympic Cycling Coach

with Ed Pavelka

VELO-NEWS
BRATTLEBORO, VERMONT

Contents

Thanks to the following persons and companies for their help in our production of this book: Mark Hodges, Hank Lange, Jeff Baird, John Sipay, Steve Bishop, Fred Matheny, Ed Burke, Roy Knickman, Rebecca Twigg, Alexi Grewal, Mary Cappy, Mountain Safety Research, W.L. Gore & Associates Inc., Biotechnology Inc., Bicycle Parts Pacific, Attivo Corp., Velotech, Tsuyama Mfg. Co. Ltd., J.T. Actif, Skidlid Manufacturing Co., Brattleboro Nautilus, Brattleboro Fitness Barn.

Credits: Illustrations by Jude Roberts-Rondeau.

Photos by Robert F. George pages 9, 14, 20, 23, 25-27, 38, 42, 51, 57, 59, 65, 101, 111, 125, 160, 164, 165, 167, 201, 205, 216, 245; by Cor Vos pages 112, 142, 143, 145, 147, 152, 163, 171, 173, 187, 190, 200, 215, 224, 226, 228, 240, 244, 246, 247, 260, 263; by Michael Chritton pages 28, 124, 157, 161, 166, 170, 179, 189, 231, 254, 257; by Jeff Baird pages 49, 67-69, 108, 176, 243; by Bernard Thompson pages 36, 130, 156, 226, 232, 251, 253; by Sergio Penazzo pages 26, 129, 136, 151, 193, 222; by Ed Pavelka pages 62, 63, 71, 211, 230; by Tom Moran pages 122, 229, 252; by John Libera page 41; by Tom Moorhead page 16; by UPI/Bettmann page 180; by USCF page 93; by Les Woodland page 194.

About the Authors

Edward Borysewicz was born on March 18, 1939, in Lithuania before it and the eastern part of Poland were absorbed by the Soviet Union. Running, not cycling, was his first serious sport. As he became a national-caliber schoolboy competitor in the 400 meters he did ride a bike, but only for recreation. It wasn't until his mid-teenage years that cycling's high standing in Poland caused him to consider bicycle racing. Once he gave it a try he knew he had found his sport. Before long he was a national pursuit champion and a member of Poland's Junior team.

As a Senior he raced in approximately 100 events per year for 11 years, six of which were spent as a member of the Polish national team. He competed throughout East and West Europe in events like the Poland/Czechoslovakia Peace Race, Tour of Austria, and Tour of Poland (he had three top-15 finishes). He won more than 70 one-day road races in Poland and was a member of a winning 100-kilometer time trial team 19 times, including two national championships.

After receiving his master's degree from Poland's Academy of Physical Education, he became a teacher and started to coach cycling at the club level. During the next 10 years he guided two of his country's largest clubs to great success and produced several world-class riders. At the same time he worked for the Polish Cycling Federation, specializing in Junior development. He twice turned down the chance to become Poland's national team head coach, a position he assumed with the U.S. Cycling Federation in late 1977, one year after he emigrated to America.

During his first six years at the helm, Coach Borysewicz led the U.S. to unprecedented accomplishments and a place among the elite countries in world cycling. His reign has seen American amateur riders win 26 world championship medals, including eight gold; eight Pan American Games medals, including seven gold; and numerous team and individual victories in events throughout Europe and Latin America. Among the many successful riders he and his USCF staff have helped develop is Greg LeMond, the 1979 Junior world road champion and 1983 professional world road champion.

Coauthor **Ed Pavelka** holds a degree in journalism from the University of Florida and has been a cycling writer since 1977 when he joined the staff of *Velo-news*. He has authored, coauthored and edited seven books on various aspects of cycling. He has ridden a bike since 1972 and raced at the District level.

Pavelka and Coach Borysewicz worked together for 60 hours to record the information that now makes up this book. The coach is not quite fluent in English, so

Eddie B at the 1983 Pan American Games in Caracas, Venezuela.

it was Pavelka's task to draw out all his instruction and advice, then write it down clearly. His goal was to express the coach's ideas in English as well as the coach would have expressed them in Polish. Before publication virtually every word of the manuscript was read back to Coach Borysewicz for his approval.

Preface

Who is Edward Borysewicz? You have a right to know, and I want you to know before you read my book. If you are going to do as Eddie B says in cycling, you must have faith that what he tells you is the right way. When times are tough, when you are tired, when you finish training and cannot make one more pedal stroke, you must believe in me. You cannot doubt my wisdom.

This book contains my road racing program. It is the same information I have given to the very best cyclists in the United States since 1977. If you read it carefully and learn it well, and if you stick with the program year by year, I can promise you one thing: You will reach your potential as a bicycle racer.

I am from Poland, a country that takes pride in its athletes and treats those who study athletics as seriously as students of any other science. I attended the Academy of Physical Education and earned a master's degree in physical education and physical therapy. I became qualified to teach 26 different sports and to coach one, cycling.

It is a much different type of education in Poland. I would like to have gone to school in the U.S. because it is not as hard. I decided this shortly after I arrived in America and met Ed Burke, who has become my good friend and the technical director of the U.S. Cycling Federation's national team program. Burke told me he had recently gotten his master's degree in exercise physiology. I laughed. "You? That's impossible! With a stomach like that and no muscles? How can you pass the physical test?" That's when I found out that American universities do not require physiologists to actually be able to do physical things. To me that is very strange.

By the time I got my degree I looked like a gorilla. All my fellow students did after five years of muscle development. In Poland, practice is as important as theory. One day there would be six hours of class and four hours of training. The next day four hours of class and six hours of training. This is how I learned sports, six days a week for 10 months a year for five years.

I learned *every* muscle in the human body by both the Latin and Polish names. The same for every bone. I had to know the answers at 12 o'clock at night and at 6 in the morning. If there was a 30-minute test and I forgot one little thing, I was in trouble. If I did not pass my second chance, maybe I would have a third chance . . . or maybe I would be put out of the Academy. They had no need for bad students. When I took the entrance examination I was one of 1,400 people trying to get 92 places. I took no chances. I studied and I learned, and at this same time I also achieved some of my greatest cycling success. It was during my student years that I was a member of Poland's national team.

When I turned 19, in 1958, I was the Junior national pursuit champion and a member of the national team. Then it was time for the army. Whether you liked it or not, when you reached 19 in Poland you were a soldier for the next two years. I didn't like it at all, especially when they assigned me to the "misfit battalion" instead of the sports division. This happened because my father, who was an army officer and a farmer, was also an anticommunist. His name was on the blacklist. He was even sent to prison in Siberia for a while. So they gave our family a hard time. I had done nothing wrong but they put me with the robbers, the bandits and the bums. It took one year for my coach and the people who knew me to get me transferred in with the athletes. For that whole time I could not ride the bike at all.

Finally I was able to train again, but it lasted for just six months. Then it was time for Berlin and Cuba and I had to trade the bike for a machine gun. It was back to being a full-time soldier. After a total of 28 months I was able to get out of active duty and into the reserves.

It took half a year of training to again become one of Poland's top riders, this time as a Senior. I began to win national-level road races and I was put on the national team. I was like an exploding bomb. I made incredible progress and got lots of publicity. I was on the short team for the Peace Race, which was even greater than being a member of the Olympic team. As early as February that season I was feeling the best of my life, like gold. My ergometer tests showed an ability to recover from maximum work that astounded my coaches. They were sure I would have a fantastic season. I remember being so enthusiastic as I went with the team to Bulgaria for an early season training camp and physical testing.

Then my life fell apart. During the chest x-ray the technician said to me, "Has anyone ever told you that you have a spot on your lung?"

Those words started a chain of events that wound up depriving me of reaching my potential as a cyclist. I am certain of it. The technician saw something at the very top of my lung that had actually always been there. In earlier years it had apparently been hidden from x-rays by my collarbone. I was young and skinny and I stood slightly bent like cyclists tend to do. Now I was a bull, strong and straight and tall. The x-ray machine had a new perspective.

"When was your last chest x-ray?" asked the tuberculosis expert. I told him I'd had one almost every six months for several years as a soldier and cyclist. No, I said, no spot had ever been seen before. "You're a lucky man," he told me, "because the process is just beginning. We can give you treatment."

I had to lay off all hard training. It was a shock because I felt so good. Now all I could imagine was the danger of becoming a terrible weak person who coughed all the time. I told the doctor to do anything to cure me—do the best and do it fast. Since I was living alone he said I might just as well enter a sanitarium. The next thing I knew I was lying there in the middle of sick people. I began getting shots and other treatment.

I almost decided it would be better to die. I refused to talk to anyone for the first two weeks. All I did was listen to the radio and sleep. They ran many tests and everything came up negative. In fact, that hospital had never seen such a healthy body. After six weeks of treatment, x-rays were taken and the spot was still there.

The doctor, who was young and inexperienced and probably afraid to admit he might have made the wrong diagnosis, said my body was so strong that it was not allowing the medicine to react with the TB bacteria. His solution was to give me maximum doses of the most powerful medicines in existence. He was a stupid man. I found out how stupid later when this treatment made my liver very sick. I only wish I had realized what he was doing from the beginning.

After six more weeks of maximum drugs and treatment I was supposed to be fully cured, but the chest x-ray still showed the spot. No change. They would not let me out of the hospital. But finally I got lucky. The man who was moved into the bed next to me was a doctor, and as we talked he became very interested in my case. He personally looked into my records and then took them to the hospital director. It was plain to these men that a big mistake had been made. The spot on my lung was a scar that may well have resulted from contact with TB when I was young, but it was only a scar—there was no active disease in my body. The hospital gave me a certificate of good health and released me.

But it was too late. For almost four months I had swallowed pills and been injected with strong drugs for a disease I didn't have. I was the victim of an incompetent doctor and my liver paid the price. Before this episode I was a rider who always felt stronger after 100 km. Now I felt weaker. Now I felt fatigue and I felt pain from my liver. No longer could I be a super stage race rider, no longer would I have a chance to ride the great Peace Race.

Four months after finally leaving the hospital I began winning races. I was even put back on the national team. The coaches gave me every chance because now they knew I was never sick to begin with. At age 24 I was once again competing at the top level. I had again made great progress. But I knew I was not the same cyclist as before. I realized I was not going to be the star that I was once becoming. Bad luck had killed my career. I still loved cycling, though, and I knew I wanted to stay involved with it. The best way was to become a coach, and that's when I decided to try for the Academy of Physical Education.

My schooling took five years. For the first three I continued to ride for the national team. It wasn't an easy combination because I didn't have the option of leaving school to race during the spring term. I had to be a full-time student or lose my place in the Academy. I always studied in my spare time instead of listening to music and playing cards like the other riders. I didn't mind because I enjoyed my books, but the coach minded. He felt school work detracted from my concentration and energy for cycling. I must say that today I agree with him—I prefer it if a rider is not going to school full-time during the spring and summer.

My studies progressed well—I wound up as the No. 2 student in the class of 1968— but my racing career stagnated. During my third year as a student/cyclist, the national team coach came to me and said, "Eddie, you are not improving. You are good but we are looking for development. Sorry, but we must pick up somebody else. This is your last year." He was 100% right. It is the way a national program must be run.

I continued as a club rider and even continued to win, but as soon as I graduated I was told by the cycling federation that my racing career was over. Now I was to start coaching, they said. Just like that—today a rider, tomorrow a coach. I was 29, finally out of school, and I felt I could devote all my effort to riding and have a couple more good years. I pleaded my case, but I had no chance. They said I had a first-category master's degree, I had six year's experience on the national team, and I was getting old. They said Polish cycling needed me as a coach, not a rider.

It was time to begin a new career.

For the next five years I taught physical education at the university in Lodz, Poland's second largest city, and I took over the cycling team of a large and wealthy club. When I arrived this team was in shambles. All its riders were about my age—no Juniors, no Intermediates. I was faced with a major rebuilding job.

Not long after beginning I got a surprising proposal from the president of the Polish Cycling Federation. He asked if I would like to be the national team's head coach, the No. 1 man. I turned him down. I told him it was too early. Who had I produced? Nobody yet. If I took over the national team I wanted it to be because I had proved my ability to produce top riders, not because the federation president handed me the job. That's the way it always must be to have the respect of the cyclists and the coaches working under you.

My four club assistants and I selected about 150 young riders (road and track) and then we organized races to begin teaching them the sport. We started with 100 Intermediates the first year and out of that group came 20 good Juniors. From them came five good Seniors. Year by year we progressed, and by the fourth season we had produced Mieczysl Nowicki. We had developed riders for the Junior Worlds and riders who won national track championships.

This is Mieczysl Nowicki, who was born in my hands as a bike rider. His development was 99% my influence, and he became the best amateur rider in the world for several years. After I traveled from Poland to watch him win two medals in the Montreal Olympics, my next stop was New York City. That was the beginning of my life in America.

If at this point I had been asked to coach the national team, I would have accepted. But the job wasn't open. So I decided to go back to the club I had ridden for during my career. It needed a new coach and again I found myself at square one. This club had gotten into the same sorry shape as the one I had labored four years to rebuild. Hard work and good planning paid off once more and it, too, developed into as good a club as any in Poland. Some riders I had coached before gave me a headstart by transferring to the club with me. It was my coaching philosophy to help them accomplish what I couldn't do when I was riding. A crazy doctor ruined my potential, so I took satisfaction in helping my riders reach theirs.

Almost 10 years after the federation first came to me it came back. Before it was too early, but now it was too late. I was upset with cycling. The great amount of time I devoted to it was the main reason my marriage had just ended in divorce. Also, during years of part-time work as a national Junior development coach I'd seen firsthand the corruption and favoritism within the federation. Politics was always involved. Often the selection of coaches and riders was simply not fair. I turned down the head coach position for the second time, and I told them I was finished as an assistant.

I continued to teach physical education from October to May, as I had throughout the years since my graduation, and I took summer work as a tour guide. I could speak Russian well and I led sightseeing trips into the Eastern bloc countries. This job was fun and it filled the time I used to spend with the federation. I also continued to coach the club, but not with the same commitment.

I'm sure that to many people my life at this time seemed very comfortable. I had a good salary, I had a very nice apartment, I drove a much better car than I've had in the U.S. My teaching job was a prestige job—only the elite people get to be instructors at a university. It was an easy job, just two mornings a week and the rest of the time I was free. Yes, I had money and I had position. But my family was gone. Losing my wife and my daughter hurt me badly. I loved them. Now I was no different than most coaches who seemed to get divorced one or two times. When it happened to me I went crazy. Everything became nothing. I began to drink cognac and I drank it every day. I could not sleep without it.

Eventually my personal life improved, especially when I met Lucy, the woman I later married. Around came 1976, the year of the Montreal Olympics, and Nowicki made the team. I had the time and I had the money, so I decided to go and watch him ride. I went as a cycling fan, not as a member of Poland's coaching staff. It was a personally rewarding trip to see my young rider win a bronze medal in the road race and a silver in the 100 km team time trial. He accomplished the latter with Mytnik, Szozda and Szurkowski, riders you will read about in this book.

After the Olympics I visited New York City to find some old Polish friends. The university had given me a one-year leave of absence. I had never been in America before and I'd always wanted to go. I arrived with one suitcase and my visa. What a shock! In Poland the United States is the magic country, but New York was the worst city I had ever seen in my life. But my friend, a former bike rider in Poland, had a nice apartment and I decided to stay with him and find out more about the country. It certainly was a different world.

Two months passed and I began wondering about returning home. I'd been having a pretty good time but it seemed aimless. My friend and I played tennis, went swimming, and he took me sightseeing. Then one day we came upon a bicycle race. The Veterans were on the course. The field was terrible, horrible. Fat guys with mustaches. I said, "What *is* this?" You know, I had not seen any cycling in eight weeks and I had been away from it during my last three months in Poland. My blood started to bubble a little. Later we went into a couple of bicycle stores we accidentally found. My friend asked if I might like to go over to Teaneck, NJ, where a man he knew named Mike Fraysse had a shop.

Fraysse was at that time a vice-president of the U.S. Cycling Federation. Back in 1974 he had attended the Junior Worlds in Warsaw with the American team. Somehow he remembered my face and my position as national Junior coach in the days when Poland's cyclists were the best in the world. We did not get acquainted then because I did not speak English, but now we discovered a common language — French. We talked about 1974, and he invited me to attend a meeting of the North Jersey Bicycle Club to take a look at the riders. I said I would like that.

My first experience with U.S. riders came when I was invited to a meeting of the North Jersey Bicycle Club. I found a lot of enthusiasm for cycling, but not much knowledge.

When I rode with those Americans I could see right away they needed a lot of information. It was fun for me to work with them. I had come from the fat to the lean. The riders were not good but they were very nice, they had enthusiasm for learning, and they loved to ride a bike. Their attitude was so different from the one I was used to in Poland, where cycling was a commercial production. Over there if you weren't good, goodbye. Nobody would pay attention to you.

By now I had a different feeling about the U.S. After my big shock in the city with its pollution and deterioration I got a chance to see upstate New York and Pennsylvania. The country was beautiful. The people I met were friendly. I began to say to myself, "Forget Poland. There is a nice life here." I decided to try to stay longer. I filled out various forms at the immigration office for residency and employment.

My six-month visa was extended and I was approved for labor in the spring of 1977. I decided to take a job with the construction company my friend worked for. I made $100-$150 a day high in the air painting huge gas tanks and high-rise superstructures. The big jets flew right over my head. Luckily, I am good with heights. To me, 50 stories up is the same as being on the ground.

It was good to have a job because my savings were getting low, but was painting my destiny in America? I didn't think so. I hoped I could get a hospital position as a physical therapist, or perhaps put my education to use some other way. Coaching also began to cross my mind.

When I left Poland I was really tired of cycling. I said no more ever again in my life. Bicycle, go to hell. Forget it. But after one year it was a different story. I was again feeling hungry for cycling. I had been in the sport too many years to stay away. So when Mike Fraysee came to me in the summer of 1977 and said, "Eddie, we want you to coach at the national team camp in Squaw Valley," I was happy to accept. Now that I'd decided I wanted to stay in the U.S., I also wanted to return to my sport.

It was the time of preparation for the World Championships. I was surprised that I would start at such a high level. Here I was in this great country and I would be working with the best coaches, the best riders, and all their training plans. I expected the sport to be very organized at the national level.

But when I got to Squaw Valley they told me, "You are the coach." *What?* I could not believe it. Who even knew me? They told me the actual Worlds team coach was in New York and he was not coming to the camp. He was going to meet the riders at the airport for the trip to Venezuela, the site of the championships that year. *What?* He trusts *me* to prepare *his* riders? Why, he never even met me. It was incredible! I could never leave my riders to anybody. Another coach might come to help me, but if I am taking the team it must be my plan from A to Z.

I began by setting up a weekly training program, but it was very hard because of the language barrier. Everybody said I spoke English like Tonto; if so, the Lone Ranger must have known Polish pretty well. I brought an 11-year-old Polish boy from New Jersey to do the translating, but it didn't work too well. Still, I felt it was a promising start. After all, American cycling was incredibly empty. No coaches, no program, no position on the bike. Riders didn't know about training, about race tactics, about nutrition. I talked about massage and the women said, "No, no, no!" I couldn't understand — maybe they thought this Eddie B does some kind of sex massage or something. After one week I finally convinced Mark Pringle and Paul Deem to come for massages. The women watched through the open door and some even got brave enough to find out the benefits for themselves.

The most important part of this experience was that I found out the riders needed me. They gave me a very positive reception and five weeks later they had quite a successful Worlds. Pringle finished 10th in the men's road race and Connie Carpenter won the silver medal in the women's road race.

At the end of that year I decided to accept the USCF's offer to become its first national coaching director. American cycling needed help and I felt there was a lot I could do for it. I wanted to see American cycling grow up. I wanted to make a foundation so it would continue to grow long after my work for the federation was finished. From that beginning in Squaw Valley, American cycling and I have shared an incredible six years. They've certainly been the happiest years of my life.

I love America. My U.S. citizenship should be approved in the summer of 1984 and then I expect to live here for the rest of my life. Before I came I spent time in every country in Europe. I know France, I know Germany, I know Italy. It would be impossible for me to live in any one of them. Why? Because they are so nationalistic. All European countries are. A foreigner has a very tough time getting accepted — maybe even no chance at all. But it's not that way in America. When you are a foreigner here you are almost typical.

I love the freedom in America. I am sorry to say, however, that there might be too much of it. I see many people abusing freedom, not appreciating it. They cheat on welfare and they cheat on Social Security. The educational system is worse than in Europe and for one main reason: not enough discipline. I feel that when the national government controls a country's education it is much better. It's the same for medicine and medical insurance. In America if you don't have money you don't pay the doctor bill; if you have lots of money you pay it easily. It is the middle class that has the hard time.

When I look back I realize I stopped in America for a number of reasons. Freedom was very important. Opportunity was very important. And there were so many little things, like a friendly nod by a stranger on the street. Do you realize how wonderful that is? In many other countries you never acknowledge someone you don't know. That is the tradition, the habit. To me one of the nicest things about America is smiling at a stranger, saying "Hello," and having a smile come back to you.

Now I have a lot of pride in America, especially when I'm overseas with a team and I see how others respect me and the progress the U.S. has made in cycling. Believe me, they are afraid of us. In New Zealand at the 1983 Junior Worlds, the Russian manager came to me and said, "I remember you. We raced against each other. You son of a bitch—you made America strong. You are giving us a hard time. We beat America so badly before, now we don't. For you everything is excellent. For us, we are having worse results this year than last year. We are in trouble."

Many people in the Eastern European federations and in FIAC (the governing body of amateur cycling) know me better than do members of the USCF's board of directors. The Polish government keeps a very close watch through its embassy in Chicago. I'm sure they have a file on what I do. You see, there is a feeling that the success I have helped bring to American cycling has come at the expense of communist cycling. They were once so strong and now the U.S. is beating them. This is one reason I haven't been able to go with our team to the Peace Race—the Polish government might give me some trouble. My work in American cycling is reported in the newspapers over there. Many people remember me for developing good Polish riders and now they see me doing the same thing for the U.S. They remember that it was me who sent Greg LeMond to Poland for two months to get his first European racing experience. I am very much looking forward to returning with an American team, but it can't happen until my citizenship is approved.

Let me close with a story to help explain how a lot of my knowledge of cycling developed.

In Poland when my generation of riders came to be coaches we produced a wonderful national team, the best team in the world for a few years. We had learned from our coaches, who killed us more than once. But cycling was still just average when Poland experienced great success in two other international sports, weightlifting and track and field. Poland had the best lifters, including Waldemar Baszanowski, and we had the best woman track-and-field athlete in history, Irena Kirszenstein.

It was then that the people at the National Sports Institute looked at the cyclists and said, "You are not the best. There is something wrong with you. We will give you a running coach for the national team because our runners are so good. We have world champions and European-champions. Running long distance is similar to cycling. A running coach can make you the best."

So first thing in the morning we had to run 5 km and do calisthenics. In the afternoon, more running. And cyclocross with running. Our breathing was fine and the step test results were good. Everyone was happy—we were running and riding and we seemed to be doing well. Then along came April and our first competition in the big fields of 200 riders. We weren't good. Our best riders were dead flat. The preparation had been wrong.

The next year the National Sports Institute came up with a different brilliant idea to fix the cyclists. They decided to give us a weightlifting coach. They figured this would work because cycling deals with power. So we lifted weights three or four times a week. They came and measured our muscles and tested us in all the exercises— bench press, leg press, and so on. After three weeks they came again, tested us again, and increased the weights. Test, test, test, every three weeks. The newspaper wrote a story about how well all the cyclists were doing, how big our muscles were getting, the incredible weights we were lifting. This must be the right way. Then came April, races, same bad results. It didn't work.

The third year they came again and said they had figured out why running and weightlifting didn't make us great cyclists. It was because those sports didn't put us in the same position as riding. Similar sports to cycling, they said, were speedskating and cross-country skiing—these would be the best preparation for us. So for the third year in a row we had a new head coach. The ideas of the first two had failed, so they were out. Out with the runner, out with the weightlifter. It wasn't long before it was out with the skater/cross-country skier.

But there was some good that came of all this. I got experience with these different training methods and collected the written material we were given. Not all of it was wrong for cyclists, not everything failed to work.

At last the riders and coaches that were left just said, "Hold it. We are cyclists. We are not runners, we are not lifters, we are not skaters, we are not skiers. We are cyclists. Get on the bike, everybody. We will make a program for ourselves." A smart man took charge, a former bike rider with the toughness of Hitler. He said, "When I am here, you listen to me. If this doesn't work you see to it that I am fired after one year. Right now everybody shut up and I will tell you what we are going to do. We are going to change, and we are going to improve."

And we did. The cycling program really began to work. He went to great lengths to design a racing calendar that would continue to develop us month by month. He put emphasis on winter preparation and the use of weights, cross-country skiing and running at that time of year instead of during preseason training. We used the elements of those sports that worked, but we emphasized the bike.

Above all, this coach made sure that our preparation matched our individual racing schedules. This is what I have tried to do for the USCF. I can send any rider to the Tour de l'Avenir, for example, but if he is not ready for it then it will probably break him. The U.S. had gotten beat up so badly in that race that we did not even dare enter a team for a couple of years. Then in 1982 we returned with our new blood and we finished. The l'Avenir was won that year by a young American pro who had been in our amateur program several years. Who produced Greg LeMond? Not Eddie B, but the coaching staff of the U.S. Cycling Federation. His parents produced his body, but if he did not have his few years in our basic program, he would never have become Greg LeMond.

I say this for several reasons. One is that in 1977 LeMond had a big problem with his position on the bike. He was pedaling pigeon-toed and we made several changes to help him. We worked with him in many other ways. He listened and worked for us. Two years later he was the Junior champion of the world. In 1980 he beat all the Russians and Poles in France's Circuit de la Sarthe. How was this possible for an American? It must have been good preparation.

When this U.S. team took third place in the 1978 Junior Worlds team time trial, it was the first medal for American roadmen in world championship history. I was proud of that, but I am even more proud that all four men were still racing—and winning—in 1984. This is one reason why I am sure that my program is correct for the long-term development of riders. From the front: Greg LeMond, Ron Kiefel, Greg Demgen, Jeff Bradley.

I don't say this to talk about myself, but I know my assistant coaches and I do it the right way. When you make a racing schedule that's too hard for the riders, you kill them. In the end you produce only negative results. Why have we not lost our good Juniors from the late 1970s? Because we do not push so hard. It's possible for a national federation to get good results in the Junior class and wind up with no Seniors. But all four of our team time trial riders who won the bronze medal at the 1978 Junior Worlds—the first Worlds medal in history by U.S. roadmen—are still in competition and they are winning. That's Greg LeMond, Greg Demgen, Jeff Bradley and Ron Kiefel.

That is some of my background. I am not just some guy who has dreamed up a cycling program. I know the reasons behind everything this book tells you to do. What follows has worked for me, and it has worked for many good riders. It will work for you.

Introduction

The national coaches of the East European countries are killers. They are incredible pushers. But over there it is a different story than for me in America. They don't care how many riders they destroy during preparation for major road races like the World Championship or Olympics. They need only six for the team and they have tens of thousands of riders to choose from. Each year in East Germany, for example, they test about 85,000 children 12-13 years old to identify which ones are worth developing as cyclists. How many thousand riders do I have? In 1983 there were 119 Category 1 Senior racers in the U.S. I can't kill any. I can't push for the maximum like an East European coach. I can't risk ruining 15 guys by saying: "This is the program for everybody. Only those who can handle it make the team." For those coaches, 15 riders is nothing. But I must avoid losing even one. That's why I have different programs for different riders, and that's why this book is written for individuals. Everyone who reads it should take the information and apply it to his or her own special abilities and goals. This is no East European system where you must do it only one way or fail.

A SPORT WITH A FUTURE

In many ways it is a big gamble to try to become a top cyclist (or top athlete in any sport). You must gamble the time you would use for schooling or the income you would earn from a job. Thankfully, we are now into a period when our best amateur riders are well supported by the sponsors of their teams. The possibility of reaching that level makes it worth it for you to try to become as good on the bike as you possibly can. More than ever in the U.S. there is a worthwhile future in cycling.

Why do you want to be a bike racer? What is *your* reason? Why has Greg LeMond become a great professional, and why did Thurlow Rogers emerge as the best U.S. amateur in 1983? The underlying answer must be enjoyment of the exercise of riding the bike. I know that's the way it began for these two riders and for almost everyone I have coached. I know because I've asked them, both in the U.S. and back in Poland when I was doing research for my master's degree. Whenever I asked, "Why are you a racing cyclist?" the most common response was, "I like the exercise." The second answer: "I like competition." Further down the list: "I like to be a winner," and, "I want the publicity." Finally, "I like the prizes."

On the other hand, why do riders quit the sport? Thousands start racing each year, but only one can be the world's best in each event. When you have 100 Intermediates you will get maybe 10 good Juniors. Perhaps in that group you will have a diamond, a Greg LeMond or a Roy Knickman, but not every year. The selection is natural, and each coach must do the best with the talent he has. But why do so few riders become stars?

When you start to ride a bike, you love it. When you start competition, it is fun. But next you are either successful or you're not. When you fail you lose interest, at least in racing if not in riding. Only those who compete successfully make the next step, which is publicity and money. Then the best of the best amateurs have a chance to make their living by racing professionally in Europe. Some do it simply because they have no better alternative and they ride as domestiques (a harder life is difficult to imagine). Only the most dedicated and talented pro will join the tiny group of stars at the very top of the sport.

For cyclists in East European countries it is different. They are not amateurs, they are pros supported by the state. Only their classification is amateur. But finally they aren't alone. Top American amateurs are now essentially pros, too, and there is nothing at all wrong with it—we are merely catching up to the strongest cycling nations. Of course, in the U.S. it is all private rather than government support, but the benefit to the rider is the same.

Some of our best-sponsored amateur teams are now giving their riders $15,000 a year. That's a good contract, but it's far from super money when you consider what it takes to live. After all, a rider must eat like four regular people, he must have a place to live, he must have clothes, he must have a car, he must have insurance, he must have everything necessary for life. How can he be called an amateur when he must spend six to eight hours each day on cycling-related matters? After three hours of hard training he is not ready to go to a job for eight hours. He is ready for a massage, a meal and rest. Recovery and nutrition are just as important as training. But somehow a rider must be able to pay for food, housing and equipment.

That's why sponsorship money is so important. It is absolutely necessary in order for U.S. cycling to continue to attract and develop its athletes. When the money is not there, the rider quits. When he falls and ruins his $1,500 bike and there is no money for a new one, he quits. When he breaks his arm and has big hospital bills, he quits. The sport is not without danger, and costly problems can result. Especially for a young rider living at home there can be a lot of pressure from parents. They become afraid for their child's safety and for the family budget. I can't blame them. The body does not have spare parts like a bicycle, and a bicycle's parts are fairly expensive.

Our best amateurs are now on their way to an even better future in professional cycling. At least I hope so. The development of an American pro class is very important to me because it is the next step for my riders. I want to see big money in cycling because it is what makes the years of hard work worth it. The question in the U.S. has always been: Why should I settle for $100 a week racing a bike when I can make $300 doing easier work in a factory? But now the question is becoming: Why should I settle for $300 a week from a factory when there is the chance to make $500 on a bike?

A love for the exercise of riding may be the basic reason athletes decide to devote themselves to cycling, but then it helps a lot to be able to make a living from it.

A SPORT FOR THE INDIVIDUAL

Above all, cycling gives you the chance to make yourself a star. It gives you opportunity as an individual to do your best. An athlete suffers in a team sport when he is very good but the team is bad. He gets few personal results and no victories to build his pride. Cycling is different. It cuts out every excuse. You can't blame others for your failure. A soccer player can say, "I would have made the goal if my teammate had only passed the ball to me correctly. It was his fault." In cycling there is only one reason you go off the back: You are not strong enough, period.

Cycling demands self-discipline. You are working for yourself, so it is up to you to become as good as you can be. When the hills come, nothing can help you get up but your own two legs. When some riders fail they get mad and try to rationalize. They come up with a story—"I have a bad stomach" or "I have a headache" — but they are mainly fooling themselves. A smart coach will see through such words very quickly. One time a problem might be true, but not the second time. An honest excuse is rare in bicycle racing.

The rider who will be a star does not spend time trying to justify his failures. He must have a different psychology. He knows that success is up to him. If he has a team it can only help him if he is good. So he *must* be good. He must show that he is worthy of the other riders' support. When they lead him out in the sprint he must win or go blind trying. If he does not it is only fair that next time he works for one of them.

Physical and mental demands

Cycling is a hard sport. The American people think football is tough, but they do not recognize what it takes to be a bicycle road racer. There are such intense physical and mental demands.

You start the race in the midst of 150 other riders, each one trying to beat you. The speed hits 80 k.p.h. down hills, 50 on the rolling road, 42 on the flat, 25 on the climb. While keeping this pace you must remain aware of everything that is hap-

A basic rule of bicycle racing is to stay near the front. When you don't, there is a greater risk of being caught in a crash and missing the breakaway.

pening around you. You have to know where you are on the course and how much time is left until the finish. You must have studied the race description and memorized where the hills are, where the road turns into the wind, where to be ready for opponents' moves, and where to make your own. Everything is important for your tactics. You must ride offensively or defensively, depending on the situation. And you must do all this without a break for four or five hours.

What this means is that racing takes great power of concentration. Many a rider has failed to concentrate for one moment and suddenly found himself at the rear of the field. This is the most dangerous position because there is no self-determination. There is nothing you can do against the riders in front, nothing you can do if the group splits, nothing you can do about crashes. But it is so hard to stay near the front. The riders in the lead are up there for one very simple reason: They are the best tactically and physically. They have the concentration and the strength. You must be one of them. It is your responsibility, because only at the front can the race be won.

Now consider the requirements on a rider's body. They are amazing. You may burn twice as many calories in a four-hour road race as a factory worker will burn in a full day. To replenish these calories you must eat food that is *necessary* as well as food that you like. For example, I never ate horse meat in my life until an eight-year period when I was racing. Horse is considered a very good meat because it has no fat. In Europe riders eat it a lot. It is also much cheaper than beef and pork. But *horse* meat? It didn't sound good at all. At first I ate only a little, then more, and then I was eating a lot. I rode well on it. When I stopped cycling I stopped eating it.

It takes some craziness to be a bike racer. You have to dedicate your life to the sport if you want to be good. You must also have some luck. The rider who becomes the best is not necessarily the one who has the best body, it is the one who works best, who concentrates best, who has the smartest program, and who is lucky. You are dealing with machinery and speed, so you must be willing to accept whatever type of luck comes your way each time you ride.

One mark of a good cyclist is the ability to shrug off the bad luck that turns apparent victory into defeat. When you can't deal with this it can break your psychology. It can stop your career. You must always be ready to lose. Good riders, however, generally have good luck. The reason is simple: They stay on the front of the field. This lets them avoid the road dangers that puncture tires and break wheels, and they are safe from crashes that often happen in the middle of the pack. In this sense, a good rider makes his own luck.

Body types

It takes three years of development to be a good Junior, then two more to become a decent Senior. That's the general rule, but it varies depending on your physical capacity and how fast you learn. It has been different for riders like Greg LeMond, Roy Knickman, Greg Demgen, Jeff Bradley, Thurlow Rogers and Ron Kiefel. All of them were world-class Juniors who had the talent to win immediately upon turning Senior at age 18.

LeMond and Knickman are absolute diamonds. They have grown up and developed incredibly fast. Right now everybody knows who LeMond is. Soon you will know Knickman just as well. But he was nobody when I first saw him four years ago and began to call him the next LeMond. It brings to mind the first time I saw Greg in 1977 and I was asked what I thought about him. I was certain when I replied, "A diamond, a clear diamond." But, of course, a diamond will not become a champion every time.

"A diamond," is how I described Greg Le-Mond in 1977. But he was a gem in need of polishing, which my coaching staff and I helped provide. For example, note his pigeon-toed foot position, which we quickly corrected when he attended a USCF training camp.

When I see a rider for the first time I am not looking for an athletic V-shape body, or huge legs, or super muscle development. These are the three qualities that are important to me:

1. Very fast recovery, what I call good physiology.
2. A love for the sport, what I call being crazy for cycling.
3. A desire to work extremely hard.

When a rider has these three things, that is what makes the potential, the talent. Talent is not a nice-looking body. In fact, after five years of development a cyclist's body does not look so nice. Check a super rider like LeMond and you won't see the slim hips and broad shoulders that athletes have in some sports. His body is developing like Merckx's, like the trunk of a tree with almost the same measurement for chest, stomach and hips. All the best riders look this way. Saronni is a tree, not a V. Hinault is a tree, not a V. Soukhoroutchenkov, the Russian who won the 1980 Olympic road race, is a tree, not a V. Szurkowski, the Pole who was the world's best amateur in the early 1970s, is exactly the same.

Eddy Merckx and Giuseppe Saronni have the typical tree-like torso of many successful road riders. The circumference is almost the same for chest, stomach and hips.

It is often said that to become a superstar you must have a short body and very long legs, like Baldini and Coppi. This is not true. Merckx, for example, has legs of average length for his height, and Szurkowski has short but huge and powerful legs under a long torso. Soukhoroutchenkov has average proportions but gigantic calves, while other very good riders have slim calves. What all this means is that there is no picture-perfect body for cycling, and a rider's potential should never be judged just by looking at him. This is especially true for someone who is new to the sport and has not yet had his body developed by the bike.

So we see many different builds on riders. We see them with chicken chests, with bow legs, with long bodies, and with short bodies. Each can be a good build for cycling. On the other hand, basketball selects athletes by how tall they are. Football selects by how big they are. In cycling size simply does not make much difference. I remember back in the mid 1960s when the Italian pursuit team competed in Poland. Their best rider, a fellow named Ursse who was world champion in the individual pursuit, stood almost two meters tall. I am not a short man but I had to

Another "tree," Ryszard Szurkowski, who beat fellow Pole Stanislaw Szozda to win the 1973 World Championship. The next year Janusz Kowalski finished first, Szurkowski was second, and Szozda was fourth. Polish riders at that time were unquestionably the best amateurs in the world.

look up when I talked with him. He used 180 mm crank arms and it was the first time I had ever seen any so long. The next best rider on the team was a little guy. It was incredible — they were complete opposites. This is what I mean when I say there is a place in cycling for everybody.

Even spiders. That's what we call some young beginners because that's exactly what they look like. There is absolutely no fat on them. They are all long bones and very little muscle. It would seem impossible that such a person could ever be good in a tough physical sport like cycling. But they can be, as two such spiders, Mark Pringle and Andy Hampsten, have proved. But you wouldn't believe how Hampsten, for example, looked five years ago when we first started working with him. When he showed up from North Dakota the bicycle was heavier than he was. But he had the physiology, he was crazy for cycling, and he was a very hard worker. That's what it takes, no matter what your body looks like when you start.

"Spiders"

Andy Hampsten used to be skinnier than his bike. This photo shows how cycling has developed this "spider's" body during five years in the U.S. national team program.

The table below is interesting. It shows the height and weight of nine great professional roadmen, and the ratio between the two measurements. Note the differences among these stars, who displayed quite a range of body proportions. See how you compare, but don't put too much importance on it.

Name	Weight (kg)	Height (cm)	Ratio
Altig	80	179	447
Anquetil	70	174	402
Gimondi	71	184	385
Karstens	74	178	416
Merckx	74	182	407
Motta	68	180	377
Poulidor	70	172	407
Simpson	69	181	381
Van Looy	76	178	427

Source: Poland's Academy of Physical Education and Federation of Sport, Cycling. 1977

Elements of success

Hard work. That's what it takes to reach your potential in cycling, plus being consistent in your program. It all comes back to self-discipline, because everything you do starts with it. Riders who come to camps at the Olympic Training Center in Colorado Springs wake up each day at 7 o'clock and go to bed each night at 9:30. They do this for two weeks, then go back home. It is then up to each one to keep the same regimen for rest, for eating, for training—the same regimen for life as a cyclist. When a rider is more crazy for the disco and girl chasing than he is for the bicycle, he is not going to be a star. Cycling requires not only ability of the body but also of the mind. Again I will say it: A rider must dedicate his life to the sport.

Dedication

It is not possible to be too crazy for cycling. There is only one danger when you are living 100% for the sport: overtraining. This happens when a rider pushes himself too far. It is one reason why a coach is so important. A coach is just like a school teacher for a beginning rider. He helps the rider find a good position on the bike, and he explains in A-B-C fashion what the rider has to do. The coach helps a rider avoid overtraining by setting up a program that emphasizes rest as much as work.

Avoid overtraining

Correct training will improve your ability to consume oxygen and recover quickly from hard efforts. We measure this in terms of maximal oxygen uptake, or max VO_2. World-class road riders have a value in the range of 80-90. This figure results from lab testing that determines the most milliliters of oxygen you can consume in one minute divided by your weight in kilograms. It tells how fast your "engine" is. Just as a car puts out r.p.m. by burning oxygen and gas, you perform by burning oxygen and glycogen. When you can burn more oxygen your engine can work faster. You have more potential in cycling. Max VO_2 can be developed, as we have seen with Greg LeMond, who has gone from 70 to more than 80.

Maximal oxygen uptake

When a car loses power, you can sometimes fix it by simply putting in a new air filter. The engine gets more oxygen and it runs strongly again. In a similar way you can help your muscles work better by increasing the amount of oxygen that is delivered to them. This is done by training to improve the size and efficiency of the lungs, plus the ability of red blood cells to transport oxygen. We experimented with this in 1981 by having a month-long team time trial training camp at 4,000 meters above sea level in Colorado. Some people called this crazy, but four of the guys—Tom Prehn, Ron Kiefel, Thurlow Rogers and Kevin Lutz—went down to New York and won the National 100 km Championship. It worked perfectly. Kiefel, for example, developed virtually the maximum number of red blood cells possible in the human body.

I recommend that you have a periodic max VO_2 test, blood test, and urinalysis. These are good indicators of general fitness and health, as well as whether your training program is producing results. A max VO_2 test may be difficult to arrange depending on where you live. Check at universities, hospitals, private sportsmedicine clinics, etc. All riders who attend camps at the Olympic Training Center are given the three tests, plus the strength test that is described in Chapter 3. The results tell the coaching staff and each individual rider what needs attention.

Regular physical checkups

THE VALUE OF A COACH

You can sit by yourself and read this or any other book about training and racing, but it is mainly theory. It may be hard to comprehend everything and apply it correctly. A coach can be a big help in turning the information into practical, on-the-road instruction. For the same reason it's helpful to train frequently with experienced riders rather than always alone.

This brings to mind two incidents during my first contact with good American cyclists in 1977 at Squaw Valley. Four riders were pedaling along side by side, spread right across the road. I told them, "Please, guys, use an echelon." They said, "Why? That's dangerous. It's better to ride against the wind so we can work harder and get better training." Of course that's not true. You can work harder in an echelon because the speed can be much faster. It puts you in a racing situation where you ride a couple of centimeters behind the next wheel. When you never do this in training you will not do it well in a race. This makes perfect sense, but apparently no coach had ever explained it to these riders.

When I announced on another day that the workout would be 60 km with intervals, the riders could not believe it would do any good to ride such a short distance. I told them, "If you have anything left after the 60K, I will be very happy to let you ride 200K or whatever you wish. First, let's see what happens on the road." It turned out that they had never before been coached on interval training. They really didn't know how it was done. After 50 km they were dead. They were used to doing what's called long, slow distance. This is training that makes people happy—when you train LSD you feel comfortable. You don't work hard, but you build your psychology: "I rode 160K today. I feel good. My pulse is down. Right now even 250K is no problem. I am a strong guy." Not really. This is just base, not the ability to race.

Do you need a coach? Absolutely. Words on a page can help a lot, but it is something more when a coach is actually working with you. He has the trained eye and the experience to personalize all the instruction. For example, during the winter of 1982-83 Rebecca Twigg stayed at the Olympic Training Center for the first time. She had perfect psychology, she was a very hard worker, she had a super body. She was already the world pursuit champion. Even so, I had to correct her in many things during that preseason period because she had never been under the full-time supervision of a coach before.

A coach's expertise

A coach must know more than just training on the bike. He must have experience with winter indoor workouts, such as circuit weight training, stretching, aerobic exercises, and using the stationary bike. He must know physiology, anatomy, psychology. If he doesn't he won't produce the best rider. And if you as a developing rider don't seek out and work with the best coach, you won't reach your full potential.

Now, I say "the best coach," but if I've discovered anything during my many years in this sport it's that there is no such thing. Nobody can know it all. I am still learning cycling every single day. I am being taught by assistant coaches and by riders and by people much below me. I listen to everyone, because when I stop listening I stop learning. But even though no coach is "the best," you must believe in the coach you have. A local coach might not have a great cycling education or very good ability as an instructor, but he is much better than no coach at all. You must trust him like you trust your doctor. When you believe the medicine is right you feel much better.

No book can substitute

It boils down to this: As helpful to you as this book will be, it is not intended to be a substitute for a coach. I don't believe any book can be. A good coach is more than an instructor; he is a manager, advisor and friend. He is the mirror that lets you see yourself the way you never can. He will tell you the truth. On the other hand, when you rely only on riders to help you, you are not likely to get 100% true information. After all, they want to win races, too. So if you are a beginning rider, please contact your nearest bike clubs and find a coach who is willing to work with you. The same goes even if you've already been in the sport several years but have never had a coach.

Someday, after gaining enough knowledge from cycling books, from coaches and from your experience, you will become your own best coach. I remember the day Greg LeMond told me, "Eddie, now I teach my father. He no longer teaches me. Now I know more about cycling than he does." When a rider displays such experience, the coach knows it is time to become less involved. The rider begins to know more about himself than the coach does. However, the smart rider will still consult his coach when he has a special problem, or when he wants an objective eye and opinion, or when he just needs someone to talk to.

A smart coach will consult with his former riders, too. I look forward to each new meeting with Greg LeMond because I can always learn something important from his experience in European pro cycling and the way his body is developing. Just as Greg became able to teach his father, he now has things to teach his old coach.

STRONG POINTS, WEAK POINTS

This book will cover all the major road events, in this order:

1. Road race
2. Criterium
3. Individual time trial
4. Team time trial (2-man and 4-man)
5. Stage race

I will tell you how to prepare for each event and race well in it, but the intention is not to turn you into a specialist. That would be wrong. I do not believe in taking a group of riders and saying, "This one is a road racer, this one is a criterium racer, this one is a time trialist . . . ." An individual may have a best event, a primary talent as a cyclist, but to be a good bike rider he must be good for everything.

Everyone has strong points and weak points; everyone is better at some things than at others. Even so, it is often the case that the weakest point of a good rider is stronger than anything an average rider has to offer. The reason isn't just "natural ability" as so many people think. It is the ability to work extra hard on the things that don't come easily.

Why are there so many riders who never win a race? There could be mental problems or tactical problems, but usually it's because they lack one of the three qualities necessary for success:

- Speed
- Power
- Endurance

3 qualities of the successful road racer

The winner is the one who has the right percentages of each.

When you are riding 160 km races you don't need endurance for 220 km. Always remember that you are dealing with limited potential energy. When you use this energy to build fantastic endurance you don't have energy left to build speed. It's

Speed vs. endurance

like the wings on an airplane: When the left one goes up, the right one goes down. One wing is speed, the other is endurance. When endurance is up, speed is down; when speed is up, endurance is down.

For example, have you ever seen a great match sprinter win a 160 km road race? If Mark Gorski and Ron Kiefel rode together in such a race it would be impossible for Gorski to win. But if they went out together for Tuesday speed training, Gorski would beat Kiefel so easily. They are both very good athletes, but they have two different types of preparation. Their programs are absolute opposites in terms of volume of kilometers. Many riders do not recognize distinctions like this. Someone will say, "I am fast because after 160K I beat Gorski." He is not fast; he only has good endurance and Gorski doesn't.

Improve the weak point

Throughout your career you must evaluate yourself and decide what to work on. Many riders need speed but they do not like sprint training because it is hard. I hear them say, "I'm not a sprinter, I'm a road rider." That's absolutely the wrong attitude. You must train to improve your weak point. You have to develop every skill if you are going to be a good cyclist.

Right now you are the aspiring racer. You want to be good, good enough to compete successfully in all of the road events. What do you have to do? The remainder of this book will give you the answers. But first here is an overview of my system so you will understand what's in store.

THE YEAR OF THE CYCLIST

Before taking even one more ride, read through Chapter 2 and make all necessary adjustments to your position on the bike. This is imperative, no matter what time of year you are reading this. Then you can proceed.

Yearly training plan

The bible of the racing cyclist is his training plan. The year is one big cycle and the plan must cover it all. Each new plan is made in mid October as the current racing season ends. This is also the start of the six-week Rest Period for recovering from the many stresses of hard training and competition.

Decide your goals for next season and how you will prepare for them. Consult with your coach, team manager or advisor. Know who you are. Is it reasonable to strive to win the District Championship? The Nationals? The Worlds? The Olympics? You may not have much choice if you are a rider with a sponsorship. If you are being paid to ride with a company's name they will tell you which races you must perform well in.

As we will see later it is possible to reach a super performance peak for a special event. This is the last step when you have built a solid base. But your main objective should not be to ride well during one small part of the season. It should be to ride well for the *entire* season. Something is wrong when you are good one week and bad the next.

Planning chart

Use a large piece of poster paper to construct a yearly planning chart based on the illustration. Write in your big events with red ink. They are your priorities. Then use a different color to write in all the other races you will enter, or at least as many as you know about at this time of year.

For a cyclist the new year actually begins December 1. That is the beginning of progressive indoor and outdoor work in the 18-week Preparation Period. It has three distinct segments and ends April 15, the start of the Racing Period.

YEARLY TRAINING PLAN

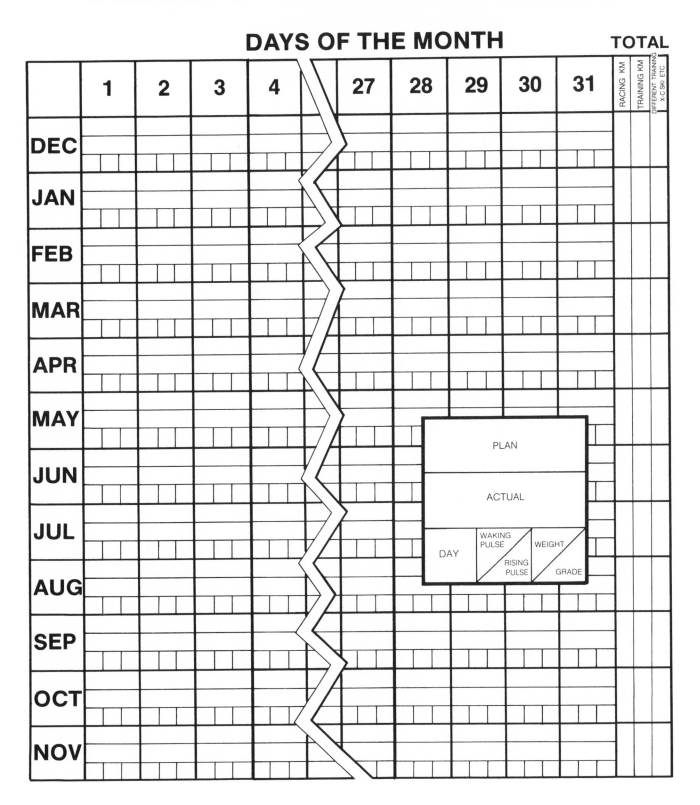

Adjust calendar for
cold weather

(Please note: Riders who live in northern climates where winter is severe will have to adjust their calendar accordingly. For example, the Preparation Period may be started around December 15 and extended to May 1 because the racing season begins later. In this book I am assuming the standard April 15 date for the beginning of racing.)

Training is done at home in November (yes, there is activity in the Rest Period) and December. In January you should attend a training camp. In March go to a warm-weather area, such as Texas or Florida, for group training and training races. By mid April you will be ready for a spring and summer of major competition. For some riders this means a trip to Europe on a USCF team, then the Coors Classic, World Championships, etc. For others it is a regional race schedule that will be the foundation for national competition in the future.

The planning chart's large boxes

Large top box for
training planned

Look again at the yearly planning chart. Between the races there are days for training and for rest. Each day has two large boxes. In the top one, write in the distance and type of ride you will do that day. Use colored ink to signify intensity. For example, green ink means it is to be a steady ride for conditioning. Blue ink means greater intensity like sprints, intervals or hill work. This gives you an easy-to-see outline for what you are going to do.

Large center box for
training accomplished

At the end of each day use the large box in the center to record the distance and intensity (signified by ink color) that you actually did. Perhaps you were tired from traveling after a race and you trained less than planned, or you caught a cold and didn't train at all. Write it in, and don't feel guilty. It's okay to do less than scheduled if there is a good reason, but never do more. If the chart says to ride 50 km at green pace on Wednesday and you feel terrific, don't do 65 km blue. Be glad you feel like an eagle and save your energy for Thursday, because that is the day for interval training. Remember that hard work on Thursday is for a purpose—to sharpen up for Sunday's race. Stick to your plan as closely as possible.

How do you know what to schedule into each of those training boxes all season long? That's what you will learn in the following chapters.

The planning chart's small boxes

First small box for
date

At the bottom of each day's space are three small boxes. Write the day of the week (M, Tu, W, Th, F, Sa, Su) in the first one.

Second small box for
pulse rates

Divide the second small box with a diagonal line and in the top corner record your waking pulse. Lie still for a couple of minutes after you wake up (especially if you've been startled by an alarm clock), then count your heart rate for 15 seconds and write down the number. Now keep your finger on the pulse, stand up, and immediately count again for 15 seconds. Write this figure in the lower corner of the box. The second figure will always be greater than the first because blood is being pulled down by gravity when you stand and the heart must beat faster to counteract this. A 15-second count shows this much better than a 30- or 60-second count, because when you are fit and have good recovery your pulse falls back to its normal resting level very quickly.

What this pulse check reveals is how tired your body is from training and other stresses. When both pulses are faster than normal, or when the second pulse is unusually greater than the first, it is a clear signal of fatigue. But the only way this can work is if you record these pulses day after day after day. Everyone responds differently to training stress, so you must know what is normal for you.

For example, in the three days before he won the Junior World Championship in 1979 Greg LeMond had pulse counts of 10/14, 10/13, 9/13. That is very good. He was rested. But when a rider is training hard he will have 13/18, 14/19, 13/20, etc. If today you have 10/14, then train, and tomorrow you have 10/14 again, you know that the training was not hard work for you. If it was, the counts might be up to 11 or 12 and 16 or 17.

Both pulses will go up when training is hard, or at least the standing pulse will. They will also go up when you are catching a cold, when you have psychological stress, when you don't get enough rest, etc. Anytime your pulses are higher than what's normal for you it tells you one thing: Your body is not ready for hard training. This is objective information.

Another piece of objective information is your weight, and that's what goes in the third small box. Again draw a diagonal line. In the top corner record your morning weight, preferably after visiting the bathroom and before eating breakfast. Wear the same clothes each time, or no clothes.

Third small box for weight

Like with the pulse numbers you are looking for a weight pattern. During the Preparation Period and early in the Racing Period it is normal to have a body fat percentage greater than the ideal. A gradual weight loss is welcome. But in the middle of the season when your body fat is already down to 3% and you begin to lose weight, watch out. There is no more fat to burn so you will begin losing muscle. I call this "negative metabolism" and it is a dangerous situation. It can be avoided if you keep a record of body weight and match it to periods when you ride strongly and feel good. This will tell you the best weight to race at each season.

It is even better to find out your exact percentage of body fat by using skinfold calipers or underwater weighing. This will help you make the best use of your daily weight checks. Senior men should strive for 3-4% body fat. Juniors can't go quite that low because they haven't matured physically. They still have what we call baby fat. Senior women usually have a high percentage of fat and this means they have a lot to lose. When they get under 10% they are good. It is possible for women to get as low as 6-8%.

If you don't know your percentage for certain there is a very simple way to estimate how much fat you need to lose. First, pinch the skin on the back of your hand. Notice how thin it is—there is no fat there. Now try this on various parts of your legs and face. Once that skin has almost the same thinness as your hand, you are like you're supposed to be.

Skin pinch test

When you look at European professionals you see every vein and muscle. There is no fat on them. It is the same for top amateurs. I remember what used to happen to me when I was in the Academy of Physical Education. They had me on the table all the time during anatomy class. The professor would say, "Eddie, come up here so we can look at your body." You could almost see through my skin. Everything showed. I didn't like this, I thought my body looked terrible. Some fat makes the body look much nicer, but it makes it work worse.

Thermal regulation is one body process that doesn't operate very well when there is the insulation of fat. This is important during hard exertion like cycling because overheating is always a danger. When I first came to the U.S. the only cyclist on

Thermal regulation

the national team who looked like an in-shape athlete was Mark Pringle. The rest had too much fat. This was an incredible hindrance to their performance in an event like the 100 km team time trial. They would sweat out a tremendous amount of water during that race. It's no wonder they were being told to drink four bottles, but what they actually needed to do was lose fat. A fit 100 km rider needs half a bottle at most.

When I first met the U.S. national team, everyone was too fat. Only Mark Pringle, shown here in the 1978 Milk Race, had the lean body of an athlete.

Weight gain is normal until mid 20s

When you are about 24 your body development is complete and your weight should stabilize. Before that you are still growing and developing muscle. This means it is normal for a Junior to gradually gain weight from season to season, and this will continue while he is a young Senior. The 17-year-old Roy Knickman and 18-year-old Rebecca Twigg were fat compared to now. But even though they have lowered their percentage of body fat they have gained a few pounds. What does this tell us? They have developed muscle.

Water in the blood

One other important point related to age: You have more water in your blood when you are young. The result is a big difference in your reaction to temperature when you are under age 24 vs. over 24. When you are 19, for example, a temperature of 90-100F degrees is incredibly hot. When you are older you can take the heat much easier. However, you will have a harder time in the cold because you lack the insulation of baby fat.

Although the planning chart doesn't call for it, blood pressure can be recorded daily as another objective way to judge fitness and recovery. There are now several low-cost, do-it-yourself blood pressure instruments on the market. By testing yourself each morning you may discover a pattern that corresponds with periods of improving form. Among riders who put a lot of value on blood pressure is former professional world road champion Francesco Moser. He uses a daily check to know for sure whether he is on track to top racing condition or something is going wrong. For him, the wider the gap between the diastolic (lowest) and systolic (greatest) pressures, the better his form.

Blood pressure

In the bottom corner of the weight box give yourself a grade (A, B, C, D) on how you feel after you're out of bed and moving around a while. This is subjective, of course, and many times it is the one piece of incorrect information on the chart. You might feel A, but when you go out on the bike you are tired. Or you feel C, then after 15-20 km you are A. This is why your pulse counts are so important. For example, let's say you have intervals planned but you don't feel sharp. If your pulse says your body is normal you know it's okay to ride hard. But if you rate yourself a C or a D and your pulse is faster than usual, you must change your plan and ride easier.

Third small box for self-appraisal

CYCLING DIARY

The seasonal planning chart is a valuable guide and reference, but it is not meant to take the place of a diary. You should keep a detailed account of each day's training performance and how your body is responding. This includes things that don't fit into the chart like diet, weather, equipment, position adjustments, etc. There should also be a detailed account of your performance in each race. Lazy riders don't like to do this writing, and neither do some older riders who have lots of experience and who think they know their body. But a diary is important for everyone. It remembers things much more clearly than the brain does.

In some countries a national team rider *must* make an entry in his notebook every day. It is this way in Poland, for example. The coach checks it monthly. In fact, the coach keeps his own notebook with the basic training plan and one page for each rider with personal information like shoe size, frame size, birthdate, etc.

When it is the proper time of year the coach goes to each rider and says, "Next week we will sit down together and formulate your plan for next season. In the meantime go through your diary completely, analyze the information, and write down your ideas." This is for experienced riders, of course. For others, the coach stands in front of a blackboard and gives them the plan they all will follow.

EVOLUTION TO A HARDER PROGRAM

It is necessary to have a yearly program that gets harder as you get older. This means harder racing as well as harder training. Year by year this builds the foundation for maximum development. In fact, as a rider matures it is natural to want to race in place of training. Alexi Grewal told me this is how he began feeling in 1983 and I understood exactly what he meant. He was just 22 then but he had been involved in bike racing for half his life. He no longer was finding the many kilometers of the Preparation Period as enjoyable as he once did.

Racing for training

This isn't bad, however. In Grewal's case he was at the point where he could benefit from more and harder racing, racing that would actually do more for his development than training. This will become true for you, too, if you are still maturing. As you get older you will want to undertake a harder racing program. You will want to add difficult races, longer races, stage races, and compete against better riders. This is a natural part of growth as a bicycle racer.

But even when that time comes, a lot of training must still be spent on improving weak points. Strong points are what produce results; weak points are what limit them. When your weak point is endurance because you are young or because school or work does not allow enough training time, your goals must be realistic in reflecting this. It wouldn't be wise to put your current hopes on long-distance road races, but you can make them your long-term goal.

If you are a first-year Senior, for example, you do not have the endurance to race 180 km. As a Junior you could do 120 km, but you cannot increase by 50% in just one year. At 130, 140, 150 km you will be much more tired than riders five years older than you. They have built endurance during their additional years on the road. Don't avoid long road races and short stage races, but ride them for training and long-term preparation, not for results. Instead, make it your current goal to excel in shorter events like criteriums.

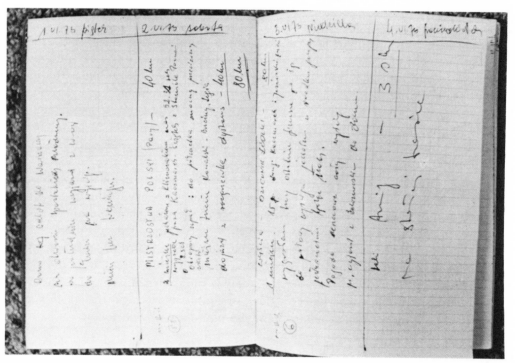

These are the personal notes made by a member of Poland's national team. You must keep a diary and learn from it if you want to make maximum improvement each year.

SUMMARY

For a racing cyclist the year has three parts. It begins with the six-week Rest Period between the end of the old season and the start of the new one. Next comes the 18-week Preparation Period, which itself has three parts. Then it is time for the Racing Period.

The general early season program of rest and winter preparation discussed in Chapter 3 is good for everybody—all riders do it the same way. Then we come to training with intervals, and that's when the program becomes different for long-distance road races, criteriums, time trials, and stage races. Also, there are differences in the way to peak for a major race in each type of event. This will be explained in detail in the appropriate chapters.

Just in case I have left any doubt: *It is absolutely essential to have a yearly training plan.* If you do not have one you cannot be organized. You will not be sure of what you are doing, and you will waste time. Self-discipline is a vital part of this. Make the plan, stick to the plan, and evaluate the plan. Racing success is never black and white, so you must develop all the information possible to design a plan for each new season. It is the only sure way to improve.

When one of my riders loses I am not mad if he knows *why* he has lost. When he is bad he must know why he is bad, and when he is good he must know why he is good. When he does know I am so happy. It means he is ready to be a good bike rider. He can tell me everything about his season—his total racing kilometers, his total training kilometers, how much cross-country skiing he did, how much weight training, how many hours in the gym . . . everything. And he knows how this is different than in past years. By himself he can design this season to be better than last season, and next season to be better than this one. It doesn't happen easily, but it can't happen at all if the information isn't kept and analyzed and used.

It all has to begin sometime, and there's no better time than right now. Okay? Let's see exactly how to find your best position on the bike, and then how to prepare your yearly plan for training and racing.

Riding Position

Newcomers to cycling have no idea how complicated it is to arrive at correct position on the bike. And they have no idea how important it is. They don't understand why the handlebars are shaped so funny and why the seat is so skinny. They never heard about shoe cleats. They don't know how to position the brake levers, the handlebar stem, the saddle on the seat post, and the seat post in the frame. And even before getting to those matters there is the question of the correct frame size.

If you are just beginning your racing career (or finally getting serious about it) I recommend a bike with a standard production frame. You will do perfectly well on a factory frame as you learn the sport. Later it might be helpful to have a frame custom built *if* you have peculiar body dimensions. For example, you may be among those with a long torso and short legs. A custom-designed frame can help put you in a better riding position. It is riders with the opposite condition—long legs and short torso, like we saw in Riviere, Baldini and Coppi—who seem to have an easier time setting up a good position on any bike. They have an easier time getting comfortable.

If you don't now have a custom frame or you can't afford one, it isn't something that should prevent good performance. Ryzard Szurkowski won the 1973 Amateur World Road Championship on a factory bike. The whole Polish national team rode absolutely average factory bikes for several years. We had no trouble getting correct positions. However, if you are built like Bill Walton it is a different story. No factory bike can come close to fitting a big guy like him. A custom frame then becomes a necessity, not just a nicety. Bill has a lot of interest in cycling and has even done some track racing in San Diego, where he plays pro basketball. California framebuilder Ted Kirkbride and I worked together in 1979 to come up with a frame that would fit a 6-foot-11 rider. As the photo shows, it's not your usual design.

Nowadays many factories that manufacture high-quality frames are in effect making custom frames. As seat tubes vary in length so do top tubes, angles, wheelbases, etc. Like individual framebuilders, factory research departments have studied the position problems of riders of various sizes and they've come up with design solutions. Unless you have a body that is wildly out of proportion, a quality factory frame should fit you fine in all respects, assuming it is your correct size.

What is your correct size? I am a coach, not a framebuilder, so my ideas are based on what I see that works. I sort of go at it backwards to decide frame size. This is my basic rule: After the correct saddle height is determined *(see below)*, 8-12 cm of round seat post should show out of the frame. The average is 10 cm, but a range is necessary because in some frames the top tube is proportional to the seat tube. For example, a 58 cm frame will have a 56 cm top tube; a 60 cm frame will have a 58 cm top tube. If you have a relatively long upper body you need a longer top tube, so you may have to ride a frame with a longer seat tube than you actually need. Not every frame manufacturer goes by this proportion, of course, so by checking around you may be able to find a factory frame with ideal seat- and top-tube lengths even if your body dimensions are unusual. If you have no luck, the solution is a custom-designed frame.

How to determine
correct frame size

It took a custom frame for basketball star Bill Walton to get a good riding position. At 6-foot-11 (210 cm) he needed something special, but most other riders can do perfectly well on a mass-produced frame.

It is not a bad idea to go for a frame on the small side, a frame that shows you 12 or even 13 cm of seat post. A smaller frame saves weight, which is an important advantage. It will also be stiffer than a larger frame. This is good for your jump and acceleration. On the minus side, a light, short frame will often be less stable on descents and in corners. It can also create difficulties in setting up your position. For example, you may have to move the saddle back in order to have a comfortable upper body, and this could put you outside the proper knee-over-pedal relationship that I discuss below. It may also require the stem to be positioned far out of the frame and/or to have an extraordinarily long extension. Either condition increases the risk of a stem breaking. To avoid such problems you must compromise. Choose a slightly smaller frame as long as it will allow your correct position, but do not sacrifice strength and handling for the sake of a little less weight.

Smaller may be better

If you are ready to buy your first pro bike, start by getting together with a friend who is close to your body size and who has a racing bike that fits him well. Carefully record his position so it won't be lost, then adjust the bike to fit you by using the guidelines in this chapter. After doing so you will be able to determine if the frame also has the correct seat- and top-tube lengths for you, or if the one you buy should be different somehow. Of course, if there is a cycling coach available ask him to give you a hand with this.

Other good methods to determine frame dimensions are the Serotta Size-Cycle and the Fit Kit. A shop that has either of these systems can help you a lot. Always remember, however, that a bike shop is a business. The people who work there want to sell you something. Be wary of anyone who immediately says, "Oh, I have the *perfect bike* for you." A shop that is really interested in helping you will let you set up your position on several bikes. A good shop will work hard to make sure the bike you finally choose fits just right.

Be your own mechanic

It is best to assemble a new bike yourself. In the U.S. the bike shop often builds it up, which is convenient but it makes you lazy. Also, you can't always trust a shop. Many times the mechanic is only average, or it is a young person who is learning the trade. He must work quickly by the hour and he can't take the time to do the thorough job you can do. A cyclist has to be able to trust his own hands more than those of the average bike shop mechanic.

Work with your bike like you handle a baby—with care and enjoyment. You should love your bike and love working on it. You should want each component to be the best and to work perfectly. I believe it is very important for every cyclist to be a good mechanic. When you come to the Olympic Training Center you will even see Rebecca Twigg and the other women working on their bikes. The only time a mechanic should be necessary is during the racing season when you don't have the time or energy to do the service. In a stage race, for example, you must trust the mechanic. But you also must carefully check the bike yourself after he has finished with it. Each morning say hello to the bike, ride it to breakfast, and make sure it is working correctly. You are the best judge of your bike.

I encourage all riders, even national team members (like Tom Doughty shown here), to do their own bike maintenance. When you know exactly how the bike works, it increases confidence and enjoyment.

When you know how every part of the bike works, it is much easier to use the bike correctly. When you have installed and adjusted each component, when you have had your hands into everything, it adds greatly to your confidence as a rider. It helps you know whether everything is perfect or something needs to be fixed or replaced. I don't include the building of wheels as part of a cyclist's expertise because it is a special talent. Not many riders learn to do it well, but some professional mechanics do it very, very well. Usually it's best to let a proven wheelbuilder handle the job, especially when dealing with unusual spoking patterns like one-cross, two-cross, and radial. It takes knowledge, experience, talent and accurate equipment to build these wheels right.

Leave wheel building to experts

When setting up your riding position do it with the bike on a wind-load trainer. This makes it easy to climb on and check each adjustment. Be certain the bike's top tube is level with the floor. Use two large mirrors so you can see yourself on the bike—one mirror for the front and the other for the side. These will show you things you can't feel. (For the same reason I recommend using mirrors when you train indoors. They let you spot problems with position and pedaling technique.) It is also very helpful to have a fellow rider or a coach work with you. His eyes may see things that you don't, and he can make measurements for you while you are on the bike.

Use mirrors and a helper

Be certain to pedal a few strokes each time you remount. This will move you into your natural, comfortable position on the saddle. Without pedaling you might only think you are sitting as you normally do while riding. If you're not, all the position adjustments will be wrong when you get out on the road.

Always pedal

NEW FINDINGS ABOUT SADDLE HEIGHT

In 1976 when I left Poland, the heels-on-pedals measurement for saddle height was correct and I used it in the U.S. You are probably familiar with this method. You pedal backwards with your heels and saddle height is adjusted until your knees almost straighten at the bottom of the pedal circle. For years this was the way road riders around the world set their saddle.

In 1980 when I returned to Europe for the first time, I noticed right away that saddle position was different. It was a logical response to changes in the length of races. When I was a cyclist I rode stages of 240 or 250 km and classics of about 220 km. Gradually the average amateur road race dropped to about 180 km, and stages were shortened to around 160 km or less. That's a big difference. There have also been changes in the condition of the roads (they used to be rougher with more cobbles) and in the weight of equipment (much lighter now). All this has resulted in faster average speeds on shorter and usually hillier courses. For this type of racing a higher saddle position is more efficient because it produces more power. The fact that a lower saddle protects knees from strain has become less important as race distances have been cut back.

Why saddles have gone up

A lot was made of it when Cyrille Guimard, the Renault director, raised Greg LeMond's saddle 5 cm or so right after Greg joined the team. Some people thought his position in the U.S. must have been totally wrong. Actually, a portion of that adjustment was necessary for one simple reason: LeMond was still a growing teenager and it had been a while since his last position check. Guimard apparently made the rest of the increase because of his preference for a very high saddle position. We should remember, however, that there can be too much of a good thing. Guimard's own career was cut short by knee problems. His best rider, Bernard Hinault, whose position is very high and who races at distances 50% longer than amateurs, had a knee injury severe enough to take him out of the 1980 Tour de France. In 1983 Hinault's other knee developed tendinitis and he underwent surgery in mid-season.

Everyone is different and we must never forget it. My knees are different from yours, and yours are different from the next rider's. One rider will handle a high saddle position easily, the next one will have all kinds of trouble. When I saw the higher saddles in 1980 I began checking bikes and riders. I measured the Russians, Czechs, Poles, Italians, French, and English. I found that most riders had a position not determined by a formula from their coach but by their own perception of what worked best.

The Hodges study

In April of 1982 our national Junior coach, Mark Hodges, who is an exercise physiologist, did a study at the Olympic Training Center that shed light on how saddle height affects a rider's oxygen consumption. This is an important relationship. We wanted to find out if there was a certain saddle height that would allow a rider to perform a set amount of work with less expenditure of energy than at any other height.

Hodges devised a hydraulic seat post so a rider's position could be changed during the test without interrupting his effort. Eleven riders participated, including Thurlow Rogers, Alexi Grewal, Roy Knickman, Leonard Nitz and Brent Emery. Each rode his own road bike attached to an ergometer-like device so pedaling resistance could be precisely set. It was a very strict procedure. An electronic metronome established a 90 cadence and a fan blew air at the same velocity the rider would have felt had he been pedaling on the road. Standing up or changing position on the saddle in any way was not permitted. Everything possible was done to make sure that saddle height was the only variable.

Each rider was tested twice the same day. He rode for 45 minutes, recovered completely, then went another 45 minutes. He experienced 10 different saddle heights, including his own. The heights were based on a percentage of his leg length, from 92% to 100%. In this case, leg length was precisely determined by combining bone measurements from the top of the femur to the bottom of the heel (see below). Max VO_2 tests were given and each rider's workload was set at 80% of his maximum, which made him pedal hard but kept him from passing his anaerobic threshold.

During each 45-minute test a rider's saddle was raised or lowered 5-6 times. The changes were randomly assigned and came every 6-8 minutes. This interval gave the rider time to reach a steady state of performance at each new height. The rider never knew what height he was using at any time. He concentrated only on keeping a steady 90 cadence and keeping still on the bike.

Each rider's oxygen consumption per minute was recorded for the 10 different saddle heights. The chart below shows the findings for the group as a whole.

What do these results tell us? Based on this group of riders, who were pedaling against a constant heavy workload as in time trialing, the most efficient saddle height was 96% of leg length. Why? Because it was where the lowest oxygen consumption value occurred. In other words, it took less energy to do the work at 96% than at any other saddle setting. It is significant that 96% produces a higher saddle than the traditional heels-on-pedals method.

Saddle Height (% of leg length)	Mean Oxygen Consumption (liters/minute)
92	3.65
93	3.53
94	3.57
95	3.50
96	3.35
97	3.58
98	3.68
99	3.78
100	3.91

Seven of the 11 riders came into the study with a saddle lower than 96%. Alexi Grewal had the lowest percentage of all and he was the only one of the seven who did not fit the pattern of benefitting from a higher saddle. A possible reason is that he has a considerable leg length discrepancy. One leg is almost 2 cm shorter than the other. At this writing, Grewal, at about 93%, has the lowest position of any leading U.S. road rider.

For you to benefit from this study you must know how to measure your legs properly. According to Hodges, by determining the trochantric leg length it is possible to closely approximate his technique of adding the measurements of various leg bones. This is how to proceed:

1. Stand barefoot on a hard surface with your buttocks and heels against the wall. The balls of your feet should be 15 cm apart.
2. Begin with the right leg. Have your helper put a mark on the center of rotation of the greater trochanter of the femur. This is the most outward bump on the hip where the leg bone inserts into the hip socket. To make sure of the center of rotation, lift your knee until your thigh is parallel to the floor. If the mark moves forward or up with the leg, the mark is not on the center

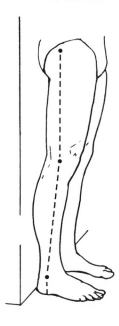

Hodges method for leg measurement.

on the center of rotation. Relocate the mark until it does not move.

3. Put a mark on the outside center of your right knee over the iliotibial tendon. This is the prominent bulge about 2 cm back from the center of the kneecap. The mark will be about halfway between the front and back of the knee.

4. Put a mark on the center of the large bone on the outside of your right ankle.

5. Repeat steps 2, 3 and 4 for your left leg.

6. Have your helper measure each leg three times, beginning from the hip mark, going through the knee mark, through the ankle mark, and to the floor. Do these and all other measurements in millimeters.

7. Average the three measurements of each leg, then find the average of both legs. Multiply the answer by 0.95.

8. Measure the thickness of the sole of the shoe at the cleat, and measure the height of the pedal cage above the top of the center section that houses the axle. Add the total of these measurements to the number that resulted from step 7.

Now you are ready to set the saddle height. Here are the steps:

1. Remove the left pedal.

2. Place the left crank arm pointing downward in direct line with the seat tube.

3. Lay a straightedge on top of the saddle, from front to back.

4. Measure the distance from the center of the hole in the crank arm to a point midway between the top of the saddle and the straightedge. Move the saddle up or down until this measurement equals the number arrived at in step 8 above.

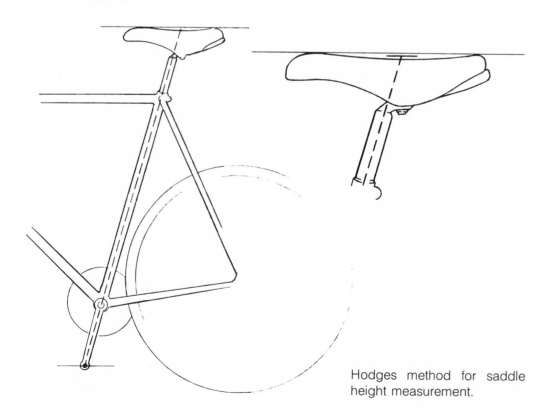

Hodges method for saddle height measurement.

When you are finished you will be very close to the 96% saddle height that was determined to be most efficient. But remember that a change in pedals, shoes, crank length and even shorts (padded v. unpadded) may make it necessary to repeat the whole measuring and adjustment process.

Now let's look at several key points Hodges makes in evaluating his study: Hodges' key points

- Once past 96% there is a rather sharp increase in oxygen consumption. A rider will be more efficient at 94, 95 and 96% than he will at 97%. This means it is better to have a saddle slightly lower than the optimum rather than slightly higher.

- Only Thurlow Rogers already had his saddle at 96%. Seven of the others were below this level, three were above it. All were found to be almost as efficient at their normal saddle height, no matter what it was, as at 96%. This points out the value of the muscle memory that develops when a rider trains many kilometers in the same position. (By the way, in order to participate in the study, all riders were required to have used the same saddle height for at least one year.)

- A saddle higher than 96% may produce even greater power, but the price is less efficient use of energy. This is why experienced riders move on the saddle. When they need more power for climbing or making a hard chase, they slide to the back. This can effectively increase saddle height by as much as 2 cm. Once the effort is over, they move forward to their normal, efficient position.

- The findings of the study are applicable to time trialists in particular and road racers in general. They cannot be extended to track riders, even pursuiters.

- The study was done on men and does not apply to women because of the difference in pelvis width, crotch height, and foot length.

- For the male rider of average height, the difference between 94% and 96% of leg length equals 18 mm of saddle height. So there is a rather large range for optimum position. The important thing is to arrive intelligently at a certain height and then keep it. Don't fool around making small changes, and don't raise or lower the saddle for different types of races. You must maintain a stable position so your body can adapt to it and develop maximum efficiency.

- It is impossible to give an exact formula that *every* rider should use to set his saddle. There are too many variables, such as saddle fore/aft position, pedaling style, foot length, shoe construction, pedal design, etc.

Most of our national road team riders are now using a saddle height about 10-12 mm higher than what results from the heels-on-pedals method. This correlates with 96% of leg length. But who knows? Maybe five years from now, because of new research or changes in the design of saddles, shoes and pedals, seat height will be based on a whole new formula. I expect computer technology to at least help us come up with ways to be more precise in using the method I'm about to outline.

HOW TO SET UP THE TOTAL POSITION

What follows is my method for finding the optimum riding position. Saddle height is the first adjustment. It is based on what we have learned from Mark Hodges' study, and from measurements I have taken on top international road riders at events like the World Championships. I advise double checking by using both my method and the Hodges method. Remember that there is a range in which the height is correct.

Here is the procedure:

1. Look at your cycling shoes. The shape of the sole has an effect on saddle height. Among the many different shoe models there is a wide range of sole thicknesses. Some, like Adidas and Vittoria, have almost a uniform thickness from toe to heel. Others, like Sidi, Le Coq Sportif and Marresi, have a sole that is thin at the toe and heel but it thickens under the cleat. When this is the case you have to compensate when setting the saddle height, as we will see in a moment.

2. Look at your pedals. Most pedals for road racing, including the widely used Campagnolo SL and Shimano DD pedals, are designed with a distinct top and bottom. Of course we want to use the top for the saddle adjustment procedure, so you must remove the toe clips and straps.

3. Look at your saddle. There should be no tilt—the area you sit on should be parallel to the top tube. At least that's the place to start, and most riders find it is best. If a *slight* tilt one way or the other seems better for you, and riding proves it, go ahead and be different. But don't be crazy. Once a rider told me he tilted the nose of his saddle down so he would feel like he was always going downhill. The saddle must be essentially level so you can use all of it. When you are pushing hard on the flat or climb, it is natural to move to the rear of the saddle to get more leverage for your legs. You are looking for power. But during a sprint you move to the nose. That's what your body tells you to do.

4. Put on your cycling shorts and sit square on the saddle in your normal riding position. Have your helper put the right crank arm straight down (6 o'clock) and hold the pedal top side up. Straighten your leg and try to touch the pedal with the heel of your shoe. *Do not move your hips to help you reach.* If you have shoes with a uniform sole thickness, saddle height is correct when 5-8 mm of space remains between the heel of the shoe and the pedal. Although this is slightly lower than some international riders now use, it prevents you from mistakenly putting the saddle too high. As the Hodges study says, a saddle that is slightly lower than optimum will still be almost perfect once your body has adapted to it.

Compensate for sole thickness

In most cycling shoes the thickness of the sole varies. Find out exactly how much in your shoes by taking out the laces and measuring with calipers. Let's say you find the sole is 5 mm thick at the heel and 15 mm thick at the cleat. That's a 10 mm difference, so the clearance between heel and pedal should be 15-18 mm. In other words, the difference in sole thickness is added to the 5-8 mm gap you are trying to achieve. If you use an insole or orthotic, leave it in the shoe so it will be included in the measurement. (You begin to see now why you must not ride in shoes that are too big for you. If your feet can move inside by even half a centimeter it will throw off your saddle adjustment.)

Compensate for foot length

Why do I have a 4 mm spread for proper saddle height? This is to accommodate feet that are relatively long or short compared to leg length. If your feet are longer than normal for people your height, you need to go toward an 8 mm gap to the

When measuring the sole thickness of your cycling shoes, make sure to put the calipers inside the cleat slot.

pedal, or even 9 or 10. If your feet are relatively small, the gap should be 5 mm or even 4. If your foot length is average, use a gap of 6 or 7 mm. The saddle height you finally settle on should be the one that feels the best and also looks right to your coach. The final decision is made on the road.

After you have gone through the adjustment procedure with one leg, do it with the other. This will help tip you off to a leg length discrepancy. Almost everyone has a difference of a couple millimeters and it doesn't cause any problems. If you find a considerably greater variation, however, you must correct it. We've found that the best solution is to use a piece of leather or rubber under the cleat to build up the sole of the shoe of the short leg. This is what Alexi Grewal, Roy Knickman and other riders have done. Without such a correction in cycling shoes and other footwear, serious structural problems can develop in the body. One is static scoliosis, a form of curvature of the spine.

Compensate for leg length discrepancy

There is an even better way to find out if you have a difference in the length of your legs. Lie down on your back and have your coach or friend pick up both your legs by the heels. He should shake them easily to loosen them, pull them gently to stretch them out, and lay them down together. Now he can see how your ankle bones match up with each other. If they are even or just slightly off, you don't have anything to worry about. But if there is a difference of a centimeter or more you should take corrective measures. It wouldn't be a bad idea to consult an orthopedist or podiatrist. Look into having a pair of orthotics made for your walking shoes to even up your legs and also eliminate any pronation problems. Build up the sole of your cycling shoe as Grewal and Knickman have done.

Saddle height remains the same for all road racing, with two exceptions. As I explain in Chapter 8, you should lower the saddle slightly after about the fourth day of a stage race. In Chapter 6 I discuss the reason you should install longer crank arms for a time trial, which has the effect of raising the saddle although it is not actually moved. In general, when cycling events get shorter the basic position on the bike should be higher. Track pursuiters sit higher than road riders, and track sprinters sit higher than pursuiters.

Lower the saddle in winter

In winter the saddle must be lowered. Why? Because of the extra clothes you are sitting on. If saddle height remained the same as in summer the clothes would make it too high. Also, raise the handlebar stem a centimeter or so. Speed is much lower in winter and there's no reason for an aerodynamic position. It is uncomfortable to bend over the bars when you are wearing lots of clothes.

Note to tourists

Finally, there are certain riders who should not use the high saddle produced by the above procedures. Tourists don't need it because they are not concerned with maximum power. For long distance a lower saddle is better — remember, one reason saddles have gone up is because races have gotten shorter. When the saddle is lower the knee is extended less. It is less active and there is less strain on it. This is an important consideration for a tourist who is making 5,000 pedal revolutions every hour, or 25,000-40,000 each day for many days in a row.

Note to riders with injured knees

Anyone who has had a knee injury resulting in surgery is usually better off with a lower position. But sometimes with tendinitis in the knee a higher saddle is better because it makes the knee push. It's hard to say . . . it simply comes down to how the knee feels. Experiment and precisely record the exact saddle heights you use. Seek the advice of a coach and the doctor who is familiar with your knee.

Note to Juniors

Juniors: Your riding position must be checked and adjusted every two months. If you let more time than that go by, it's possible your saddle position might become 1-2 cm too low. It can happen that fast when you are still growing. For example, Roy Knickman grew 4 cm during one season. He was going from correct position to incorrect in a matter of weeks.

Cleat adjustment

After saddle height has been set, adjust the shoe cleats. There are two variables: (1) location of the cleat front to back; (2) rotation of the cleat to align the foot on the pedal. There is also the matter of the angle of the foot when it is at the bottom of the pedal stroke. This is determined in large part by saddle height — a higher saddle means a higher heel.

Fore/aft location

For a normal foot with toes of normal length, the cleat should be positioned to put the center of the ball of the foot over the center of the pedal axle. This is the minimum position. Riders with relatively long feet and anyone who rides long distances will find it best to cross the line and have the center of the ball of the foot slightly forward of the axle.

I believe the type of riding you do is what actually determines correct fore/aft foot placement. Track riders, especially the sprinters, tend to do best with their feet back slightly so they are more on their toes. Road racers usually prefer to be deeper into the pedals, to have the center of the ball of the foot as much as 1-1.5 cm in front of the pedal centerline. Position your cleats with these guidelines in mind and then ride the bike. The most important thing is what feels best to you.

Rotation

When setting the rotation of the cleat you must consider whether you have excessive pronation or supination of the foot — that is, how much your foot tends to roll inward or outward, respectively, during pedaling. Also important is the size of the ankle bone and the basic structure of the legs—whether you are bowlegged, knock-kneed, or have normal straight legs. These things affect the position of the knee in relation to the bicycle. If your legs and feet are normal, rotate the cleat to the point where your ankle bone has 5 mm clearance when it passes the crank arm.

Do you have a problem with pronation or supination? You can tell by looking at the sole of your cycling shoes. In front of the cleat is an imprint made by the pedal cage. If this line is uniform across the width of the sole, everything is fine. But if it is deeper toward the crank arm side and less visible toward the outside, you are over-pronating. That is the usual problem. Much less common is insufficient pronation (what could be called over-supination), which makes the imprint heavy toward the outside edge of the sole and lighter toward the crank arm side.

To remedy a pronation problem you can try over-the-counter arch supports or get custom-made orthotics, which are much more expensive but eliminate trial and error. Or you can modify the slot of the cleats. This was easy to do in the old days when cleats were made of leather. The pedal cage would cut into the leather until there was even contact all the way across the slot, and you could use a knife or file to help the process. Today it is more difficult with plastic or alloy cleats. Very little material remains under the slot, and what is there is hard to modify.

What you are striving for is super contact between your foot and the shoe, and super contact between your shoe and the pedal. Always do your testing out on the road and make adjustments as necessary. No position is good unless it feels comfortable during the full range of riding conditions. Be aware that the best position for your left foot may not be a mirror image of the right foot.

Best of all, have your cleats professionally aligned with the Fit Kit's Rotational

Pronation and supination

Test by riding

By using the Fit Kit's Rotational Adjustment Device, shoe cleats can be precisely positioned to eliminate twisting forces that might injure the knees.

Adjustment Device. This instrument, invented by former racer Bill Farrell, can be found in many good bike shops around the U.S. We have been using it at the Olympic Training Center since 1982 with very good results.

(For more information about cycling shoes, please see the Appendix.)

Fore/aft saddle position

Now that saddle height is set and cleats are adjusted, you can determine the correct fore/aft position of the saddle.

How to place the plumb line

Put the clips and straps back on the pedals. Climb on the bike, strap in your feet, and pedal for a few moments to let your body move into its normal posture. Sit exactly in the center of the saddle and lean into the bars as you usually do. Stop pedaling with the crank arms perfectly horizontal. Leave the position of your front foot just like it would be if you were riding along on a flat road. Pay attention to the elevation of your heel and be certain it is normal. Hold everything steady.

Now have your helper locate the tibial tuberosity on your forward leg (the tibial tuberosity is the bump at the top of your shinbone just below the knee). Have him hold a plumb line to the rear of the tibial tuberosity in alignment with the shinbone. In other words, eliminate the bump because its size can vary quite a bit from rider to rider. Now see how the plumb bob lines up with the centerline of the pedal axle.

Zero position

For those who ride mainly short road races and criteriums, the string should bisect the axle. This is called the zero position. Move the saddle forward or rearward on the seat post until you get it perfect. As always, be certain to sit dead center on the saddle and pedal a few strokes each time you remount. (The zero position is also correct for track pursuiters. For track sprinters, however, the plumb line should

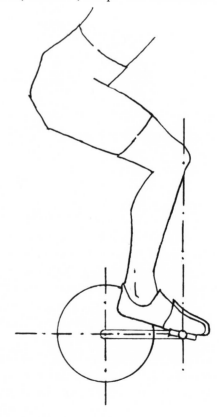

This is the zero position. The plumb line from the knee bisects the pedal axle.

fall 1.5-2.5 cm in front of the center of the pedal axle. This is called a positive position. The longer the sprinter's legs, the farther forward the knee should be.)

Your personal feel on the bike makes it okay to deviate slightly from the zero position. A road racer should not use a positive position, but some riders, especially those who compete often in long-distance events, prefer a negative position by 1-2 cm. That is, their plumb line is 1-2 cm behind the center of the pedal axle. It should never be more than that.

As a final step, recheck saddle height to make sure it hasn't been appreciably changed by the fore/aft adjustment. If it has, correct the height and then recheck fore/aft. Take your time and get it right.

Once you have set the saddle and cleat positions using these guidelines don't just put them out of your mind. Always be aware of how you feel on the bike during the first few rides and make further adjustments accordingly. If possible, have someone shoot a videotape so you can see for yourself how everything looks. It can take as long as two seasons to arrive at the optimum position, but never make a change just for the sake of change. Make it because your body tells you to. As soon as you do feel very good, stop the refinements so your body can develop maximum efficiency.

Toe clips

Toe clips come in four lengths—short, medium, long, extra long—but if none of these sizes is exactly right you can easily create one that is. Do it by putting small washers between the clips and the pedals, or by putting the flange of the clips behind the pedal cage rather than in front. If you have the toe straps in the normal position and they hurt your foot, route them through the pedal in a different way. What is right is what works best for you. Don't let the equipment make you accept a less-than-ideal situation.

Handlebars

For road racing, the width of the handlebars should equal the width of your shoulders. Too narrow restricts the expansion of your chest in breathing; too wide opens you up to catch more wind. Use bars with a flat, straight top, not those that bend forward from the center like most track riders prefer. The curve of the hooks must be deep enough for good support across your palms when your hands are in there. I used to custom bend my bars a little so my hands would fit better. This is not necessary today because there are plenty of different shapes available.

Position the bars so the drops are parallel to the ground. Smart riders cut off the last several centimeters because that part is never used. Your hands should always be somewhere in the hooks when you're riding in a low position. Then you can quickly reach the brake levers by moving only the fingers. This is essential in racing situations.

About 70% of the time you will be riding on the tops with your hands resting on the lever hoods. The levers should be positioned to make this comfortable, but they must also be easy to reach when your hands are in the hooks. Usually both needs will be met if you line up the tips of the levers with the drops of the bars, but this can vary depending on hand size and finger length. When the lever position is finally decided, tighten them enough to stay in place during all normal riding, but not so tight that they can't move without breaking in a crash.

Stem

The height of the stem out of the frame is determined by the height of the saddle (the part you sit on, not the high rear lip some models have). In general for road racing, the top of the stem should be 2-4 cm below the top of the saddle. It may be as much as 6-8 cm below for short races like criteriums and time trials. Comfort is the best way to decide exactly what stem height to use.

How to determine correct extension

The forward extension of the stem is figured in centimeters, not millimeters, because it does not have to be super precise. You can effectively shorten or lengthen the stem during riding simply by changing the angle of your elbows. To determine if the stem extension you have is basically correct, assume a normal riding position with your hands on the brake lever hoods. When you roll your eyes downward to look at the axle of the front hub, it should be blocked from view by the handlebars.

Long training rides and road races will tell you for sure if the stem is right. Should you develop soreness in your trapezius muscle it means the stem extension is too short; when your deltoids and triceps hurt it is too long. In general, a stem as long as 10-12 cm is safe, but 13 cm or longer is getting dangerous. It could break in certain conditions. If you need a stem that long it tells you the top tube of your frame is too short.

Putting it all together

What does a good riding position look like? The elements include

- Straight back
- Slight bend in elbows
- Head tilted slightly to one side to take strain off neck
- Knees close to the frame
- Heels close to the crank arms
- Heels elevated slightly at bottom of crank rotation

Ankle movement

On the last point, a slight amount of ankle movement is normal during the pedal stroke, and some riders will have more than others. Ankle movement, or lack of it, should happen because it is natural. You should *not* consciously try to make your ankles rotate through the pedal circle. Concentrate on making a smooth stroke and your ankles will take care of themselves.

Most riders have a relatively fixed foot position with the toes slightly down. Others, like Roy Knickman, have a very flat foot all the way around. A few, like Leonard Nitz, have an extreme toes-down position. Whatever is natural is good, except if your heel drops lower than the rest of the foot at the bottom of the stroke. If that happens it's a sign the saddle is too low or your foot is not far enough into the pedal.

The descriptions and pictures in this chapter should help you find a very good riding position. But it is still a difficult process, maybe more difficult than you believe. I want to emphasize 10 points that will help you get it right.

1. The bike must be perfectly level. After you set the bike on your wind-load trainer check it with a spirit level on the top tube. Adjust the bottom bracket support if necessary.

2. Have your coach or a cycling friend help you through each step.

3. Check the length of each leg to find out if there is enough of a discrepancy

to require a correction of some type.

4. Sit square in the saddle *every* time you remount the bike. Remain square in the saddle when you do all position tests.

5. Double check everything. Check your right leg, spin a few revolutions, stop, check again. Then do the same for your left leg.

6. Test ride your position. A long road race will tell you the most. Refinements may have to be made for a season or longer, but don't go crazy constantly making miniscule changes. Give your body a chance to adapt.

7. Carefully measure and record all elements of your position as soon as it is basically correct. Update the information whenever a change is made. Then if anything happens to your bike you will save a lot of trial and error in setting up another one.

8. Equip your training bike as much as possible like your racing bike. Use the same model saddle, handlebars, pedals, and shoes, and duplicate saddle height, stem height, etc. A different frame may mean that some position measurements aren't the same, but your position on both bikes must be virtually identical.

9. If you change to a different saddle or shoes or pedals, you must go back and check your position from the beginning. A slight change in one measurement can upset another.

10. Take your time. You can't make your position fast and make it right.

Yearly Training Plan

Each autumn, as soon as you know the dates of winter training camps you can attend and the races that are important to you next season, write them into your planning chart *(see Chapter 1)*. Also write in what you will do in training every day from December 1 to November 30—the racing cyclist's year. It is not as complicated to do this as you might think. This chapter and the one that deals with each specific event—road race, criterium, individual time trial, team time trials, stage race—will give you all the guidelines you need.

The yearly schedule that follows is for riders whose key events come in July and August. This is the time of the USCF National Championships and the Worlds. The schedule is not right if you live where it is warm and you start racing in February and March. If this is your situation, you will have to make adjustments. The same goes if you live in a very cold area and don't start racing until May. But for the majority of American amateurs who begin competing in mid April, who want to perform well thoughout the spring and especially in the big midsummer events, and who continue to race into the early fall, this is the schedule to follow. It is very similar to what is done in European cycling:

1. Rest Period—October 15 to end of November
2. Preparation Period—December 1 to April 15
3. Racing Period—April 15 to October 15

REST PERIOD

What do I mean by Rest Period? Lie down, drink beer and smoke? No. The athlete's life is different. This is an important time for tuning up. After a season of racing, a cyclist's body is tired and so is his mind. An active racer may have competed 100 times. He looks forward to the Rest Period like a worker looks forward to vacation.

Begin by visiting your doctor for a complete medical checkup. I mean *complete*—general tests and special tests. Have an EEG to identify any type of concussion from a crash. Have your blood analyzed. You may have a low red cell count after a hard season. A high white cell count could mean an infection somewhere in the body. Have a urinalysis. Check your heart with an EKG. If you have ever had a broken bone, tendinitis or a similar injury, have this area looked at. Get an eye exam. Go to the dentist—you *must* see the dentist twice a year.

Cut your mileage drastically during the Rest Period. Ride the bike for training

A mountain bike is an ideal way to continue riding during the Rest Period while avoiding the onus of training. Let it take you away from the pavement, the traffic, and the familiar routes. Once the Preparation Period begins, a mountain bike can be used for cyclocross training and for road training in sloppy conditions. The important point is to duplicate the saddle position of your road bike as closely as you can.

three times a week, four times maximum. Seniors should do 50-90 km each ride. These are not fast rides, not hard rides. You can even do some of them offroad in parks and forests. Use your mountain bike to get away from the routes you have used for training all season. Besides this riding it is fine to have casual daily contact with the bike. If you are going to see your friend, forget the car and ride over. If you are going to school, don't drive the car or a motorcycle, ride the bike. Nice and easy.

Reduce length and intensity of rides

From October 15 to the end of November do only what you want to do. Don't go to the gym for weight training and other work—that is coming soon enough. Right now your body is tired, so give it a rest. Enjoy some parties, but stay away from beer, wine and other alcohol. It is bad for your liver. I don't mind if you go disco dancing, but not in places where all the windows are shut and the air is filled with smoke. It will kill your red blood cells. Stick to your good diet so you won't pick up lots of fat and have trouble later when you need to lose it. You won't get fat eating good food because you won't eat as much as when you are racing and training hard. Since you are exercising less now, your appetite will be less. Realize, though, that often the vitamin and mineral content of food is not what it should

Continue eating a sound diet

be at this time of year. Fruits and vegetables might still look pretty, but many times they have been frozen or in cold storage and they are several months old. This is why the blood and urine tests are important—they help make sure you do not have any deficiencies, particularly iron. For safety have a second blood test about late January. If your blood is not good, you won't be able to handle a super program.

Enjoy some other sports in the autumn. If you were once a swimmer, go for some swimming. Go boating and fishing and water skiing. Do you like tennis? Play tennis. Soccer? Play soccer. Hiking? Go hiking. Running? Hold it. Running can be good, but it can be bad, too. In fact, right after the season you can't run. You can hardly walk. If you've seen professional riders they walk like ducks. It takes time to be able to use the legs differently. Personally, I don't like running when it means going to the track or out on the road just to run. It can be too much like bike training. A half hour out, a half hour back. You won't clean your mind that way. Instead, play soccer or basketball. These sports are fun so you don't consider the running, but they make you run a lot. Volleyball, handball, touch football, aerobic dance—play what you like. If you want to stay in the bed, forget it—that's not the right way. There are some restrictions.

During the last two weeks of the Rest Period (November 15-30) you must begin to get ready for the Preparation Period. Lift very light weights once every three or four days to begin waking up the body for serious weight training. Continue enjoying some other sports and riding the bike, but never do anything strenuous two days in a row. You are still resting. You are getting ready for something big.

PREPARATION PERIOD

December 1. The alarm clock rings. The games are over. The fun is done. It is time to work.

Does this sound too early? It is not, believe me. You will see as I explain the program. Besides, you can't let yourself lose too much. If you take a lot more time off, you will fall from the top of fitness to the bottom. That is one stress for the body, and then there is another stress, a bigger one, when you build back up. In my program you take only six weeks off and during this period you sweat when you are hiking, you sweat when you are playing soccer, and you are still riding the bike. You are leading an active life even though your body and mind are being refreshed. A smart rider will not allow too much loss. You might not believe it, but when December comes you will again be hungry for training. Six weeks off is enough.

Now the Preparation Period. How you work from December 1 until April 15 will determine how good you will be during the season. It is a long period, four and a half months, so it is divided into three stages of six weeks each:

1. Body Conditioning—December 1 to January 15
2. Cycling Conditioning—January 15 to end of February
3. Specialization—March 1 to April 15

Diet

Before we begin strenuous work, I want to again emphasize diet. Your body is going to be pushed to the limit at times, perhaps beyond a point of exertion you have

Enjoy other sports

Begin the transition

The three stages of Preparation Period

ever reached before. Why? For the only reason that matters to an athlete: to make the body stronger. But work is only part of the program. Rest is just as important because it is necessary to let the strength develop. And then there is nutrition. Without high-quality fuel, the body cannot function at its best. It cannot develop to its maximum potential. Winter is the time to set the pattern for good eating habits.

You must eat the best food possible. You must also eat a lot, like a farmer. When you are racing or training super hard you can burn 6,000-9,000 calories a day. Your diet must give back this amount or you will lose weight — first your fat will go and then your muscle. This will cause you to become tired, weak and overtrained. So you must eat well, but rather than two or three very big meals a day, eat a minimum of four small meals, or even five or six. This is customary in many countries. The idea is never to overload your system but always to have a supply of energy. There is no question that this eating pattern is better for your health and athletic performance. Research has proved it, and so has the experience of many riders. The meals spaced among breakfast, lunch and dinner can consist mainly of fresh fruits and salads. Knowing that you will have a little more to eat in a couple of hours will keep you from stuffing yourself. I agree with those who say you should always leave the table feeling like you could still eat some more.

Eat 4-6 small meals each day

The day doesn't begin with a big steak for breakfast. When you wake up, record your pulses and then go clean your mouth. Have half a glass of water mixed with a squeeze of lemon and spoonful of honey. This glucose is good for the heart and it wakes up the stomach. Do the deep breathing and stretching exercises I talk about below, visit the bathroom, record your weight, then you are ready to eat. Have some

Breakfast

These European pros, shown at a prerace breakfast, are eating a variety of good food that should be on the table of all cyclists: juice, milk, cereal, eggs, potatoes, pancakes and steak. Your goal at every meal should be to eat the best food possible.

cereal with milk, toast, an egg with lean meat, cheese, juice. Feel satisfied when you leave the table, but not too full.

Breakfast should end about two hours before you go training. Now, I realize that you might train very early in the morning because of work or school. It may be impossible for you to eat and then wait two hours before riding. If so, you simply cannot do strenuous training in the morning. You must never ride on an empty stomach, and yet you can't go hard if you have just eaten. You will have to arrange for afternoon training. Later in the season when competition begins, what to have for breakfast on the morning of a race is simple: Eat exactly what you are used to before hard training. Don't change anything.

Importance of
quality meat

There has been some question in the U.S. about the need for meat in an athlete's diet. I have no reservations about my answer: You must eat it. You must eat better meat and many different kinds—rabbit, mutton, pork, poultry, fish, beef, elk, etc. This variety is important because it gives you a wide range of amino acids. These are the building blocks of protein. They are to the body as bricks are to a house. The various animals have different muscle structures and each type supplies its own assortment of amino acids. The greater the variety you eat, the better. You will get the quality protein necessary for maximum muscle development. For this reason it is wise not to slip into a routine diet. You must not eat only beef, for example. Variety is better for your body and for your appetite.

You have to spend three or four times more money for your nutrition than a nonathlete. You can't eat hamburger and ground junk meat just to cut expenses. That's not good economy. Instead of hamburger you must eat filet mignon and T-bone steak. The meat must also be as fresh as possible. It is best to buy it directly from a farm so it hasn't been subjected to steroids and other chemicals. In addition, go to a farm for all your chicken, eggs, milk, vegetables and fruit.

The best way to eat meat is raw, not cooked at all. Beef prepared like this is known as tartar steak and it is popular in Europe. It is the best meat for your body if you are used to eating it. If you aren't, it can upset your stomach. I won't fault you if you cook your meat, but avoid having it well done. Rare is better than medium, and medium is better than well. The less meat is cooked, the more nutrients it retains. When you cook steak for half an hour, it is about as good for you as the sole of my shoe. The same goes for other meats like fish and poultry, which should always be baked or broiled, never fried. Fried foods are terrible for your digestion.

I believe there are big individual differences in the ability of riders to produce glycogen from the foods they eat. Many bodies can make this muscle fuel very easily from carbohydrates. Some can produce it easily from the fat in meat, which has a lot of energy but is harder to convert. Different bodies can do different things. I still don't think we know everything there is about physiology. So I say that if you like meat and do well on it, you should eat a portion every day (the leaner the meat the better). There is nothing wrong with this, but also nothing wrong with eating meat only four times a week if that's what you feel is best. For sure, meat makes a heavy meal and there are times when it shouldn't be eaten—like two hours before a criterium. However, a diet without meat altogether is very boring and it is likely to lack enough quality protein.

Always emphasize *fresh* vegetables and fruits. These are among the best sources of complex carbohydrates, the No. 1 energy source for an athlete. Grains and grain products like pasta are another. I don't think it's necessary to get too complicated about nutrition, but it is important to understand a couple of basic points. First, the calories in an endurance athlete's diet should break down this way: 60% from carbohydrates, 25% from fat, 15% from protein. If you want to figure out exactly how your meals compare, calculate on the basis of one gram of carbohydrate equaling four calories, one gram of protein equaling four calories, and one gram of fat equaling nine calories. Some sports nutritionists are now saying that any change in the above percentages should go toward more carbohydrates and less fat. But don't make the mistake of thinking this means it's okay to include a lot of sugary foods. These contain very few nutrients and they aren't good for your performance or your health. On the other hand, the complex carbohydrates supply vitamins, minerals and some protein along with the best raw material for formation of glycogen.

Choose unprocessed foods as much as possible. Eat fruits and vegetables raw rather than cooked, and drink their juice—a bike rider must have a juicer. Don't be lazy and get everything out of a can. Buy fresh produce and prepare it yourself. Eat lots of salad made with every different type of vegetable you can find. Breads are good for you, too, but forget those made of white flour. Go for heavy rye breads at a European-style bakery.

Any food will work in your body, but the question is how well it will work. You can't just eat everything great the day before a race and eat junk the rest of the week. You have to eat right month by month and year by year. When it comes down to it, I think the two most important points about nutrition are to eat a wide variety of good foods and always listen to your appetite. When you feel like eating a certain food it is because your body is asking for it, your body needs it. So eat it.

Body Conditioning

Okay, let's go! Body Conditioning. This means rebuilding your base, your foundation. This is your body. You need to strengthen it with indoor training because cycling causes certain weaknesses and damage. Consider how many hours you spend on the bike. Your legs work very hard. Your back works hard or not at all, depending on whether there are hills. It is the same for your arms, but generally they are always in one position. Your abdominal muscles never work. The result is a peculiar build and posture for cyclists. A West European doesn't need to tell me if he was a bike rider. I know by looking at him. When he sits his back bends and his shoulders go forward and down in the same position as when cycling. This posture does not look nice and it damages the body. It closes the chest and that restricts breathing.

Cycling develops the latissimus dorsi and longissimus dorsi because of the work done over the handlebars. These are the large muscles that fan across the back. The former extends and rotates the arms, the latter extends the spinal column. When these muscles are strengthened out of proportion to the abdominal muscles it makes an S shape of the spine. When the S becomes bigger and bigger, it causes pressure on the nerve roots between vertebrae. This pressure causes pain. The usual response is, "Oh, I have to do exercises for my back because it hurts." Wrong—you must do exercises for the stomach and only stretch the back. Now is the time to make this correction, to move the body in opposite ways from riding the bike. The objective is to set your shoulders back, raise your chest, and straighten your back.

Next, tumbling. I was in many crashes when I was racing but I never got a concussion. Why? I know how to fall. As a coach I've always taught my riders how to

Breakdown of calories for an endurance athlete

Emphasize unprocessed foods

Why riders tend to have poor posture

Tumbling

protect themselves and they've had almost no head injuries. Use mats on the gym floor and practice tumbling over the right shoulder, left shoulder and straight ahead. Set up a box or something else a couple of feet high so you can run up and dive over. Extend your arms, tuck your head, and roll across your shoulder and back as you land. If you do this as part of each indoor workout you will develop instincts that can save you from a bad injury in a crash.

Practice diving and tumbling during indoor training to develop the correct instincts when falling from a bike.

In the Rest Period you rode the bike for recreation. Now it is a different story. Now you begin riding for training. During each of the six weeks of Body Conditioning the bike is used a little differently. The first week is easy riding, the second is harder, the third is hard, the fourth is hard, and the fifth and sixth are even harder to make you ready for the Cycling Conditioning period. During these last two weeks, indoor training is decreased. This gives you the extra energy to do more work on the bike.

Cyclocross

Each week of Body Conditioning has four rides, with two of them being cyclocross or climbing. Either will do a good job of increasing your power, but at this time of year I prefer cyclocross, for two reasons. First, it develops super bike handling. You ride on slippery sand or dirt or snow in difficult terrain, but if you fall it is a lot less painful than landing on pavement. (Even so, always cyclocross with a friend in case you do hurt yourself and need help.) Second, when it is winter and you go climbing on the road, you get very hot going up and much too cold going down — and the next day you get sick.

Cyclocross is an essential part of the Preparation Period. Climbing steep hills develops power. Descending rough terrain improves bike handling techniques and confidence.

The best cyclocross course for this training is one you can ride all the way around. The less you have to get off the bike, the better. But if you have to run or jump a few steps it is not bad and it may even help keep your feet from going numb when it is very cold. The difficulty of the course depends on your experience in this type of riding. You have to change once in a while to keep up with your increasing strength and ability. The weather is also a factor. If a snow comes you will have to cut the hills because it's impossible to go up steep ones and too dangerous coming down. But when it is dry, make the course difficult for yourself. Up and down, up and down. Give your muscles, lungs and reflexes some hard work. This training is excellent for developing power.

During Body Conditioning it is not necessary to ride on Sunday. In fact, it's probably better if you don't. All season long Sunday will be a very busy day for you. Make it a free day now. Here's the schedule:

Monday Road ride. Easy for two hours, maybe two and a half if it is warm. Use a fixed gear if you have flat roads to train on. This is economical because it saves your derailleurs and freewheel from being ruined on dirty winter roads, but there are more important reasons: (1) It helps develop a nice 360-degree pedal stroke, which is especially helpful to beginning riders; (2) It is good in the cold because it keeps the legs working all the time; (3) It gives you better control on the snow and ice because you can brake with your legs as well as the calipers; (4) A fixed gear makes the training harder when the roads are bad, the wind is blowing, and the temperature is low. This means you can get the same benefit for less time in

Daily training schedule

the miserable conditions — 50 km in a fixed gear equals about 65-75 km with a freewheel. But you must use a freewheel and derailleur if you train in rolling terrain, since it is the only way to keep a steady pedal r.p.m. At this time of year cadence is what's important, not gears. You must pedal at 90 r.p.m. or more, no matter what size gear this requires.

How to set up a fixed-gear bike

Since track frames often don't have holes for mounting brakes, it is best to set up an old road frame for fixed-gear training. There are several ways to do this. One is to use a rear hub that takes a freewheel on one side and a single fixed cog on the other. Roy Knickman has a setup like this. By turning the wheel around he can use it for riding in rolling terrain (freewheel) or on the flat (fixed). Another way is to install a single fixed cog on a road hub, using spacers to line up the cog with the small front chainring. For training you need a 20-, 21- or 22-tooth cog. These are not too common, but a good bike shop should be able to get one for you. Take off the derailleurs, gear levers and even the large chainring if the shop can get you the shorter fixing bolts required. A third and very inexpensive way is to use an old freewheel that has been welded solid. The cog you want to use should be in a position that gives a straight chain to the chainring.

The winter bike does not need to have an expensive frame. Strength and durability is more important than light weight. It should have lots of wheel clearance and, ideally, cantilever brakes. This will let you easily install fenders. I strongly recommend using them for winter training because they keep you and the bike much cleaner and drier. The best fender for the front wheel has an extra mudguard at the bottom to help protect your feet from spray. Always use a leather saddle or one with a foam and leather covering; an all-plastic saddle gets very cold.

Tuesday　Indoor training. The best time is in the afternoon or evening. Avoid morning, if possible, because the body is still sleepy and stiff. If you have time for exercise early in the day you can do some cross-country skiing, skating of any kind, play basketball, etc., or even take a one-hour easy ride. Do this additional activity for fun, not for hard work. If you have school or a job that eliminates time for anything but the indoor training, don't worry about it. Only the full-time bike rider is able to exercise, rest for several hours, then go to the gym in the evening. The indoor training takes around two to two-and-a-half hours. I will describe it in a moment.

Value of sauna and whirlpool

After the workout take a sauna and whirlpool bath. Ten minutes in the sauna will bring up a nice cleansing sweat and increase your blood circulation. This helps flush the waste products out of tired muscles. The massaging effect of the whirlpool also aids recovery, but don't stay in longer than about five minutes or the heat will drain your energy. Finally, if you can use a swimming pool it is a very good way to end the evening. Don't swim hard, just paddle around and relax in the water for 15-20 minutes.

Warm up well before cyclocross

Wednesday　Cyclocross. It is important to ride about 15 km to warm up before starting cyclocross training. Do this even if the park you use is just a kilometer from your house — ride around town to get there. Wear a lot of warm clothes on the way, then take some off before you start training. Cyclocross for 30 minutes each time during the first week, 40 minutes the next week, then 50 minutes, and one hour. Of course, this depends on how you feel and how hard the course is. In real cold weather take a thermos of hot tea and drink some before and after the training.

If you have flat roads in your area, set up a fixed-gear bike for winter training. One way to do it is to install a rear track hub and combine the fixed cog with the small chainring.

When you are finished, put the extra clothes back on and ride a minimum of 8 km back home to warm down. Then get a hot shower right away.

A lot of riders now have a mountain bike for off-season fun on the trails. Steve Tilford, Roy Knickman and Alexi Grewal are three U.S. national team members who even compete in offroad events. A mountain bike works very well for cyclocross training and even for road training when conditions are sloppy. The 26x2.125 knobby tires are more efficient on snow, slush and soft ground than 700C tires. The important thing if you use a mountain bike is to have a riding position that is as correct as possible *(see Chapter 2)*. Putting the saddle at the right height is no problem, but the wide, flat handlebars won't allow the same upper-body position you have on the road bike. You have to compromise a little. Some riders install dropped bars, although I don't think that's necessary as long as the angle of your back isn't extremely different. Leg position is much more important.

Mountain bikes work well for 'cross training

Thursday   Road ride, same as Monday.

Friday   Indoor training, same as Tuesday.

Saturday   Cyclocross, same as Wednesday.

Sunday   Free day. Do what you like. Stay in the bed if you are tired. Lie around and watch TV or read a book. Build a wheel or work on your bike. Go to the movies. At this time of year I don't like to see you push yourself into more bike riding. If you have energy, go skiing instead. But have some self-control. You are the one who determines whether your program works or doesn't work. You must feel good during this period, not be getting tired.

To sum up the bicycles, you will need two during the six weeks of Body Conditioning: (1) a bike with brakes, fenders and a fixed gear for Monday and Thursday road training; (2) a bike with derailleurs, low gears and strong wheels for Wednesday and Saturday cyclocross training. It can also be used for climbing if a warm spell gives you the opportunity.

WEEKLY SUMMARY
BODY CONDITIONING PERIOD (DEC. 1 TO JAN. 15)

M	Tu	W	Th	F	Sa	Su
Road ride. Easy 2-2½ hours at 90+ r.p.m.	Indoor training	Cyclocross or climbing on road	Road ride. Easy 2-2½ hours at 90+ r.p.m.	Indoor training	Cyclocross or climbing on road.	Free day. Exercise if you wish, but no riding.

Winter clothing

With the beginning of regularly scheduled training rides comes the need to discuss winter clothing. It is critical to your safety. In Poland I have trained when the temperature was 5-10 degrees *below* zero (Fahrenheit). Our national team camps were very strict. There was no such thing as saying, "Oh, it's so cold. We will train if it warms up tomorrow." All of us knew how to dress for such conditions because we were educated by our club coaches. From my experience, I will tell you the steps to take for winter riding safety and comfort. This will be sort of a worst-case situation. You will not have to take all these measures when it is not so frigid. Knowing how to dress for the various winter conditions comes with experience and is part of your development as a bike rider.

Begin with hot cream

Before starting to dress, rub hot cream on your knees, wrists, ankles, elbows, shoulders, and lower back. Use Musclor 3, Capsolin, one of the Cramer formulas, etc., but be careful—they are strong. Go easy until you know for sure how your skin will react.

Underwear

Underwear should be wool or polypropylene. The sleeves of the undershirt must fit longer than normal so they will keep wrists covered in the riding position. If you can't get one with a turtleneck collar, wear a dickey or bandana. Neck protection is very important. The underpants should fit high up the waist and back, and be long enough to keep your ankles covered. A pair of cycling tights with a chamois-lined crotch work well.

Torso protection

For the middle layer on top wear a long-sleeve wool cycling jersey. Or two. Cut the stitching so you have one big rear pocket instead of two or three small ones. Insert a thick piece of wool or felt to give your lower back extra protection. Over everything wear a jacket made of Gore-tex. This is a super material because it keeps out wind and water but it allows water vapor to escape. This prevents you from becoming soaked by condensation from the body heat generated by riding. Again, the sleeves must be very long and the cuffs must not let in wind. The back must extend down to keep you protected in the riding position. There should be a drawstring for the waist, a high, snug neck, and a hood. If the jacket zips up the front, it should have a button-down flap to cover the zipper so wind and rain won't leak in. For ex-

This photo illustrates some of the clothing that helps take the cold and danger out of winter riding. Note the wool or polypropylene hood; the long, insulated snowmobile mittens; the insulated booties; the thick wool tights. Also shown is one of the new generation of Gore-tex cycling jackets. This particular model is made by Mountain Safety Research. It features a high collar, heavy-duty front zipper with snap-down wind flap, zippered underarm vents and pockets, extra-long sleeves with Velcro closures, a drawstring to snug the waist, and a fold-down rear flap to protect against spray from wet roads. The bright yellow color and reflective silver stripes increase visibility on murky days. The Gore-tex material is both waterproof and windproof, yet it permits evaporation of sweat to keep you comfortable. It has proven to be nearly ideal for cold- and wet-weather riding. My advice is to watch for the introduction of new Gore-tex cycling products, and wear them.

tra chest insulation you can put a sheet of plastic between the jacket and top jersey.

One or two pairs of wool cycling tights can be worn over the long underpants, but even better are knickers like cross-country skiers wear. These should be made of double-thick wool. You may even be able to find some that are triple thick around the knees, or you can sew on a pocket and use it as you do the big rear one in the jersey. The knickers should be cut high in the back or, better yet, have a bib top. If no bib, wear suspenders to keep them up around your waist and lower back. (Please note: To maintain proper riding position in winter it is necessary to lower your saddle. You must compensate for all the extra clothing you are sitting on. If you keep the same saddle height as during the racing season, it will be too high in winter.)   **Leg protection**

Feet are a big problem. It is hard to keep feet truly warm, but you must prevent them from becoming painfully cold or numb. Begin by installing covers over the toe clips. Wear knee-length wool socks, two pairs if your shoes won't be too tight. You must be careful not to restrict blood circulation. Shoes should be designed for winter, having high tops and fleece-like insulation inside. Put on gaiters that cover your shoes and lower legs. Gore-tex is the best material for the same reasons mentioned above. The widely available vinyl shoe covers ("booties") do a good job of keeping out salt, sand and snowmelt, but they tend to make feet damp from condensation.   **Foot protection**

Mittens will keep your hands warmer than gloves, so they are the best choice when it is below freezing. Whatever you use, make sure they extend well up the wrists.

Wear sunglasses to protect your eyes from glare, dust and wind. They should have plastic frames rather than metal so they won't freeze your skin. Put plenty of protection on your face, such as Vaseline or a lotion made for cold weather. Some riders   **Head protection** prefer to wear a wool or polypropylene ski mask and this is fine. Cover your ears with fleece-lined ear muffs or a wool hood. Then put on a wool cycling cap with a visor. Pull the jacket's hood over everything and tighten the drawstring enough to keep the wind from going down your neck.

When you protect yourself like this, 5F degrees below zero is no problem. You will be chilly when you begin riding, but the exercise will soon warm you up. Plenty of frost and icicles will form around your head to make you look frigid, and drivers going by won't believe what they are seeing. But you will be comfortable and you won't get sick afterwards.

It is no excuse to miss training just because it is cold. (The exception is later in the winter when speed work begins; intense efforts should not be made when it is below 50F degrees.) However, it's another matter when cold is accompanied by snow and ice. Training can be dangerous then unless you have plowed roads that aren't open to traffic, such as in parks. If people are out jogging on park roads, you should be riding on them. Whenever possible, use routes that have trees to break the wind. Wind makes cold temperatures even more dangerous, of course. It is always best to start out against the wind and then have it blow you back home. This will keep you from working up a heavy sweat and then freezing as the wind cuts into you.

As the snows of winter give way to the cold rains of spring, don't feel that you need to train in the rain to be able to race in it. That is, don't start out when it's raining with the idea that it is a necessary part of your development. You'll get all the wet-weather experience you need on days when you get caught by showers. Don't

In very cold temperatures, wear booties over your cycling shoes. Look for a model with a layer of insulation under a water-resistant material. Gore-tex is a very good choice for booties and for gaiters, which protect the entire lower leg.

look for rain—when you ride every day it will be looking for you. Stay out of it as much as you can. When it's dry for the start but showers are possible, stuff a light rain jacket in your jersey pocket. Be careful, because an hour or more in a cold rain can be dangerous to your health. Go on a shorter ride if rain is threatening, or use a course that has a shortcut home.

Indoor training

At least one day a week during Body Conditioning you should feel great and have a relatively low morning pulse. This will be Tuesday, which follows the free day and Monday's nice steady ride. It lets you know that you are not overtraining. You have the capacity to do more work. This is why you should push yourself hard during indoor training, just like I push my riders. When a session is over I want to see them walking on flimsy knees. They will be if the two hours are spent correctly.

Indoor training begins with 15 minutes of stretches. Do each one that's illustrated, plus any others you like, two or three times apiece. Stretch slowly to the point of discomfort and hold for 30 seconds. Do not bounce. If you are not experienced it is best to stretch under the supervision of a coach or someone else who knows the correct techniques. It is possible that the same movement may do a lot for you, or do nothing. I don't believe that a beginner who is working out alone can possibly do stretches, aerobic exercises and calisthenics correctly. Ninety percent of riders don't even know how to do something as elementary as sit-ups. In fact, they don't

Stretching

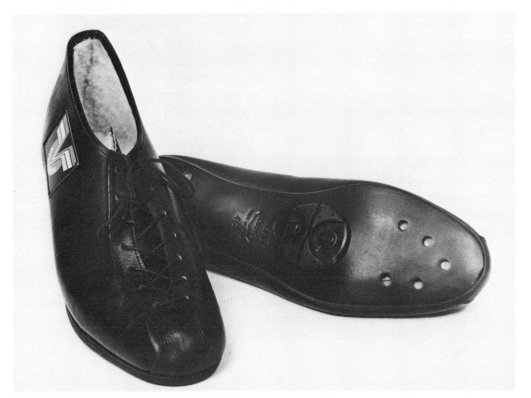

Foot comfort is improved in cold weather if you wear fleece-lined shoes, such as these made by Vittoria. Other important features are the high cut of the leather uppers and their lack of ventilation holes.

even know why they are doing them. They think they are for the stomach when actually they are for the back. (The correct technique is to lie on the floor with knees well bent, feet loose, and hands clasped behind your head. Keep your chin firmly tucked to your chest—that's where most people go wrong. Sit up once straight forward, the next time with a twist to the left, and then with a twist to the right. Alternate like this until you are done. If you can do dozens, make them harder by using an incline board or by holding a weight behind your head.)

During my riding career I never stretched. There wasn't a conscious decision not to, it was just that nobody in European cycling knew anything about it. And, for the most part, they still don't. Instead we did morning breathing exercises to exchange the air in our lungs. About 60-80% of the lungs aren't involved in normal breathing, which means there is lots stale air in there, especially after sleeping all night. The first thing in the morning we went outside for a few minutes to slowly rotate the arms way up and back while breathing deeply. This empties the lungs and fills them with clean air. It is something you should do every morning, too.

Since I've been in the U.S. I've learned a lot about stretching. I realize now how inflexible my body has always been. Generally, I feel that a coach should teach only what he has had experience doing himself, but I have come to believe that stretching is very important. I believe it is better for a cyclist to have a flexible body than to be stiff like most European amateurs and pros. I can see how stretching helps the body relax and be more comfortable on the bike, how it can prevent injury in a fall, and how it can contribute to better posture. I think the many U.S. cyclists who have been doing daily stretching exercises are actually more advanced than their European counterparts.

I recommend stretching twice a day all year round. First, upon getting up in the morning and doing the deep breathing exercise. Second, in the evening before self-massage *(see Chapter 9)*. If you have the time, stretching before and after training is good, but it is not essential. A proper warm-up with some pedaling off the saddle will loosen your body for the workout. Right after, it is more important to get a shower, give your legs a light massage, and get some food.

After stretching, do the aerobic exercises illustrated. These continue to loosen the body. They raise the heart rate and bring up a good sweat, and some of them build strength almost like weight training. They require coordination, concentration, and a partner who is about your size. You must believe in these exercises and like to do them. This part of the workout lasts 30-45 minutes.

Now it is time for 30 minutes of circuit weight training. Remember that you are not a lifter, you are a bike rider. The objective is to condition the body for cycling. You need to correct problems and imbalances, and strenghten the muscles important for riding the bike. Basically, these are the

- triceps
- deltoids
- all back muscles
- abdominals
- gluteus maximus
- all leg muscles

Not many European riders are as flexible as Roy Knickman, because most of them don't include stretching in their daily training. I have come to believe that the flexibility many U.S. cyclists have gives them an important advantage.

I do not like any super intensive forms of weight training for the road rider (as opposed to the track specialist). The best system is a circuit with 10-15 stations that strengthen everything—legs, shoulders, arms, back, and especially the stomach. I prefer that exercises aren't segregated for each part of the body but are rotated. For example, go from legs to stomach to back to arms to stomach to legs, and so on. This training works. It has been used by many riders and more than one world champion.

If you have access to a health club, it is fine to do your circuit training there on the Nautilus or Universal machines. This equipment will produce good total-body conditioning even if you can't use an exercise rotation like I just said. At the Olympic Training Center we have a building that is full of Universal equipment and free weights, but it is difficult for riders to use it when and how they need to. So I have set up a special room for them with stations composed of Universal, free weights, and equipment for stomach exercises. The circuit training illustrations are based on what we have in this room. If you can't duplicate it exactly, don't worry. The important thing is to work all of the muscles listed above, and this can be done with a variety of different exercises. Your cycling coach or a strength coach at the high school or university can help you design a good circuit program with the equipment available to you. A library will have books that show all the exercises that can be done to strengthen each muscle.

Setting up the circuit

The two key factors at the stations that have weights are the amount you lift and the number of repetitions. I want you to train with about 50% of the maximum weight you can handle for one repetition. Remember that your maximum will be more in the third week than in the first, so increase the training weight accordingly. Do 10-15 repetitions in the 20 seconds you are at a station. Take 15 seconds to change stations (or the weight on the barbell), then exercise again for 20 seconds. Go through the entire circuit three times with a three-minute rest before starting again.

Choosing the proper weight

continued on page 92

STRETCHING

The stretches illustrated should be done in the morning and evening all year round. They should also be done to begin each indoor training session. To stretch correctly, extend the position slowly until there is mildly painful resistance. Hold at that point for 30 seconds, back off for a moment, then repeat at least one time. Never bounce to increase the range of flexibility. Where appropriate, stretch in the other direction, with the other leg, etc. Do the stretches in sequence as numbered.

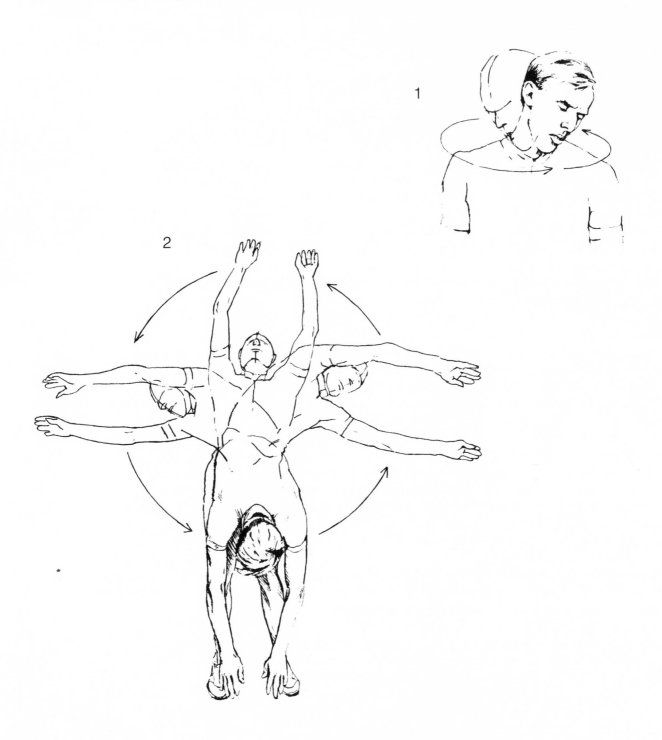

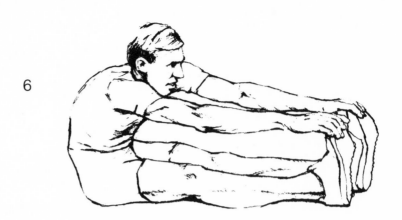

6

7

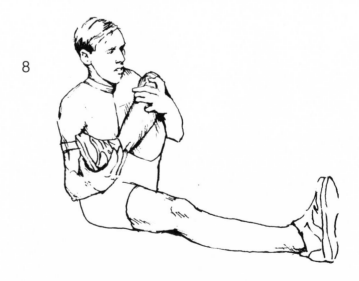

8

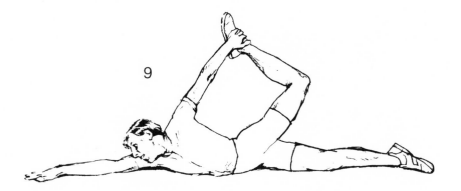

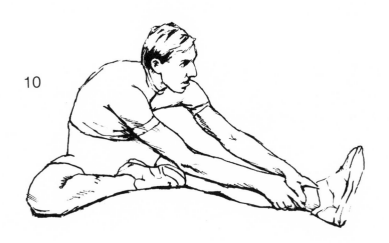

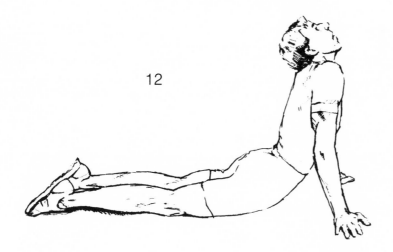

12

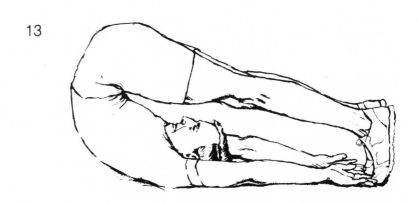

13

14

AEROBIC EXERCISES

Aerobic exercises are the second segment of each indoor training session. Included are elements of the first segment, stretching, and of the third segment, circuit weight training. The key to aerobic exercising is to work at a brisk pace so stress is put on the whole body, including the heart and lungs. Very important are the exercises at the end of this segment, which help a rider learn to coordinate body movements and control body weight. For two-rider exercises to be done correctly, the partners must have nearly the same weight and height.

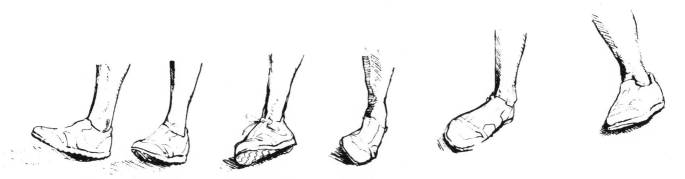

1. Begin by walking for 20 meters in each of these three foot positions. First walk on the heels, next on the outside of the feet, then on the inside of the feet. This loosens and strengthens the feet and ankles.

2. Change to a normal walk, then make a number of exaggerated strides like a cross-country skier. Walk faster, then do a series of steps with high knee lifts and back kicks. Next do some head-high kicks to outstretched fin-

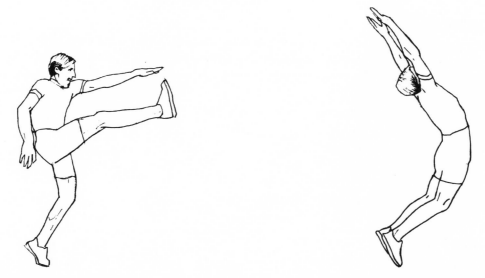

gertips, using each leg. Begin to jog. Jump up every few seconds, reaching as high as possible. Continue jogging and add other movements not shown, such as a sideways cross-over step. The idea is to loosen the body, raise a good sweat, and start breathing hard. Then it is time to begin the specific exercises, each of which is followed by 60-90 seconds of more jogging, kicking and jumping. The heart rate must be kept elevated throughout this segment.

3. Lie on back. Exhale and push hard against the floor with the lower back. Repeat 10 times.

4. Lie on stomach with legs together and arms forward. Arch the back and begin to rock. Go higher and higher. Continue for 30-45 seconds.

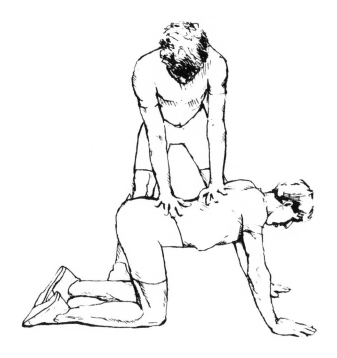

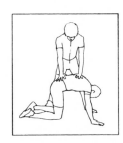

5. Rider A gets on hands and knees. Rider B stands beside Rider A and puts hand pressure on Rider A's back. Beginning from a full sag, Rider A slowly arches his back 10 times. Then the riders reverse positions.

6. Rider A lies on his back with legs together. Rider B kneels beside him and puts his hands on Rider A's chest and thighs. Rider A keeps his chin tucked and raises his legs and upper body simultaneously. Rider A holds the position for 10 seconds against Rider B's hand pressure. After six repetitions, the riders reverse positions.

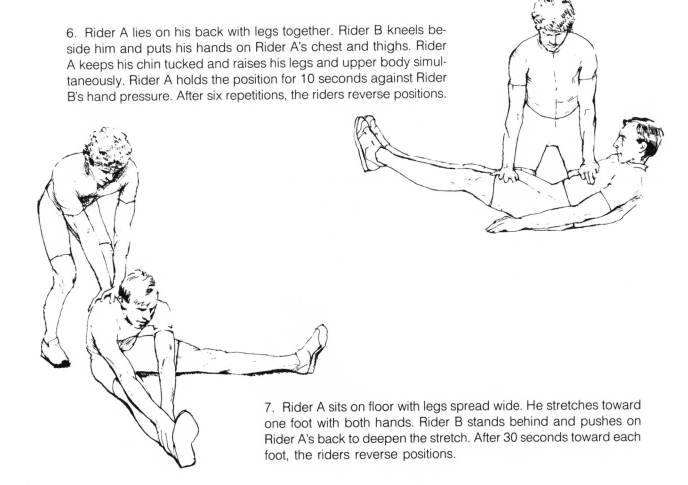

7. Rider A sits on floor with legs spread wide. He stretches toward one foot with both hands. Rider B stands behind and pushes on Rider A's back to deepen the stretch. After 30 seconds toward each foot, the riders reverse positions.

8. Rider A sits on floor with legs together. Rider B places a knee in center of Rider A's back and grasps each of Rider A's outstretched arms at the elbow. Rider B gently pulls the arms backward and upward at a 45-degree angle. After 30 seconds, the riders reverse positions.

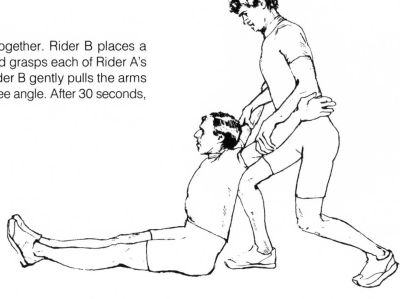

9. The riders stand back to back and interlock elbows. Rider B slowly bends forward, picking Rider A off the floor. This position is held for 10 seconds. Then Rider A picks up Rider B. They continue until each rider has been picked up five times.

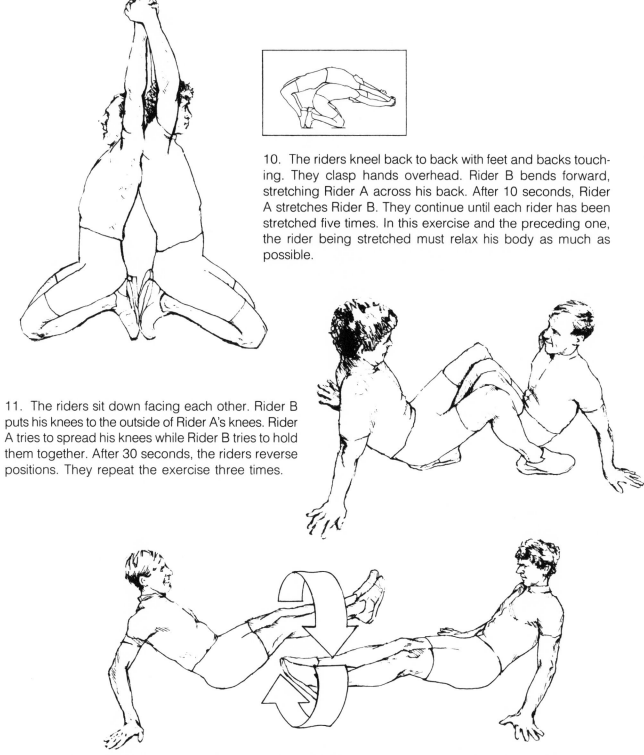

10. The riders kneel back to back with feet and backs touching. They clasp hands overhead. Rider B bends forward, stretching Rider A across his back. After 10 seconds, Rider A stretches Rider B. They continue until each rider has been stretched five times. In this exercise and the preceding one, the rider being stretched must relax his body as much as possible.

11. The riders sit down facing each other. Rider B puts his knees to the outside of Rider A's knees. Rider A tries to spread his knees while Rider B tries to hold them together. After 30 seconds, the riders reverse positions. They repeat the exercise three times.

12. The riders sit down facing each other. Legs are straight. Each rider's feet are at the other's knees. The riders lift their legs and slowly circle each other. Every 15 seconds the direction of rotation is reversed. The exercise is continued to exhaustion.

13. The riders stand side by side with legs spread wide and their feet touching. They grasp each other's wrist. Rider B leans far to the outside, pulling Rider A up onto one foot. They return to the starting position, then Rider A leans over, pulling up Rider B. After five repetitions, they reverse positions.

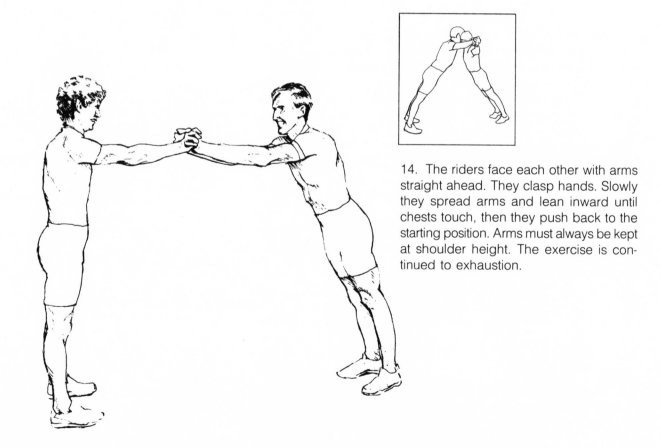

14. The riders face each other with arms straight ahead. They clasp hands. Slowly they spread arms and lean inward until chests touch, then they push back to the starting position. Arms must always be kept at shoulder height. The exercise is continued to exhaustion.

15. Rider B wraps his legs around Rider A's waist. On the count of three, Rider B pushes up hard from the floor while Rider A lifts and steps forward. He holds Rider B high in the air momentarily, then eases him down. After five repetitions, the riders reverse positions.

16. Rider A walks on his hands while Rider B supports him by the ankles. The pace is varied during several trips around the room, then the riders reverse positions.

CIRCUIT WEIGHT TRAINING

Many of the circuit weight training exercises illustrated here are used by cyclists at the Olympic Training Center. They are ideal for a road rider's winter program. If you don't have certain pieces of equipment, consult a weight training book for other exercises that you can do to strengthen the same muscle group. These exercises are not shown in a specific order; set up your circuit so that each succeeding station will work a different part of the body. Note that the first four exercises also are used for the strength test described in this chapter.

Here are the locations of the muscles listed in the exercise instructions: calf = back of lower leg; quadriceps = front of thigh; hamstring = back of thigh; gluteus maximus = buttocks; abdominals = stomach; lumbar = lower back; latissimus = middle of back; trapezius = upper back; pectorals = chest; deltoids = shoulder; biceps = front of upper arm; triceps = back of upper arm.

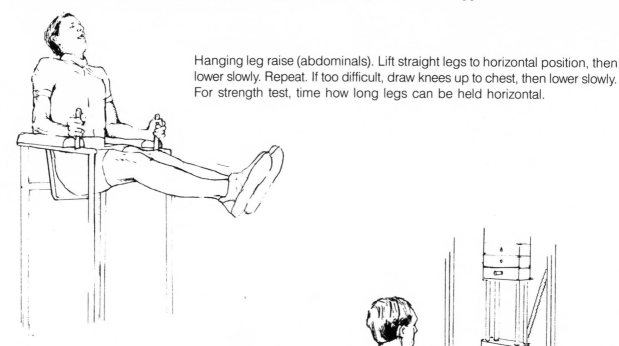

Hanging leg raise (abdominals). Lift straight legs to horizontal position, then lower slowly. Repeat. If too difficult, draw knees up to chest, then lower slowly. For strength test, time how long legs can be held horizontal.

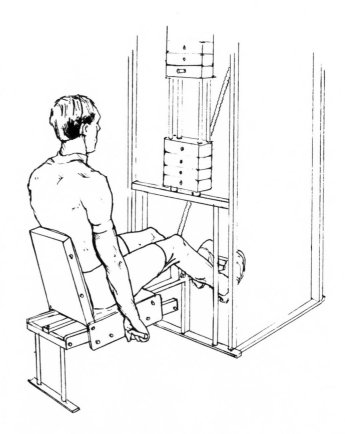

Leg press on Universal Gym (quadriceps, gluteus maximus, calf). Adjust seat so that knee bend is similar to top of pedal stroke. Keep feet parallel. Straighten legs fully and point toes to work calves. Repeat. For strength test, progress to maximum weight that can be pressed once.

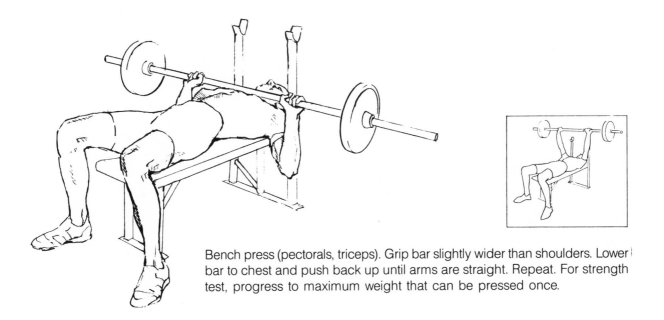

Bench press (pectorals, triceps). Grip bar slightly wider than shoulders. Lower bar to chest and push back up until arms are straight. Repeat. For strength test, progress to maximum weight that can be pressed once.

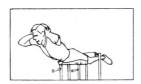

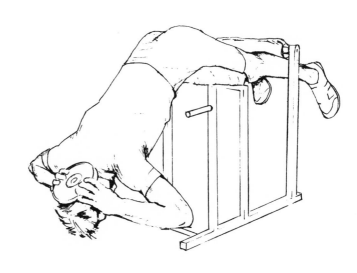

Back hyperextension (lumbar). Bend fully toward floor, then arch up as far as possible. Repeat. Hold weight behind head to increase resistance. For strength test, count the repetitions until torso can no longer be raised above horizontal.

Dumbbell kickback (triceps). Stand with one foot forward and knees slightly bent. Move arms fluidly as if cross-country skiing. Concentrate on making full rearward extensions.

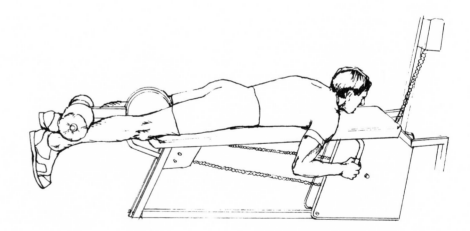

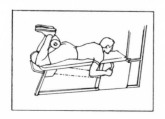

Leg curl on Nautilus machine (hamstring). Lie on stomach with knees just off end of bench. Bend knees until roller contacts buttocks. Pause momentarily, then lower slowly. Repeat.

Leg extension on Nautilus machine (quadriceps). Sit into machine with the knee and foot of each leg in the same vertical plane. Straighten legs. Pause momentarily, then lower slowly. Repeat.

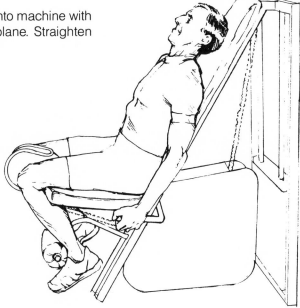

Press behind neck (deltoids, triceps, trapezius). Grip bar slightly wider than shoulders. Extend arms fully overhead, then lower bar to base of neck behind head. Repeat.

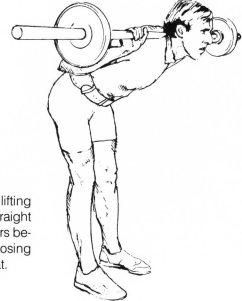

Good morning (lumbar, hamstring). Put on weight lifting belt to support low back and abdomen. Point feet straight ahead and lock knees. With bar resting on shoulders behind head, bend over as far as possible without losing forward vision. Return to starting position. Repeat.

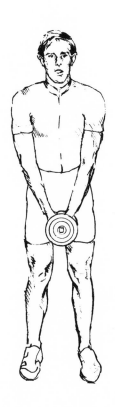

Dumbbell squat (quadriceps, deltoids). Hold dumbbell with both hands, elbows locked. Point feet straight ahead. Do a deep-knee bend and simultaneously raise dumbbell to eye level. Repeat.

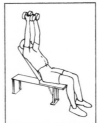

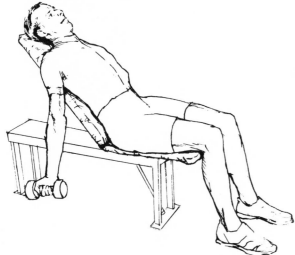

Straight-arm lateral (pectorals). Sit on incline bench and hold dumbbells overhead, elbows locked. Lower dumbbells as far as possible toward floor, then return to starting position. Repeat.

Partial squat (quadriceps, gluteus maximus). Pad the bar for comfort. Put on weight lifting belt. Position feet straight forward and the same distance apart as they are during cycling. Keep head up. Squat only to the same depth of knee bend produced by pedaling. Straighten legs and go all the way up onto toes to work the calves. Repeat.

Sit-up (abdominals and lumbar). Feet should be loose and knees well bent. Keep chin on chest. Alternate sitting up straight forward, with a twist to the left, and with a twist to the right. Hold a weight behind head or use an incline board to increase resistance.

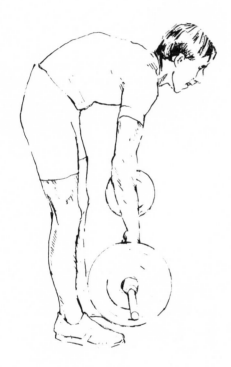

Bent-over rowing (latissimus, biceps). Bend over and let barbell hang just above floor. Pull weight up to chest, then lower slowly. Repeat.

Leg raise (abdominals). Lie on back. Lift straight legs upward to the vertical position or farther. Lower slowly. Repeat. For more resistance, increase the inclination of the board.

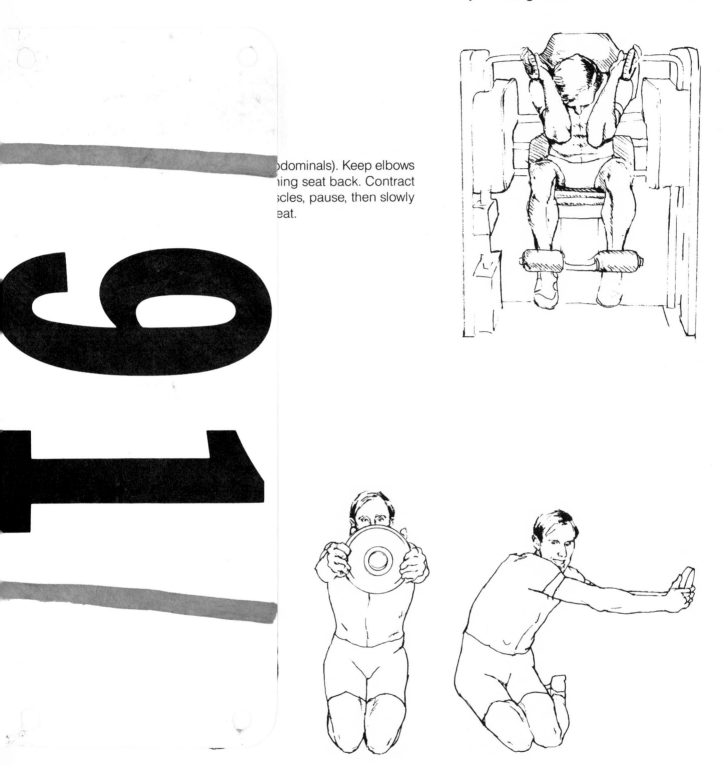

odominals). Keep elbows
ning seat back. Contract
scles, pause, then slowly
eat.

Twisting (lumbar and abdominals). Move hips from side to side past the heels while swinging the weight plate in the opposite direction. Keep plate at head level. Motion should be slow and continuous.

continued from page 71

A word of caution about the squats: They are *not* done with a deep knee bend. Go down only as far as the knees bend when you are pedaling. Keep your legs the same distance apart as they would be on the bike, and point your feet straight ahead.

Weight progress chart

Keep a chart on this training. For every circuit you complete, write down the total number of pounds you lifted. For example, if you used 100 pounds for the squat and you did 12 reps, that's 1,200 pounds. If you used 50 pounds in the bench press and you did 12 reps, that's another 600. I would like experienced Senior riders to total about 15 tons (30,000 pounds) for each circuit training session. That means about five tons for each of three circuits. Juniors, Veterans, women and beginners of any age should total at least 10 tons. It must be a good, hard workout. It must make you tired.

Ending the workout

The next 30 minutes is for basketball, volleyball or whatever you can play with your workout partners. This is for fun and more aerobic work. Then 15 minutes of low-resistance spinning on the wind-load trainer or ergometer. Finally, a short sauna, whirlpool bath, and swim.

I can hear some of you now: "But Eddie, I don't have the facilities to do everything you've said." Are you sure? If you are a serious athlete it is almost a requirement to be a member of a health club. If there isn't one in your town, check to see what is available at your high school or college. Look for a YMCA. You must find something. If it takes driving 20 miles to a bigger town, it is worth it. I realize that you may not have an ideal situation — few riders do. But you do have ingenuity and determination. You can come up with solutions. For example, even if there is no sauna and whirlpool you still have a bathtub. Fill it with warm water and pour in some mineral salts. Lie in there for 10 minutes and massage your legs. This is very good after training. The heat will relax you both mentally and physically. If you don't have a club with Nautilus and Universal machines, it's not a major problem. You can set up super circuit training in your basement using free weights. Even with only one barbell and two dumbbells you can have a dozen stations. Be creative. Work hard with what you do have, and you will get results.

Indoor cycling

I don't have to tell you the two big problems with winter: bad weather and early darkness. What should you do if these conditions force you to miss a ride? First, I must say that nothing is as good as road riding. No indoor machine is better than cyclocross. But when you absolutely cannot ride outside, use the wind-load trainer or ergometer. These will give you similar benefits to the training you are missing, and that's exactly what you must try to do — duplicate the training you would be doing outside.

When you can't make a Monday or a Thursday ride, set your bike on the wind-load trainer, fill some water bottles, open the window, put on your stereo headset, and go for it. Warm up, pedal steadily at 90-plus r.p.m., and cool down. Try to ride for the same length of time and with the same effort you had planned for the road. I know it's no fun pedaling inside a room for two hours, but what can you do? You must stick to your daily training schedule.

When you miss cyclocross or climbing on a Wednesday or Saturday, make up for it with hard work. This is also a good opportunity to test yourself. Set your bike

A wind-load trainer is the key to consistent on-bike work during the Preparation Period if you live where winter weather is severe. It also is a helpful device when setting up your riding position. This scene is from the Olympic Training Center in Colorado Springs, with Andy Hampsten, Alexi Grewal and Bill Watkins working out on TurboTrainers.

on the trainer, strap your watch to the handlebars, open the window, but forget the music. This time you will need attention.

Start by warming up for 15-20 minutes. The workout then consists of two nine-minute sets. The idea is to increase the gear every three minutes while keeping pedal r.p.m. at 90. For example, begin in 53x16. After three minutes, shift to the 15. After three more minutes, shift to the 14. After three minutes in that, stop and immediately take your pulse. Do it with your fingertips on the carotid artery beside your Adam's apple. Count for six seconds, then add a zero to get the one-minute rate. If it is 170 beats per minute this schedule is perfect. If it is 160 or less the work was too easy and you should use bigger gears (try 15, 14, 13). If you get 180 or more the work was too hard and you should use lower gears (try 17, 16, 15). When your pulse exceeds 180 on the first set you won't be able to handle the second one.

Now pedal easily for about 10 minutes, keeping 90 r.p.m. in a small gear. Loosen your legs. When your pulse has fallen off to about 110, you are ready for the second set. Put it in the big chainring and go. Duplicate the gear pattern of the first set. When you can complete the second set with a pulse of 180-190, you are doing super work. If you can't finish the second set, this tells you the first set was too hard.

It will probably take a couple of workouts to find the gears that give you a first-set pulse of 170. If you are on a Monark ergometer, try 2, 3 and 4 kiloponds. Or maybe 2, 2.5, 3. It's hard to say—it depends on how strong you are. It also depends on how old you are, because the optimum pulse rate becomes lower as you grow older. The figures I have given are generally accurate for 25-year-old men who are fit, who are good bike riders already. But pulses are highly individual. Two Seniors of identical age may have maximum heart rates quite different because one started cycling when he was 16 and the other started at 19. The younger you begin, the greater will be the development of your heart muscle. Exercise makes it grow. The

Special workout of two nine-minute sets

pulse becomes low because the heart is so big and strong. A large pump can maintain the necessary pressure with a slow rhythm, but a small pump must work faster to accomplish the same thing.

After taking your second-set pulse, see how long it takes your heart to drop back to the average resting rate of 72. The faster this happens, the fitter you are. When you can use a greater resistance and recover just as quickly, you have become stronger. You should start to see improvements in your performance after about three weeks. It is possible to get some incredible results. For example, consider Mieczysl Nowicki, one of the best Polish riders of the 1970s. He won a silver medal (team time trial) and a bronze (road race) at the Montreal Olympics. Twice I saw Nowicki take this test on an ergometer using resistances of 3, 4, and 5 kiloponds. His pulse was back to 72 *one* minute after he finished the second set.

Although this test is good for conditioning, I would rather have you out on the cyclocross course or the hills doing natural work on the bike. But even when the weather is consistently good, stay inside once every three weeks and test yourself. It will provide some very hard work, and it will give you objective numbers to judge how your training is progressing.

Test yourself once every three weeks

One last point about indoor cycling: Forget rollers. They are the old style. At one time rollers were the only way you could use your own bicycle for indoor work, but now we have the TurboTrainer, Racer-Mate and other similar wind-load devices that supply pedaling resistance. Rollers cannot compete with these for worthwhile training because they do not make you work harder when you shift to higher gears. However, if you already own rollers don't throw them away. They can be helpful to your sprint if you use them just a little. Here's how: Warm up for 10-15 minutes, then do 10 minutes in top gear with 4-6 jumps to maximum pedal r.p.m. (each jump should last 10-20 seconds). This develops your ability to pedal at high speed and stay in control of the bike while doing it. It will improve your acceleration. Incorporate this workout on days you ride the wind-load trainer or ergometer, but don't do it more than once a week or for more than half a dozen jumps at a time. If you do, the lack of resistance will harm your pedaling technique.

How to benefit from riding rollers

Strength test

Every type of winter training that can be tested should be tested. Otherwise, since there are no races, it is difficult to know if your program is working or if something is wrong. If it is too easy or too hard, you will not have improvement. When you can see positive results, it helps you believe in the program and keep working at it.

Take a strength test soon after the Preparation Period begins. Do it in place of your second regularly scheduled circuit training workout. It will tell you exactly how strong you are at the beginning of your program. If you have a record of the previous year's winter training, it will show how much strength has been lost during the season. The tests are simple and they do a good job of determining strength throughout the body. Before testing, do the usual stretching and aerobics to get thoroughly warmed up.

Legs   Test with squats or leg presses. The idea is to find the maximum number of pounds you can do for one repetition. Start with a weight you know you can handle, then go from there. Do each weight one time, then add some more. If, for example, you can do 475 in the leg press but can't quite complete a rep with 500, 475 is your amount. The next time you test, do the same sequence of weights so your fatigue will reach the same level, then see if you can make 500. If so, go for 525.

Arms Do exactly the same procedure with the bench press. To test correctly you must have someone to take the bar off when you reach the weight you can't quite handle.

Stomach Use a ladder attached to the wall, parallel bars, or a special gym stand made for exercising the stomach. Or you can make do with two desks or two sturdy chairs. Support yourself with your arms, then raise both legs until they are horizontal. Count the seconds you can hold them that way. When you can hold at 90 degrees for 10 seconds, your abdominal muscles are good. When you can hold 15 seconds, they are excellent. When you can hold only five seconds, you need to work. But don't be discouraged—I have seen riders who can barely get their legs up that high, let alone hold them in place for even one second.

Back Lie face down across a table with your legs held by a strap or a workout partner. The edge of the table should come right under your hips (use a pad or a folded towel for protection). Put your hands behind your head, bend toward the floor, then arch back up until your torso crosses the horizontal. Seniors should hold a 5- or 10-pound plate behind the head so they won't be able to do it a hundred times. I'd rather see about 20 repetitions before it's impossible to get all the way up anymore. Use the same weight each time you test and go for maximum reps.

That's it. After four weeks do all four tests again. Then a final time around February 1. Now no one will be able to tell you that circuit weight training doesn't work. You will have in black and white how many reps, how many seconds, and how many pounds you are better. You will know you are stronger. But if you should find no improvement, watch out. You may be wasting your time by not working hard enough, but usually it is just the opposite—you are working too hard and becoming overtrained. Bad results also can come if you are sick or injured. Never test in either case.

When to test again

Progressive ergometer test

When I came to the U.S. I introduced a special way to evaluate cycling fitness. It is called the progressive ergometer test and today nearly all top-level USCF riders take it. Very few of them like it because it is tough, but cycling *is* tough. The test is done to the end, to the point where you become too exhausted to turn the cranks at the required r.p.m. It finds out how much work you can do, and how fast your heart recovers. It is the single best way to determine your muscle power and cardiovascular efficiency. The test was developed for riders weighing 72-75 kilograms (158-165 lbs.) who already have a strong body. It has been used about 15 years in Poland, where the riders usually are big like in America. We have been using it at the Olympic Training Center in Colorado Springs since the USCF began operations there in 1979.

This test should be taken three times during the Preparation Period: (1) around January 15 after Body Conditioning; (2) at the beginning of March after the six weeks of Cycling Conditioning; (3) in mid April after Specialization. It is a more complex test than the one described above for the wind-load trainer, but it is not

When test is to be taken

all that difficult after some experience. It involves precisely timed heart rate readings, which makes it necessary to have at least one helper.

A difficulty some of you will face is getting the necessary testing equipment. You must try, because it is such a good way to judge your progress each year, as well as from one year to the next. Certainly every cycling club should own the items listed below. A sponsor should be happy to provide the money because it is a good investment; season after season the equipment can be used for rider development. Once the equipment is available, it is a simple matter for the coach and riders to learn how to perform the test correctly. Ideally, testing will be done by the same people each time so there will be consistency in the technique. It is a bonus if the club can enlist the help of someone experienced in working with heart rates.

The better the equipment, the more accurate the test results. Here is the list of what is needed:

Equipment

1. Two stop watches
2. Monark ergometer with toe clips, racing saddle, dropped handlebars
3. Electronic heart beat counter (sphygmometer)
4. Metronome for establishing pedal cadence

If there are several helpers, the various jobs of testing can be divided as follows (or one person can do them all if he is experienced):

Personnel

1. Person to change metronome and ergometer workload
2. Person to monitor pulse
3. Person to record data

To take the test, a rider wears cycling shorts and cleated shoes. The ergometer saddle must be adjusted to the correct height. After being fitted with the heart rate sensor, the rider sits quietly on the ergometer for five minutes, then his resting pulse is recorded. Next he warms up easily until he breaks a sweat and feels ready for the hard effort ahead. Once the test begins, the heart rate is recorded at the end of every single minute. Here is the test schedule:

Test schedule

Time of Test (Minutes)	Resistance (Kiloponds)	Cadence (r.p.m.)
0-6	3	60
6-11	4	70
11-16	5	80
16-end	5	90

As soon as the rider can no longer maintain 90 r.p.m. despite his most intense effort, he stops pedaling. Immediately the elapsed time and heart rate are recorded. Then the rider remains sitting on the ergometer and his heart rate is recorded on this schedule: (1) at one minute following test completion; (2) at two minutes; (3) at three minutes; (4) at six minutes; (5) at nine minutes. The test is then finished for that rider.

Draw up a large worksheet like the one illustrated with places to record all the test information. Make plenty of photocopies. Then it's a simple matter to fill in the blanks for each rider tested.

PROGRESSIVE ERGOMETER TEST

End of Minute	Heart Rate	Blood Pressure	Resistance (kp)	Cadence (r.p.m.)
(Resting)	_____	_____	0	0
1	_____		3	60
2	_____		3	60
3	_____		3	60
4	_____		3	60
5	_____		3	60
6	_____	_____	3	60
7	_____	_____	4	70
8	_____		4	70
9	_____		4	70
10	_____		4	70
11	_____	_____	4	70
12	_____	_____	5	80
13	_____		5	80
14	_____		5	80
15	_____		5	80
16	_____	_____	5	80
17	_____	_____	5	90
18	_____		5	90
19	_____		5	90
20	_____		5	90
Stop time _____	_____	_____	0	0
+1	_____	_____	0	0
+2	_____	_____	0	0
+3	_____	_____	0	0
+6	_____	_____	0	0
+9	_____		0	0

Total Work Accomplished:

3 kp	×	6 min.	×	60 r.p.m.	×	6 meters	=	6,480 kpm
4 kp	×	5 min.	×	70 r.p.m.	×	6 meters	=	8,400 kpm
5 kp	×	____ min.	×	80 r.p.m.	×	6 meters	=	____ kpm
5 kp	×	____ min.	×	90 r.p.m.	×	6 meters	=	____ kpm
						Total	=	____ kpm

Percentage: time of test _____ ÷ 16 min. = _____

Total Heart Rate: (1st min.) _____ + (2nd min.) _____ + (3rd min.) _____ = _____

$$\text{Points} = \frac{\text{Total Work} _____ \times \text{Percentage} _____}{\text{Total Heart Rate} _____} = _____$$

Body Weight _____

Date of test _____

After hundreds of tests it has been determined that a good rider in good shape should be able to last at least 16 minutes. But not many will make it past 20. The test is designed to be intensive and short so that large groups of riders can be tested in reasonable time. To pool all the data and increase its usefulness to riders and coaches, a point system has been devised. It is based on (1) total work accomplished; (2) heart rate during the first three minutes of recovery; (3) the percentage that the time of the test represents to 16 minutes, which is considered 100%.

With the Monark ergometer it is simple to calculate the total work accomplished. Its gearing is such that one revolution of the crank moves a point on the wheel's circumference six meters. If the rider is pedaling at 60 r.p.m. then the distance covered would be 360 meters per minute. The friction belt around the wheel supplies resistance that is read on the ergometer's gauge in kiloponds. When this resistance is multiplied by the distance pedaled each minute, it gives us the total kilopond meters (kpm) of work.

Okay, here's an example to show how all this is used. Let's say our rider completes 18 minutes of work. If 16 minutes represents 100%, 18 minutes is 112%. He has post-exercise heart rates of 156, 132 and 108 on each of the first three minutes, which when added together equals 396. His total work accomplished is figured like this:

Formula for total work accomplished

3 kp	×	6 minutes	×	60 r.p.m.	×	6 meters	=	6,480 kpm
4 kp	×	5 minutes	×	70 r.p.m.	×	6 meters	=	8,400 kpm
5 kp	×	5 minutes	×	80 r.p.m.	×	6 meters	=	12,000 kpm
5 kp	×	2 minutes	×	90 r.p.m.	×	6 meters	=	5,400 kpm
						Total work	=	5,400 kpm

Now we have all the numbers. The rider's points are figured with this equation:

$$\text{Points} = \frac{\text{Total Work} \times \text{Percentage}}{\text{Total Heart Rate}} \quad \text{or} \quad \frac{32,280 \times 112}{396} = 9,130$$

Evaluation of point scores

This is a fine score for a Senior—9,130 points says he is very strong right now. The figure will also be useful to him in the future (even future seasons) when he tests again. His point totals will tell him if he is improving, and by how much. On the other hand, points can be misleading when they are used to compare one rider to another. The problem is body size—on the ergometer a bigger rider can usually do more work than a smaller rider who is just as fit. A more meaningful comparison between two riders can be made by taking each one's figure for total work and dividing it by his body weight. This helps negate the advantage of size. But remember, the principal purpose of the test is to judge how each individual rider is developing within his own program, not how he compares to everyone else.

From experience we know that a Junior who reaches 5,000 points or more is super fit and powerful. A Senior is good if he passes 8,000; if he scores 10,000 in the first test of the winter it makes me very happy. This is the proof of his program. His Body Conditioning has in effect produced power conditioning. He is then ready to get the most benefit from the next logical step, Cycling Conditioning. If that goes as well, the third step, Specialization, should produce excellent racing form. Each step uses the preceding one for its base.

The test procedure is exactly the same — except for the kilopond settings — for all women and for Veterans who are either new to cycling or up in age. For them the workload is not as great. Rather than 3, 4, 5 kiloponds, these riders should use 2, 3, 4. However, if any of them become able to last for, say, 25 minutes, then they should try 2.5, 3.5, 4.5 or even go up to the Senior-Junior men's level. They must work hard, but they have to be honest with themselves and not overdo it. The resistance should never be so great that is impossible to get close to 16 minutes.

Test procedure for women and older men

As it was used by the national team when I was in Poland, the test also included precise monitoring of blood pressure. For the record, I will briefly describe how blood pressure fits in. I have provided space for it on the test chart, which tells you exactly when the readings should be taken.

Blood pressure, though not part of the points formula, is still very worthwhile as an indicator of fitness. The best way to use it is to plot a graph that shows how blood pressure and heart rate correlate. The normal situation during a test is for both to increase. What we look for is where the line representing blood pressure and the line representing heart rate finally cross. The later this happens, the better the rider's fitness. Once the heart rate starts increasing at a faster rate than the blood pressure, the end of the test is coming; when the heart rate is increasing and the blood pressure is not, the rider is finished. By comparing all the intermediate numbers for heart rate and blood pressure from test to test, the picture of a rider's fitness becomes more complete.

How to include blood pressure

There are two problems with recording blood pressure: (1) the difficulty of taking accurate readings on a hard-working rider; (2) the expense of a quality blood pressure instrument (sphygmomanometer) and stethoscope. For these reasons I do not make blood pressure a mandatory part of the test. But if the equipment and a skilled technician are available, use them and gain this extra information.

One final point: Do your best to arrive for each test with the same degree of freshness. Be as consistent as possible. If one time you test the day after a hard cyclocross workout and the next time it is following a nice recovery ride, this will throw off the results. Since the test is very hard work, it is always best to take it following a day of easy training. Your morning pulse should be low and you should feel good.

Be fresh for the test

Transition from Body Conditioning

During the second week of January (the final week of Body Conditioning) begin the transition to Cycling Conditioning by cutting the number of weight training circuits from three to two. For Seniors, this means a total of 10 tons per session rather than 15. It is the same for the third week of January, then it drops to one circuit per session (five tons) in the last week of the month. After that, take a final strength test as described above. It has been two months since you began weight training and your body should be significantly stronger. Now this phase of your conditioning is over if the weather is good enough to begin riding daily. If not, weights can be continued for another week or two at the reduced level.

Reduce circuit weight training

Strength maintenance
exercises

Stop weight work with
legs

I know what you are saying: "Eddie, if I quit the weights I will soon be as weak as I was in the beginning of December." That's true, so you do not completely stop Tuesday/Friday body conditioning. On each of these days from now to the end of the season you should spend 30-60 minutes doing stretching and aerobic exercises, plus sit-ups and push-ups. None of these exercises require equipment, so you can do them wherever you travel for training and racing. If you operate out of your home most of the season, it's fine to use the same barbells, dumbbells, etc., that you have in your basement for circuit training. If you belong to a Nautilus club, continue to work out there.

One set of each upper body exercise plus stretching will keep your muscles in good tone. But starting from the time you are fully into Cycling Conditioning you must not do any work with the legs other than pedal the bike. Your riding program will be incredibly hard for them. They don't need more work. You must always remember that you have only a limited amount of energy. You can't change this, you can only use what you do have for the maximum development. When you cut back on the weights, you can put the extra energy into different training. To begin, you use it for long-distance rides that increase in length every week.

During the last two weeks of January, Monday and Thursday road rides should cover 80-100 km. Distance depends on factors like the weather, if you are alone or with a group, and if there is a vehicle to pace you. (In winter at the Olympic Training Center riders often motorpace behind a station wagon. We open the tailgate and turn on the heater full blast. This makes it quite comfortable for the riders even when the weather is very cold.) Be intelligent, think about your own situation, and make a smart decision about the length of the rides. For example, 100 km in a double echelon of 8-12 riders (the best size group for training) equals about 65 km when you are riding alone. The effort is about the same, and the time for the ride is about the same.

I recommend group riding in winter. I have no doubt that it is better than training alone, because it helps you learn drafting technique and the speed is much closer to racing. The only danger comes when you are below your partners in strength and ability. When this is the case it can lead to overtraining, since you always have to ride very hard to keep up. Leonard Nitz realized this potential problem one winter when he came to a training camp in Colorado Springs. He was not as fit as the riders who were already there, and it took a month before he was 100% competitive in the training. He was smart and did not push right away. If he had, he could easily have broken himself.

Cycling Conditioning

Daily training takes on a whole new look for Cycling Conditioning, January 15 — February 28. Now you start riding every day, including Sunday, which becomes the hardest day of the week. Here is the schedule:

Monday   Recovery. Do only what you feel like doing following Sunday's very hard training. Perhaps take a sauna and whirlpool bath, then go for an easy ride if the weather is nice. Keep it to 25-30 km—you probably won't feel like going any farther. If the weather is bad do indoor exercises or spin on the wind-load trainer. Swim, play table tennis, read a book, go to the movies. Whatever you do, don't get tired.

During winter it is best to train with a group. Speed will be faster and you will sharpen your technique in a paceline.

Tuesday Cyclocross or climbing until mid February, then speed work. The climbing can include power work that I call "finishing the hill," which means going hard on the last section to the top. This is natural in a group because of the riders' competitive nature. Everyone wants to test his own strength and find out how he is doing compared to his friends.

When speed work starts it consists of several jumps during a 50 km ride. It may be five jumps or maybe only two—it depends on how your legs have recovered from Sunday's effort. Introduce yourself to speed work with short, quick 50- to 100-meter bursts on slight downhills, preferably with a tailwind. Use the big chainring and the 19, 18 or 17, depending on the grade of the road, wind direction, and how your legs feel. Each Tuesday lengthen the jumps by about 50 meters. The correct way to jump is to get out of the saddle, sprint to maximum acceleration, sit down, and hold top speed for the distance. Caution: If it is below 50F degrees (10 Celsius) do not do speed work. The cold air will be painful to your throat and lungs during super deep breathing at sprinting speed. Instead, go climbing. When it feels too cold for that, go for 30-60 minutes of cyclocross. You must be smart.

How to jump during speed work

In the evening, do strength-maintenance exercises for 30-60 minutes, as outlined above. Do them at least two hours after dinner and finish an hour before bedtime.

Wednesday Long ride. The distance is always the same as you rode the previous Sunday. But on Wednesday the pace is slower and steadier, and the terrain should be flatter. In other words, this day's training is not as intensive as Sunday's.

Thursday Cyclocross or climbing, but never speed work. (Tuesday is the main day for sprinting, although there will also be some in the Sunday ride—Sunday has everything.) Thursday is a hard day. Ride tough cyclocross for one hour, or ride 50 km in the hills. I prefer hills at this time of year, but the weather is what determines it. Climb with good effort and try different techniques—in the saddle, out of the saddle, bigger gears, smaller gears. Think about what you are doing. The best hills for this are 3-8 km long. Avoid extended grinds. In Colorado Springs we use Cheyenne Canyon, which has 3 km gradual followed by 5 km steep. This is excellent. Use the most ideal terrain that you have and work hard on it.

The best hills for training

Friday Easy ride. Go for about two hours on flat ground. The time of day will depend on your personal schedule, but if you have a choice ride in the warmest part of the day. In the evening, duplicate Tuesday's strength-maintenance workout.

Saturday Same as Monday. Do a short, easy ride and some light recreational exercise. Enjoy yourself and rest up. Next is the toughest training of the week.

Sunday Long group ride with variety. This is the longest ride each week, and each week it goes a little farther. It is also the hardest ride because it should include varied terrain and all types of effort—fast group rolling, hill jams, short time trials, sprints, etc. Most Seniors should be able to do 80 km the first Sunday, 90 km the next, then 100, 110, and so on. Ten kilometers is a nice increase. The rides should get more intensive as they get longer, so that by the last three Sundays in February you are really working hard. Distances by then should be up around 130 km, 160 for some riders. At the end of a Sunday ride you will be *tired*.

WEEKLY SUMMARY
CYCLING CONDITIONING PERIOD (JAN. 15 TO FEB. 28)

M	Tu	W	Th	F	Sa	Su
Recovery. Short, easy ride or light recreation.	Climbing or cyclocross until mid-February, then speed work. Upper body workout in evening.	Long ride. Same distance as previous Sunday, but easier pace and terrain.	Climbing or cyclocross. Work hard.	Two-hour easy ride in flats. Upper body workout in evening.	Short, easy ride and light recreation.	Long group ride with variety of hard efforts. Mixed terrain.

Sometimes Sunday training might take you beyond the correct distance—not all courses are perfect—and you will begin to feel very tired before the end. If this happens, slow down and eat. Throughout the Preparation Period you must carry food on any ride that will last longer than an hour and a half (50 km or more).

Get ready for the Sunday and Wednesday rides like you will for long road races. Eat a meal about two hours before riding, then start out carrying a banana, an orange, dried fruit, cookies, some special race sandwiches (*see Chapter 4*)—whatever you enjoy—and tablets of glucose, dextrose or fructose. Get used to eating these things so you will have confidence in them in competition. Count this food as one of your meals for the day. Also carry at least one thermos or insulated bottle full of a hot glucose mixture. This is the time of year to experiment with your formula for this drink. It's a good idea to take it on *all* winter rides for the energy and warmth it provides. Later in the season you will use it for long-distance training and racing (the mixture is not drunk hot in the summer, of course).

How to make glucose mixture

To make the glucose mixture, brew your favorite caffeinated tea and dissolve in a 1,000-milligram tablet of vitamin C and a multimineral tablet. Squeeze in some lemon, then add enough honey (natural glucose) to make it sweet enough to taste good. Don't use too much—the drink must be acceptable to your stomach. You can find out what works best by trying different mixtures during winter training. Once racing begins, you should have developed an excellent drink to keep your body supplied with energy plus the minerals and liquid lost through sweat. Glucose is the most important carbohydrate in body metabolism.

I recommend drinking more glucose mixture after training (made with caffein-free tea if you wish). One glassful should do it if you carried the proper amount on the ride and sipped it frequently. I don't like to see riders guzzle a lot of liquid after training or racing, especially not plain water—it has so little in it to benefit the body. It's much better to have glucose mixture, a commercial sports drink, juice, milk, etc., and to have only a small amount. Too much will fill your stomach and kill your appetite. It will keep you from eating good meals and digesting food properly.

Transition from Cycling Conditioning

During the last two weeks of February, Cycling Conditioning begins the transition to Specialization. This means more race-like activity. For example, at the Olympic Training Center we allow riders to make efforts like sprinting to road signs. We do some group interval training. On Thursday we might have two-man time trials. These are short (1-3 km) and repeated as many as five times, depending on how the riders feel. This is like the first competition of the season. The last two Sunday workouts usually become more like racing than training. The important thing is to reach this point by gradual preparation. Everything must be step by step, not forced.

Before we start Specialization, I want to emphasize a couple of things to certain riders.

First, for those of you who live in the North. If you can't go to the Sunbelt for winter training, you will have to wait longer than February for the warm weather necessary to do long-distance rides, hill training and speed work. Perhaps continue weights and cyclocross until early March. Then, as conditions allow, begin longer road rides, climbing and jumps. You must be flexible, you must think, you must do the best you can. But you can't work out hard when it is cold. Your season is later, so it's okay if your Cycling Conditioning starts later. You mustn't try to hurry things by going from weights and cyclocross directly to sprinting when you finally get a spell of warm weather. First there must be long distance and climbing. I believe it is better to arrive at the first races a little bit below good form rather than try to force hard outdoor training in cold weather.

Northern riders must adjust program

Next, for those of you who live in an area without many riders. You must do what you can to get people together for group training. Some winter workouts are best done with others, for reasons I've already mentioned. For example, Tuesday's climbing or speed work is better with at least one other rider because competition will make you work harder. Wednesday's long ride should be with 4-12 riders to allow practice in a pace line, if not a double echelon. On Thursday you don't need anyone because you are going to push yourself to the end; the end is different for you and for the next rider. Friday's nice and easy ride will be more enjoyable if you have someone to talk with. Saturday can be solo, and so can Monday. On Sunday you need competition. It is the one training ride each week that absolutely *must* be done with a group.

Training partners are necessary

Specialization

Now it's March 1—time for Specialization. Finally you can get out your beautiful racing bike. Clean your winter bikes well, put on some heavy grease, and tell them

Switch to your racing bike

thank you and goodbye. You may use the winter road bike occasionally during rainy spells, but in general you are finished with it and the cyclocross (or mountain) bike for this season. From March 1 to April 15 it is the summer bike and a summer program. Now you ride each and every day (sometimes twice a day) seven days a week. Now you deal with the bike full time. No car rides around town — all your local transportation must be by bike. You live with the bike, you are married to the bike. I'm sorry for you if you don't think this is necessary. Believe me, it is what it takes to be a top rider.

These six weeks are to polish yourself for the racing season. This is your final preparation. Part of the program will be training races (or real races that you ride for training). You are ready for them in March if you have kept to my schedule since December 1 — in fact, you will have been all but racing each of the last few Sundays. Our program for U.S. national team riders goes at it just this way, with a March full of training-type races in Texas. Each race is a little longer, a little tougher, and by April the riders are ready for a month of international events in France and Italy. In turn, those races are preparation for major early summer events like the Peace Race, Milk Race and Coors Classic, which help build form for the National and World Championships, Pan American Games and Olympics. This season-long racing development begins with Specialization training.

The definition of Specialization

Why do I call it Specialization? Is it because you will specialize as a road racer or a criterium racer or a time trialist? No. As I have said, that is the wrong approach to the sport. You must be as good as possible for everything. Instead, Specialization means the period when the yearly program begins to emphasize the speed work and interval training that makes you ready to race. It specializes you for competition. Perhaps "specialization" is not the best word because it can cause confusion, but that's what it is called in European cycling so I continue to use it. Please keep this definition in mind when you encounter the word in this book.

Here is the daily schedule for the six weeks of Specialization. It is also the basic schedule for the entire six-month Racing Period. You will see that it requires some very intense work. Now is the time to begin self-massage after training if you haven't been using it already. The technique is described in Chapter 9.

Monday   Recovery. Ride twice nice and easy. Do 30-60 minutes in the morning and again in the afternoon. Spin a small gear at 90 r.p.m. or faster. After the second ride take a sauna and whirlpool bath, or sit in a warm tub with mineral salts. You will be tired from Sunday's hard work, so don't exert yourself today. Just keep the blood moving to loosen your muscles and rid them of waste products.

Tuesday   Speed work. The time of day for this training depends on how you feel, your morning pulse, and your weight. It's possible to have lost four pounds on the long, hard Sunday ride and still not regained it. When you can, wait until the afternoon to ride. This will give you an extra 6-8 hours of recovery.

Total distance should be about 50 km. After warming up well, do at least two sprints whether you feel like it or not. Do them like you are going for the World Championship, like for $100,000. Each one must be a maximum effort for the entire 150-200 meters. Use your best gear for sprinting. Perhaps jump to top speed in 53x17 and then push in the 15. After the first sprint your legs will feel like they've become twice as thick. That's natural. Change to a small gear and spin easily. Ride slow, relax. If it takes 10 minutes for your breathing and pulse to return to normal, fine. If it takes 15 minutes, fine. Then go one more time. Do you feel better or worse than after the first sprint? When worse, training is over—pedal back home in a small gear. When you feel better, go for a third sprint. On a day when you're sharp you might wind up doing five or six, but never 10 or 12. Remember, tomorrow you have a long ride.

In the evening, do your upper-body strength maintenance. You should be using moderate weights (or your body weight in the form of sit-ups and push-ups). Do enough reps of each exercise to feel fatigue in the muscle, but don't push to the maximum. The time is over for building strength; now you are just trying to keep what you've got. This workout must not steal from the energy you need to ride the bike.

Wednesday Long-distance ride. Use flat or rolling terrain. The distance is the same as the previous Sunday. Use the big chainring as much as possible and keep a steady pace of about 32-34 k.p.h. In general, this is the day you should feel comfortable. It is the third day after Sunday's hard ride, so recovery should be complete. When it isn't, you must cut the distance. When you could handle only two sprints on Tuesday and your pulse says you still don't have full recovery on Wednesday morning, don't ride 110 km if that's what is scheduled. Maybe go 100, maybe only 85. If you are riding with a group, stay behind, don't pull through. But when you feel good, do your share of the work and go for the full distance.

Thursday Intervals. This is the hardest workout of the week. Afterwards, take a sauna and whirlpool bath, or use a warm tub with mineral salts. See information about intervals below.

Friday Middle-distance ride. Go out with some friends for about two hours. Keep your legs turning at 90 r.p.m. or faster in a moderate gear. No strain, no pain, just enjoy the scenery and conversation. After the ride or in the evening do upper-body strength maintenance.

Saturday Short ride with jumps. Do only 35 km easy in the early weeks, then gradually increase the distance to 50-80 km and include about three sprints of 200-300 meters with complete recovery between each. This works better than steady riding to warm up your body for Sunday's hard training or training race.

Sunday Long, hard group ride. Steady work in a pace line or echelon should be spiced with fast climbing, attacks, chases, sprints for road signs, etc. This evolves into a full-fledged training race as the weeks go by, with each rider trying to be first to the finish. (Of course, no training ends with a sprint or any type of hard work. You must pedal a small gear for 5-10 km to cool down and regain normal breathing.) The length of the ride should increase each week by about 10 km, beginning with 80-90 km the first Sunday. By the end of Specialization, Senior men may be riding as far as 150 km. The long distance plus the intensity means you will be very tired Sunday evening.

WEEKLY SUMMARY
SPECIALIZATION PERIOD (MARCH 1 TO APRIL 15)

M	Tu	W	Th	F	Sa	Su
Recovery. Ride 30–60 minutes in morning and again in afternoon. Low gears, easy pace.	Speed work. At least two sprints of 150–200 meters, but not more than six. Upper body workout in evening.	Long, steady ride in easy terrain. Distance same as previous Sunday. Use big chainring.	Intervals.	Two-hour easy ride. Upper body workout after ride or in evening.	Easy ride of 80 km or less, including three sprints of 200–300 meters.	Long hard group ride or training race. Increase distance by 10 km each week. Mixed terrain.

Active rest is the best rest

You will notice that there are no days away from the bike during these six weeks. The only exception is for illness or injury. It will be the same for the entire six-month Racing Period—no days off. Your rest comes on Monday and Friday when you go out for easy rides. Spinning in a small gear is better than complete rest. It helps maintain your metabolism and prevents you from getting stiff, from getting lazy. It actually gives your muscles better rest than no exercise at all. Active rest is the best rest for an athlete. You must be smart, though, and stick to your plan. For example, don't let Friday's ride turn into work. You must ride *easy* for the whole two hours. Speed doesn't matter and distance doesn't matter, so leave your bike computer at home. Take your mind off those things. Ride with a friend who shares your purpose and have a nice chat all the way. Enjoy the ride. It is the same for Monday.

Safeguards against overtraining

Don't worry about overtraining if you stick to my schedule. It won't happen. You might think that if you start getting tired and keep riding daily the fatigue will snowball. But remember all the safeguards. Sunday will kill you, but Monday is very easy. The first two jumps Tuesday will tell you if you are recovered. If not, go back home. Wednesday can be shortened as much as necessary if you still aren't sharp. After another 24 hours you must do intervals, but then you have Friday and Saturday to recuperate before making the next big effort. There is plenty of work in this weekly program, but also plenty of low-gear spinning to refresh your body and your mind.

Interval training

Interval training is somewhat complicated to set down as a program because it must change from week to week as you become more fit. And it must change depending on the type of event you want to have a peak performance for, as I'll discuss in coming chapters. Also, interval training differs from one individual to the next—what's right for you might not be right for the next rider.

Benefits of interval training

But there's no question at all about one thing, and that's the necessity of interval training for road racing. It helps you in several important ways. It improves your acceleration and high-speed endurance. It adapts you to a constantly changing pace—a feature of all mass-start racing. You must have a good jump to attack successfully and go from group to group. When the breakaway leaves, you must catch it by yourself, not make a bridge with everybody behind you. That's not jumping, that's pulling.

A jump is when you are gone, like a bullet. If another rider starts after you from two meters behind, that's where he must stay. When he can't get your wheel he has to work just as hard as you. This is so important in the final kilometers of a race. When you attack and don't give him the advantage of your draft, you have earned the opportunity to win.

It's super when a bike rider can jump and hold a speed of 50-55 k.p.h. for 3-5 km. The way to escape the pack is to have (1) a very quick jump to high speed, then (2) the strength to maintain that speed until the race is won, the breakaway is caught, or whatever the objective is. The first ability comes from speed work, the second from interval training. You can't succeed without them. When you have done the work, you will know you have what it takes to make important racing moves. Without it you will be a defensive rider, unable to create any meaningful action.

In general, U.S. road riders do best with what I call decreasing intervals. These are done by time instead of distance, which is the usual measuring stick in Europe. Over there most roads are marked every 100 meters, but we don't have that benefit in America. We do have inexpensive sports watches, though, and every rider should have one for interval training.

Even better is an electronic cycling computer that mounts to the handlebars. There are now a dozen brands on the market and the price has become very reasonable. A computer that tells elapsed time, speed and distance is great for training. One that also tells heart rate is super. I recommend a computer for every type of training so you will know exactly what you are doing. It will teach you a lot about pace and speed, which is a big benefit if you are still in your first couple of years on the bike.

The first rule of interval training is to understand what it is. The terms speed work and intervals are often used interchangeably, but actually the concepts are entirely different. It's important to get this straight so training on Tuesdays (always speed work) and Thursdays (always intervals) is done correctly throughout the season.

These are the four main distinctions between speed work and intervals:

1. Length of jumps (interval efforts are longer)
2. Speed reached during jumps (top speed is greater during speed work)
3. Pace between jumps (faster during interval training)
4. Recovery before jumping again (much more complete during speed work)

Each jump during speed work begins from a *slow* roll after *full* recovery. Your heart rate should be below 90 beats per minute and you should feel very comfortable. Then the jump is made with *maximum* effort, accelerating all the way. Go, go, go as fast as you can and then hold that speed just for a moment as you complete the distance. This develops your ability to sprint, in both the technical and physiological senses. Speed work jumps should be only 50-100 meters long when you begin doing them in mid February, then they are lengthened as you get better. When you can sprint through 200 meters you are good. When you can accelerate to your maximum speed and hold it through 300 meters, you can't expect to do any better. That's the human limit. In a race, if you try to jump with 500 meters to go you can't win. No way. Nobody can accelerate for 500 meters. Riders will catch you, draft you, and then pass you. Speed work will teach you how long you can accelerate, how far from the line you can begin your sprint. This knowledge, plus knowing the strengths and weaknesses of opposing riders, is what determines the best tactics to use at the end of a race.

Use a bicycle computer

Intervals vs. speed work

How to do speed work

An on-bike computer is essential equipment for today's racing cyclist. It is a great aid to training, particularly speed work and intervals. It mounts on the handlebars, runs off the front wheel, and accurately tells you speed, distance and time. Some models provide a great deal more information. Pictured is an assortment of computers available in 1984 (clockwise from top left): the Velotech Sport Computer; the CycleCoach by Biotechnology, Inc.; the Cateye Solar; the Push by Attivo Corp.; the Coach by Biotechnology, Inc. The Coach has the very useful heart-rate function.

How to do intervals

Each jump during interval training starts from a relatively *high* speed. This helps simulate racing conditions. Roll along at 90 r.p.m. in 42x16 or 17 instead of the 19 or 21 used between speed work sprints. The pace should be similar to Wednesday training. When the jump is made, acceleration is to a *steady* high speed (faster than average race speed) but *not* maximum speed. This speed is held for the duration of the interval, which should coincide with considerable muscle fatigue. In general, if you can hit 55 k.p.h. at the end of a speed work sprint you should do intervals at about 48 k.p.h. The shorter the work interval, the closer to maximum speed you can try to go.

The key to interval training is knowing when to jump again. Heart rate is what tells you. Count the pulse in your neck or look at your heart rate computer. When you fall back to about 110-120 beats per minute, shift into the big gear and take off. (For some riders the proper level is 100-110 b.p.m., for others it is 120-130. You have to decide based on how you feel. You shouldn't be fully recovered, but you shouldn't still be winded, either. Your breathing rate should be close to normal.)

The decreasing type of intervals

Here is the most simple form of a decreasing intervals workout:

Warm up thoroughly for about 15 km. When you feel ready, jump and go hard for one minute in 53x16, 17 or whatever is appropriate for you. Your speed should be such that you can maintain it for the full 60 seconds but not for 70. When the time is up, shift into 42x16 or 17 and keep a 90 cadence. As soon as your heart rate falls to 110-120 b.p.m., shift into the big gear and go for 50 seconds. Recover to 110-120 b.p.m., then go 40 seconds . . . recover, go 30 seconds . . . recover, go 20 seconds. Fifteen seconds is about the shortest effort that still has benefit.

Interval training is usually not so cut and dried, however. Let's say that after going down to 50 seconds you find recovery is very quick. In this case you might go back to 60 seconds for the third interval. Then down to 50 seconds for the fourth. If recovery is still good, do 50 seconds again for the fifth. Then go to 40 seconds.

Stay there two or three times if recovery remains quick. Be certain, however, that it is your recovery that's fast and not your effort that's lacking. When your pulse does not reach at least 160 b.p.m. at the end of each interval you are not doing it right. Your heart must be working close to maximum. I'm talking about 180, 190, or even 200 b.p.m. Because you should approach your physical limit at the end of each interval, that's why I say Thursday training is the hardest and most important of the week.

How do you know what your maximum heart rate is? In general, a young rider will have a higher maximum than an older one, but there are other variables besides age. The best way to determine your maximum is to train with an electronic heart rate computer (the pulse is too fast to count accurately any other way). After a good warm up, test yourself by doing several all-out jumps or hill climbs. Go as hard as you possibly can. This will give you a figure for judging how close to 100% you are working on Tuesdays and Thursdays. Don't be surprised if you see your maximum heart rate increase slightly as training progresses. It may even increase from one season to the next despite the fact you've gotten older. If last year you could reach 190 and this year it is 195, this is good. When everything is going well, the maximum heart rate rises and the resting heart rate falls. Month by month and year by year, the heart muscle becomes stronger from training and it works better.

How to find your maximum heart rate

Why decrease the length of the work intervals? So you will be able to maintain near-maximum speed and effort throughout each one even though you are getting tired. When a Senior can hold 55 k.p.h. he is a super-fast guy; 52 k.p.h. is wonderful; 48 k.p.h. is very good. Of course, the grade of the road, the type of surface, and the wind direction can add or subtract several kilometers per hour. To accurately judge progress you must do intervals on the same course.

It takes experience to know what you can handle. Generally, a Thursday interval workout should cover about 30-40 km, plus 25 km total for warming up and cooling down. At the end you will be absolutely tired, even more than after Sunday's long, hard ride. Even when you win a road race you won't be so tired. But next Thursday, if everything is going well, you will make it harder yet by doing the first interval not for one minute but for 1:10. A strong rider may be able to start at two minutes by the end of specialization. The decreases must be bigger when you get that high. For example, a sequence might be 2:00, 1:45, 1:30, 1:15, 1:00, :50, :40, :30, :20.

To make sure you will always go at the highest speed you can sustain, it's best *not* to do interval training with other riders. The exception is if you are shy about staying on a wheel when making a full effort. If so, it's helpful to do intervals with a friend occasionally. Take turns leading and sitting in.

When there are small hills on the course your speed will go down, but your effort should be just as great. It is the effort that counts. Once you are fully involved with interval training, you must push your body extremely hard. You must not reduce the length of the work interval until you know it's impossible to make it all the way through again without losing speed.

Motorpaced intervals

Interval training offers a lot of variety. One way to work out is with a pace motorcycle. Do half the intervals without it and half behind it. Or alternate: first behind, next in front, behind, in front, etc. Another way is to begin each interval in front, then have the motorcycle pass and pace you when your speed starts falling off. This is excellent for drawing out a maximum effort. A mixture of such techniques is better than always doing the same type.

Riding in the draft of a motorcycle also develops bike-handling ability at speeds even greater than you'll experience in a race. This improves reflexes. Bike handling is different at 80 k.p.h. than it is at 65, and different at 50 than at 35. When you train at high speed, racing speed is no longer the maximum. You will be more comfortable and confident in competition.

At the Olympic Training Center, a coach often uses a motorcycle to accompany riders on Tuesday and Thursday training. Perhaps your club coach can do the same. On Tuesday, for example, he can assist the speed work by leading out riders and then letting them pass with a final burst. Or he can go up the road and park, then wave a flag or jacket to signal the riders to sprint to him. Another technique is to drive behind the group and beep the horn to start a sprint, then beep it again to end it. This improves the riders' reactions.

By the way, if your club does have a motorcycle be sure it is used on each Sunday's group ride. It is good for setting the pace at certain times, like into a headwind or late in the ride when riders are tiring. If you must ride alone on Sunday, a motorcycle is a great help in establishing a variety of race-like conditions. Behind it and in front, fast and slow, jump and steady—this is the preparation for racing.

Climbing intervals

A great way to develop your ability to race in the hills is with climbing intervals. They are also the best way to increase your power. Do them on hills 1-3 km in length, not longer. The idea is to work hard going up, then turn around and ride down slowly to recover. If necessary, do a few easy loops at the bottom until your pulse returns to 110-120 b.p.m. Then go again. Repeat as many times as you can.

Here is a basic workout for a hill that is 3 km long. First, as always before hard training, warm up very well. Then do the first climb in a gear you know you can handle fairly comfortably in the saddle, say 42x20. For the second interval use the 19. Now it is hard. When you reach 500 meters to go, shift to the 18, get off the saddle, and give it maximum effort. After this, maybe you can do one more interval the same way, maybe not. Maybe you can do three more. Be honest with yourself and do what feels right.

For the first several workouts it may be best not to go all the way to the 3 km mark before turning back—one time up might finish you. So go only to the 1 km mark and do it several times. As the weeks pass and your power improves, work further up the hill until you are finally reaching the top. Then it's possible to do decreasing hill intervals: go all the way up, then to 2.5 km, 2 km, 1.5 km, 1 km, 0.5 km. I encourage you to be creative like this and make the best use of the terrain you have. Your biggest hill is only half a kilometer long and it isn't very steep? Then do as many repeats as you can, going again as soon as you reach the bottom. Work your heart rate up as high as you can each time.

While doing these intervals use various climbing techniques. This will improve your ability in hilly races. Don't make the mistake I see from many riders: They begin a hill in 42x17, then shift to the 18 part of the way up, then the 19 in the final stretch. Or 19, 21, 23—whatever they are using. This is exactly the opposite of what

A motorcycle (or car) is invaluable for training. Among the many variations is sprint work in which the rider is paced up to high speed before he swings out of the draft and tries to pass.

should be done. Climbing is always a matter of increasing the gear size, never decreasing it. When you go to a lower gear you slow down, and then you get dropped. Instead, start the climb in the lowest gear that lets you keep up with those you are training or racing with. Closer to the top, shift to a higher gear and keep the same pedal r.p.m. The result: Your speed increases. Shift up again when the crest is almost reached and go even faster. Sure it's harder to pedal the bigger gear, but the distance remaining is not great. If you train this way you will have the strength to race this way.

Generally, good climbers in competition change to a one-tooth higher gear and increase speed after the first half of a hill. They stay fresh early by using a gear that's lower than they actually need. On the other hand, those who use a relatively high gear early develop fatigue before the top. Not only can't they speed up to stay with the leaders, they usually slow down. The rule is always to go slower at the bottom than you know you can. By the top you will be able to climb at your maximum. When it's a long climb, say 10-15 km, good climbers will sometimes shift to a one-tooth bigger gear for a different reason: It allows them to stand up for a while and not lose speed. The bigger gear is necessary since pedal r.p.m. is slower when standing.

Climbing is powerful work. It takes strength in the arms, back, buttocks, and legs. When standing during climbing you also must have the coordination to use your weight correctly. Proper out-of-saddle technique requires the bike to stay on a straight line while your body moves over it. This coordination is developed by climbing intervals.

The point to remember is that climbing intervals should be used to simulate the race condition. Ride the first half of the hill steadily. Next increase both the gear and effort. Then get out of the saddle and ride the last couple of hundred meters almost like a sprint.

You say you live in Kansas and have absolutely no hills? I know what that's like because I lived in the center of Poland where it's flat like a table. There is always some place, such as a park, with enough terrain for cyclocross training, but without real hills during Specialization you will have to use the wind instead of climbing to develop power.

The technique is to pedal big gears into a headwind. This is done as intervals, with recovery as you turn around and go downwind. It won't give you the same development as hill riding, but it is the best you can do under the circumstances. Use heavier training tires and wheels for even more resistance. Meanwhile, take every opportunity to go to a hilly area for training or a camp. Also travel to some hilly road races once the season begins. You may not do too well, but by riding them you will increase your power.

When Greg LeMond reaches his rear derailleur lever he will move it forward. For good climbers the tactic is always to increase the gear, never decrease it.

Criterium intervals

Decreasing intervals are good for road races and climbing intervals develop power, but what should you do on Thursdays to improve for short, fast criteriums?

They are called criterium intervals, naturally. A workout consists of 10-15 jumps that cover 200-300 meters apiece. This sounds like Tuesday speed work, but it's not. The reason is that you let your heart rate drop only to 110-120 b.p.m. (not 90 or lower) before accelerating again. This prepares you for the jump after jump of criterium racing. When doing these intervals use a watch instead of trying to measure distance. Twenty-five seconds is about how long it takes to sprint 300 meters. Go hard for 25 seconds, recover, go for 15 seconds, recover, go 25 again, recover, go 15 again, and so on. Remember to keep a brisk pace during recovery periods.

Group intervals

There can be many modifications to interval training. Think about what you can do each Thursday to improve your weak point or prepare better for the type of race you most often compete in. Use your head. Customize the intervals. Whatever you do, work real hard at it.

To complete this discussion, here is how intervals can be done during group training. This is a good way for a team to work as a unit, and a good way for the riders to begin interval training during Specialization. Group intervals develop coordination among teammates and they give everyone some hard work. They simulate the race condition when riders must jump away from one group and bridge to another.

I will describe three basic training formations for a team of 12 riders who have fairly equal ability. As with individual intervals, there are many variations of group intervals. I encourage teams to be creative.

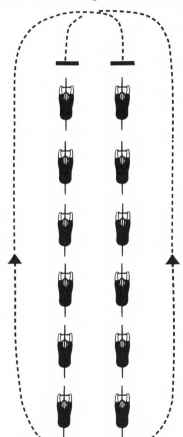

GROUP INTERVAL TYPE 1

In the first type the team members ride two abreast. During the warm-up kilometers they trade the lead in the usual way: both riders pull off simultaneously and drift back to the end of the line. The coach follows in the car or motorcycle and uses the horn to signal the beginning of the intervals. When the last pair of riders hear it they jump and go hard to the front of the group. They cross positions when they get there so the effect of the wind is balanced throughout the workout.

This is the easiest type of group intervals and the first type a team should do. Each rider gets draft from the line of teammates and it is a short distance to the front. The coach can make things harder by ordering a faster group speed. If everyone is going 40 k.p.h. the jumping riders will have to go 45-48 k.p.h. to get to the front quickly. As soon as they are back in formation the coach honks to start the next ones. In general, each rider makes 4-6 hard efforts in group training just like he does when doing individual intervals.

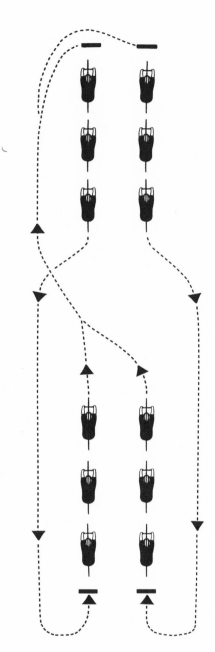

GROUP INTERVAL TYPE 2

The riders are paired by strength and then divided into two groups at least 100 meters apart. The coach follows the second group. When everyone is ready to start the intervals he blows the horn. The front two riders of the second group accelerate and chase down the first group, trading pace as in a 2-man time trial. When they catch the group, they go right to the front of the lines.

When the last two riders of the first group see the riders go by, they slow down and drift all the way back to the end of the second group. As they are dropping past the first two riders of the second group, those riders immediately jump and bridge to the front of the first group. And so on. Both groups should roll along at about 32 k.p.h., which makes it necessary for the bridgers to go 50 k.p.h. if they are to cross the gap quickly.

This formation works well because each pair of riders gets sufficient rest before they have to bridge again. The gap between groups can be as much as 300 meters. As it gets wider the bridging riders have to work harder, but they also get a longer rest.

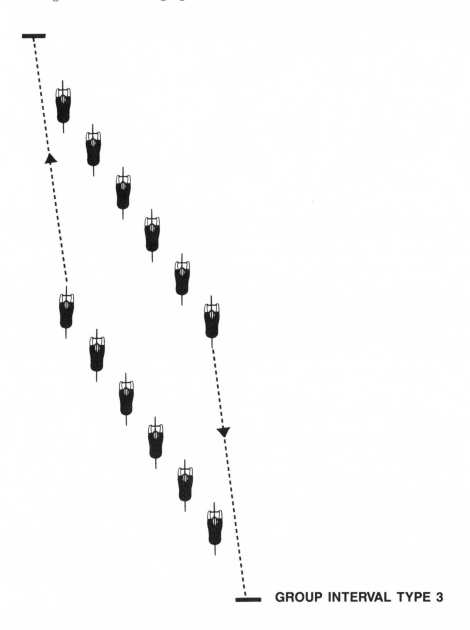

GROUP INTERVAL TYPE 3

The third type is based on the echelon. It is the hardest of the three because each rider makes his effort alone. Again the team is split into two groups of equal size. The groups form single, nonrotating echelons about 100 meters apart. The exercise begins with the point man on the second echelon jumping and bridging to the point position of the first echelon. As he catches it, the last man in the first echelon slows down and goes back to the last position of the second echelon. As he is about to join it, the new point man jumps to the first echelon. And so on.

RACING PERIOD

Finally it's April 15. Most Americans don't like this date because the income tax is due, but cyclists love it. The Racing Period is beginning. The next six months are what you have been working so hard toward since December 1.

The most important thing now is a progressive schedule of competition. Some riders are so hungry for winning that they choose only local races — little towns, little races, very little competition. They feel like they are big stars, but they are nothing. Local races are fine until you start winning, then you *must* move up to regional and national races. If you don't make this step to harder, stronger competition, you will not improve. Learning comes by racing against riders who are better than you. You learn nothing from riders worse than you.

Why do we send our best riders to Europe each spring? To learn cycling. For these riders there is no competition in America. Many U.S. races are short and the fields have only 70-80 riders. This cannot prepare anyone for international competition. It won't produce world-class riders. It won't make the U.S. the top cycling country, which is our goal. For this reason we travel long distances to be in good races. We are now getting international experience for enough of our riders to compete respectably in the toughest European stage races, like the Tour de l'Avenir. In fact, in 1983 we were able to have national teams in two major stage races held at the same time, the Milk Race and the Peace Race. To prove our progress, Matt Eaton won the former event and Thurlow Rogers placed fourth in the latter.

It is the same process for you. After April 15, racing becomes an even bigger part of your development than training. By chosing events that expose you to new challenges, you will grow as a cyclist. You will become the best you can be.

Training schedule

The daily schedule for the Racing Period is generally the same as for Specialization, except there will now be actual competition on Saturday and/or Sunday. Thursday remains a very important training day. It is used to work on problems with speed or power, or to focus on the type of event you are emphasizing — road race, criterium, time trial or stage race. This will be discussed below and in each specific chapter.

The key to the Racing Period is to cultivate one or two spells of peak performance that coincide with the events you want to do your very best in. One or two periods, not eight or nine. More than two genuine peaks is almost impossible for a road rider (but not for a track rider). Also, when you are trying for two peaks there should be about two months between them. For example, a national team rider might peak for May's Peace Race and then again for August's World Championships. Between the two he will slow down, rest, and do only one-day races for at least one month. Then he will ride a short stage race and begin final preparation for the Worlds.

Select 1-2 events to peak for

You can't keep a peak indefinitely. Every rider must decide when he needs to be at his strongest. What is the goal? District Championships? National Championships? Worlds? The peak needed for the Nationals and Worlds always presents a problem for the best U.S. riders because the events are less than one month apart. The tendency is to peak for Nationals because the U.S. championship jersey is very important to riders and their sponsors. Also, they often feel that their chance in Worlds competition isn't very good. This attitude is changing, though, and I am glad to see it. For example, Mark Gorski says that Nationals are not so important to him since he's already won a jersey. He sees the possibility of being one of the best match sprinters in the world. What's sad is that he and other top riders have to decide between the two competitions. They can't be at their peak for each one. This will remain the case as long as the present schedule exists. After you peak for Nationals, you need to rest and get away from pressure, but what do you have? The World Championships. When is there time to rebuild the peak? A rider needs at least a month and a half between major competitions, except when they are so close together that one peak can span both.

Preparation for a major road race

The peaking process for criteriums, time trials and stage races will be described in those chapters. Right now, in order to understand how training works in the Racing Period and how to reach optimum form for a major one-day road race, let's examine a situation that may be common to many U.S. amateurs: You are an up-and-coming Senior whose main goal this season is a top-10 finish in the National Road Championship. But first you must qualify for that race by finishing in the top three, for example, in your District Championship. So you need two peaks—one in early June for Districts, the second in early August for Nationals. How do you go about it?

When the Racing Period begins April 15 you have about seven weeks until the Districts. During the first three weeks you must test yourself to determine your strengths and weaknesses. Racing is by far the best way to do this. Start with criteriums because they are short, then add road races (not long ones) and begin competing twice a week. For example, ride a training criterium with your club on Tuesday, then go to a road race on the weekend. I do not recommend racing on both Saturday and Sunday yet, because it is likely you won't have full recovery for the second event. Strength is still a question mark at this time of year. There is no sense in risking your form. If there isn't a training criterium, do your regular Tuesday speed work and Thursday intervals, then race once on the weekend.

Make each succeeding race a little longer, a little closer to the District Championship distance (approximately 160 km). Push yourself. Try to join in every worthwhile break and take your pulls. Go hard on the hills. Contest the finishing sprint. If you win, fine. If you lose, fine. The important thing is to find out how your condition is, how good you are. See how you rate in the three main qualities that a successful rider must have: speed, power, endurance. As soon as you know, begin specific preparation for the Districts. With one month to go, don't think at all about training for each weekend's race, think only about the major goal.

How to remedy weak points

What should you do about a weak point? First, get clear in your mind exactly what is wrong. If you are having trouble on the hills, it means you have a power problem. If you try to win primes or the finishing sprint but are not really in contention, you have a speed problem. If during the last 10 km of a road race you feel worse and worse, you have an endurance problem. As soon as you suspect a weakness, get busy with the remedy.

Speed Many times this is a shortcoming early in the season. It is hard to develop speed in cold weather, and most preseason training is designed to build endurance and power. To correct a lack of speed, each Tuesday and Thursday should be devoted to speed work. Tuesday may be just a few jumps if it is only the second day after a race. Do what feels right. Wednesday's distance is cut back to 100-110 km. You do not need to ride longer because you already have endurance. Also, you must be fresh for speed work. Each Thursday do 15 all-out jumps of 150-200 meters, allowing yourself full recovery between each one. This will make you faster. On weekends race in a criterium.

Power It is past time for developing power with cyclocross. Maybe you did not do enough of it in the winter. That's a shame because it is such good power training. Or maybe you did not do enough ergometer-type work or weight work with the legs. Maybe you haven't done enough climbing. Perhaps you are still a little heavy, too. Improve your power by using Wednesdays for a steady ride in the hills. On Thursdays do decreasing or climbing intervals. Monitor your pulse and go every time it drops back to 110-120 b.p.m. Each weekend choose a hilly race rather than a flat one. It's best if the opposing riders are not so much stronger that you can't stay with them the full distance.

Endurance Ride long distance on Wednesdays. Go farther than the distance where you begin to have trouble, but don't make the increase too big. If 100 km is your limit, don't go out and try to ride 140 km next Wednesday. Try 120 km. A Senior with four or five weeks remaining before a 160 km race can still build some endurance if it is done sensibly step by step. Each weekend choose a road race that complements the distance of your Wednesday training. If you are training 100 km, pick a race of 115-120 km (or motorpace if no race of this distance is available). Generally, you can race about 15 km longer than you train. Once you are up to 145 km on Wednesday, you should be able to handle a 160 km race.

Of course, it is possible to have a problem in two areas or even all three. When this is the case you have to examine your training diary to find out what has gone wrong. Maybe you did not train enough in the Preparation Period, or maybe you trained too much and now you are overtrained. Either mistake will cause bad performance. The difference is that when you are overtrained you don't even want to see the bike. When you haven't trained enough you are still hungry for riding.

The final push

Three weeks before

During the third week before the District Championship, begin the final push for a peak performance. Ride long distance every third day. How long depends on your fitness and how you are feeling from the training and racing you've done in the prior 10-14 days. Although these rides will enhance your endurance, you must already be able to race almost the District distance. If you've been riding road races of only 100-115 km, you are going to have a hard time. Right now power must also be close to your maximum. However, if you still lack speed, three weeks is enough time to do something about it. Keep using the remedial speed work just described.

Two weeks before the championship, ride a short stage race or simulate one with three or four days of very hard training. Motorpacing is best because it makes you work at racing speed. Another technique is to race on Saturday and Sunday, then motorpace on Monday and Tuesday. This equals a four-stage race. Be cautious here until experience reveals what is right for you. Some riders benefit most from three hard days, some from four, some from five. It is an individual matter, and that's what makes a perfect peak so difficult to achieve. Only a foolish, inexperienced coach would list an exact program for everyone to follow. However, when no suitable stage race is available, substitute this general training pattern:

Two weeks before

First day Race or motorpace the full District Championship distance, 160 km.

Second day Race or motorpace 160 km, or 145 km if you feel tired. The effort should be as hard as on the first day, which means very hard.

Third day Less distance than the second day but no less effort. Sprint past the motorcycle, climb very fast. Never go slower than 40 k.p.h. when pacing on flat roads.

Fourth day Optional, as is a fifth day. I don't recommend more than five days, except for a very experienced rider who knows he needs the work. Such a rider will always have a blood test two months before the big event. This is a good idea for everyone. If you have a problem it can be remedied in time. Otherwise, all the hard training may wear you down rather than build you up.

For the same reason, during peaking there must be special attention to nutritional needs. I recommend a daily iron supplement and tablets supplying minerals, B-complex, and vitamin C. These help your body cope with stress. Even better, during the stage-race period have an injection containing B-1, B-6 and B-12. Shots are better than pills because they supply larger, faster-acting doses. However, shots must be administered by your team doctor or personal doctor. Do not inject yourself—it can be dangerous. A good cyclist must work closely with a medical person. If it can be a specialist in sportsmedicine, so much the better.

Nutritional needs
during peaking

Why are B vitamins so important? I can explain with an analogy. When you put wood in a fireplace it burns at a certain rate and lasts for, say, 30 minutes. When you also put in gas, the wood burns only 10 minutes but the fire is very big and has lots of energy. The body reacts the same way after a shot of B vitamins. They are a catalyst that helps your body quickly break down and utilize both carbohydrates and fats—the two primary fuels. Right now in Europe, all good riders get injections of vitamins and minerals during hard training and racing. As a big event approaches, they get a shot three days before, two days before, the day before, and on the morning. Some riders also take a glucose injection. All this is perfectly legal and you can do it, too. On the other hand, you must be certain never to use anything that appears on the Union Cycliste Internationale's list of banned substances.

How peaking works

The stage race or simulation is the key to the peaking process. Done correctly, it can produce great results. For example, Greg LeMond used it before the Junior World Championships in 1979 when he won the individual road race. That event was 120 km long, so he began by riding 125 km the first day. He did 110 km the second day, 100 the third, and 80 the fourth. There must be a decrease. It allows the rider to maintain a super effort throughout each day's distance even though fatigue is increasing. You know this training is being done right when your morning pulse goes up, when you feel bad, when you lose weight. If this isn't happening, that's when you extend the training a day or two.

Right now I can imagine what you are saying: "Eddie, why do you want me to make myself so tired less than two weeks before the big race?" The answer lies at the heart of all athletic training: The body's capacity to do work will increase only when it is stressed beyond its usual limits. Since December 1 you have been training hard and recovering, training hard and recovering. You have grown strong because of it. Now you are putting yourself through a period of extreme work, more work on consecutive days than you've experienced before. You are pushing beyond your previous barriers, you are getting closer to 100% of your potential. You are going for a maximum positive response to physical stress. At the same time there are psychological benefits. Once this training has been done, you will know that nothing in the race will be too hard for you.

Think of the body as a factory. If the usual demand is for 500 items a day, the factory produces that very comfortably. When an order comes in for 800 a day, the factory starts working harder. When demand climbs to 1,000 a day, the factory is at near-maximum production. When the order hits 1,200 a day, the machinery is shaking and ready to break. It can't keep up. Then, all of a sudden, the orders stop. No more demand. But intense production doesn't end so fast and that creates excess items. These go into storage, building a reserve that can be used to fill future needs. In the same way, the body increases energy production to answer the demand caused by very hard training day after day. When this training suddenly ceases, energy is replenished and the overflow is stored, increasing the body's potential for work. This is sometimes called "supercompensation." Now we have the complete equation: First there must be super work, then there must be super rest. However, if demand for energy does not restart soon enough, the increased production will stop and the energy level will return to normal.

Learn from the experience

So, after the stage race or simulation ends (about 10 days before the Districts), follow it with an easy ride of 30-60 minutes on each of the next two days. On the third day extend the ride by about 15 km and throw in a jump or two to find out how you are really feeling. This is a vital part of self-coaching. It is what gives you experience. I respect experience very much, and I respect the differences among individuals. Each rider must determine the effect of the hard training so that next time the program can be even better. This really can't be emphasized too strongly. There is a fine line between work that produces a rebound to peak performance, and work that causes so much fatigue that form goes into a tailspin. You must dare to approach this line, but not touch it, each time a peak is attempted.

(How important is this self-knowledge? Believe me, even the greatest athletes can become victims of ill-conceived training. For example, Beth Heiden in 1980. The year before, she was absolutely the greatest woman speedskater in the world. She was the big favorite for the Winter Olympics. Everybody expected her to win a medal in each event. Eric was second to her. What happened? Pressure, pushing, and overtraining. She and her coach made a big mistake in preparation. It's very easy to do, and you can bet that it'll happen many times again. One of my assistants has a very good education, a good heart, and he would like to be a great coach. But he is a very hard pusher and he does not recognize overtraining. The mistake by young coaches and most athletes is almost always too much work, not too little.)

Finish the week with easy rides for recuperation, then on the final weekend go to a road race or criterium of 80-100 km. If there isn't one that is right, motorpace this distance.

The week of the race

Now it is seven days before the championship. Resume your regular training program but cut the week's distance to 70-80% of normal. For example, if you usually ride 500 km a week, do only 350-400. Use your morning pulse to determine how you are recovering. This will help you to know how long and how hard to train. *Be careful.* Don't overdo it. You must be very fresh for the event you have prepared so hard for. It is better to have one day too much rest than one day not enough. I've found that some riders, particularly Juniors, need 10 days between the end of hard training and the race. Other riders do best with seven days. Keep a detailed diary so you will learn your own response. It is also a big help to have a smart coach who knows you well.

Here's how the last week before the big race should go:

Monday   Easy ride for about an hour.

Tuesday   Steady ride with two jumps. If you are used to doing about 60 km cut it to 45.

Wednesday   Steady ride of 80-100 km, 115 maximum.

Thursday   Ride 50 km with intervals. Do about 80% of the usual number, but go at 100% effort.

Friday   Steady ride for two hours. Use your racing equipment so you can test it. The bike should be set up exactly like it will be ridden in Sunday's event.

Saturday   Ride 50-65 km with two or three jumps lasting about 200 meters each. Again, use your racing equipment. Do this ride on the race course, if possible.

Sunday   Do your best. You are ready for it.

After you succeed in the District Championship, how do you peak for Nationals? Exactly the same way, unless your analysis has shown need for change. After Districts, go easy for a couple of days if you need to, then resume the normal training and racing schedule. Continue to work on your weak point. Enter the final three-week period before Nationals ready to undertake a short stage race or simulation. Then rest, cut back training kilometers, and get that top-10 finish.

SPECIAL NOTE TO NON-SENIORS

Are you a young teenager, under age 18?

Are you an older rider, over 35?

Are you a female of any age?

If you belong to one of these groups, the yearly training plan and almost everything else in this book is right for you. The main exception is the training and racing distances I discuss. They are for a Senior man who is in his low to mid 20s, but you are not as strong as this rider and your races are not nearly as long. Everything is less for you. Even so, more of your training rides will come closer to (or exceed) your average race distance than a Senior man's will.

I would like to give you specific advice for your cycling program, but it is difficult. The reason is the great disparity of strength, maturity, riding experience and goals we find in each of the above groups. For example, a 15-year-old and a 17-year-old are two very different people, but both are called Juniors. A 35-year-old and a 55-year-old are far apart in capability, and yet they are grouped together as Veterans. Among women cyclists are some who are strong enough to race with (and beat) men, and others who will never be able to. So all I can do is talk in terms of the average Junior, Veteran and woman. I urge every rider, as always, to shape my advice to his or her own special situation.

Juniors

Based on talent, physical maturity and racing experience, a rider may be good enough to compete successfully against Seniors during his last season as a Junior. There are several examples of this, including Roy Knickman in 1983 and Greg LeMond

Juniors (age 15-17) should enjoy their racing and not push too fast for development. Their events are much shorter than Seniors ride, so their training kilometers should be fewer. The evolution to Senior distances takes place at 18 and 19 after the body has gained sufficient strength and maturity. This is Roy Knickman, center, as a first-year Junior in 1983.

in 1979. As final-year Juniors, their training and racing programs were virtually the same as a young Senior's. However, no Junior can be expected to (nor should he attempt to) match the program of a mature Senior. As good as the 18-year-old Roy Knickman was in 1983, he had nowhere near the career kilometers necessary to handle the training and racing schedule of a 23-year-old like Thurlow Rogers.

Generally, the transition from Junior to Senior takes one year and often two. A young rider can't go directly from a maximum race distance of 120 km all the way up to 180-200 km. Right now, eight months before the 1984 Olympics, I am positive that Roy Knickman will be very competitive for a place on our 100 km time trial team. But I don't believe that as a first-year Senior he can make the team for the 190 km individual road race. His speed, power and technique are all very good, but it is too much to expect that anyone can increase endurance by 50% in one year. Roy needs time for this development just like any young rider. Greg LeMond was no exception when he became a professional in France in 1981. He was just 19 then and fortunately his team director, Cyrille Guimard, was a very smart man. He gave Greg a progressive racing program that included harder and longer events as the seasons went by. This paid off with some big victories in 1983, including the World Road Championship (270 km). In 1984, after three full years of development as a pro, Greg was ready to undertake cycling's toughest event, the three-week Tour de France with stages as long as 300 km. This is the right way. Everything must be done smoothly step by step as a young rider matures.

Junior men should do 30% less training distance than I have recommended for Seniors. A good Senior will ride about 480-500 km a week from Specialization onward; a Junior should do about 320 km. In terms of endurance training (as on Wednesdays), the distance should be equal to the longest races that will be ridden.

Women

Even though some of their races are still much too short, Senior women are getting more and more opportunities to compete in criterium series, stage races, and road races of respectable length. Their National Road Championship is now up to 110 km. This means that women must have a well-rounded training program that develops all three racing requirements: speed, power, endurance. No longer must their preparation be aimed at short criteriums.

Generally, women should cut the Senior men's program by 30% and ride approximately 320 km a week. However, unlike Juniors, a Senior woman should occasionally exceed maximum race distance on long training days. A 20-30% increase is about right. Her average race is not quite as long as a Junior's, and she is in the prime of her athletic potential. There should be a positive response to the extra work.

Veterans

Veterans are a particularly tough group to advise, for two reasons: (1) the great range in age, and (2) the fact that many Veterans once raced as Seniors. The result is that even though their events are now much shorter, Veteran-age riders tend to go out and train at Senior distances. I understand this compulsion and the attraction of sticking with what is familiar, but it must be resisted.

Veteran races are almost never longer than 90 km, which means even shorter than

Women should follow the complete year-round program presented in this book, including weight training. The main alteration is less training distance than men do because women's events are shorter. Even so, improving racing opportunities make it important not to neglect endurance work.

the maximum distances for Junior men and Senior women. So, like those riders, you Veterans should cut the Senior men's program by 30% and ride no more than 320 km per week. Use all the energy you've been putting into needless endurance training to work on your speed and power. Emphasize quality instead of quantity. If your longest race is 80 km, you can ride 80-95 km each Wednesday but there is no need to go farther on this or any other day. Instead, put emphasis on Tuesday speed work and Thursday intervals. This will make you very fit for the usual events of 40-65 km. One good thing about having short races is that most training sessions can approach race length and yet not result in overtraining. It is a much different story for Seniors.

Okay, okay—if you occasionally want to take a 120 km ride early in the season, I won't deny you the pleasure. It can be good for your conditioning and your psychology. But remember: When endurance goes up, speed goes down. Too many long rides will kill your speed, and speed is what you need to race Veteran distances successfully. Another benefit that comes with eliminating long rides is more time for your family and profession. After all, you are no longer a young Senior whose life is full-time cycling.

Peaking process is similar

Finally, how should a Junior, Veteran or woman peak for a major road race? You know the answer by now. Use the same method I've decribed for Senior men, except make training distances shorter because the race isn't as long.

The motorpaced stage race simulation (or actual competition) begins with the same distance as the upcoming event. Only a Junior with the talent of a LeMond or Knickman will begin by riding 10-15 km farther than race distance. Training be-

Veteran-class riders (age 35 and older) must resist long-distance training and emphasize workouts that pay off in speed and power. The hours a Vet saves by omitting needless endurance training can be put to better use with his profession, family and other interests.

comes shorter each day as fatigue builds up, but effort remains very great. After three or four days, the hard work ends and the remainder of the week is used for short, easy recovery rides.

During the final week, daily training distance is reduced to about 80% of normal except on Wednesday. A Junior, Veteran or woman who is preparing for an 80-100 km event can ride close to full race distance (or even equal it). But as I've mentioned, a Senior man preparing to race 160 km should hold Wednesday's ride to 115 km or less. There is a similarity here with running. A short-distance runner can practice his event during race week, but a marathoner tunes up with workouts much shorter than 26.2 miles.

Road Race

Tactics win road races. What is a tactic? Very simple: Anything you can do to help yourself succeed, and your opponents not to succeed.

Tactics depend on who you are—what your abilities are—and who your competition is. The terrain and weather must always be considered. In fact, everything that involves the race is a tactical decision, including what you eat for breakfast, the race clothes you wear, how you warm up, and so on. It's all up to you, but there are two restrictions: Tactics must not violate good sportsmanship, and they must be within the rules of cycling.

It usually doesn't matter if the course is one big loop, a circuit, or point to point. It usually doesn't matter if the course is flat, undulating or hilly. It is a good rider with the best tactics who will be first to cross the finish line. He must always have some luck, of course, and the terrain must be reasonable for his particular abilities.

Each of the three basic terrains puts certain demands on a rider's tactics and technique. Each type more or less selects the build of rider who can do well. For example, a flat or rolling course is perfect for a big rider. It gives him an advantage. A hilly course is just the opposite—tough for the heavy rider but wonderful for the skinny little one.

By hilly I mean climbs longer than 1 km. Anything less is more of an advantage for the big rider than for a real climber. A climber is at his best on a hill of at least 5 km. When a hill is short, even though it may be steep, a big rider can handle it with his power. It is the same for undulating terrain. The big rider can use his weight to roll fast going down a hill, and this will carry him part of the way up the next one. He can coast on the descent to rest, then apply the power. A light rider, on the other hand, must work all the time.

You know your body type, but do you have a clear understanding of how you measure up as a rider? For example, this may be your analysis: "My strong point is sprinting, my endurance is good, my weak point is climbing." You need an honest and accurate appraisal like this in order to have the best tactics. Next, are you an individualist or a team player? Finally, who will be your strongest competition on the terrain of the particular event? It's impossible to know and analyze every single rider when 150 will be at the starting line, but look through the entry list. If you know some riders by their good reputation but not by their appearance, memorize their numbers. This is another part of tactics.

Tactical preparation

If you haven't ridden the race in previous seasons try to pedal around the course the day before. This should be possible if it is a circuit race, but not if it is point-to-point or one big loop. Drive it if you can't ride it, but riding is the best way to get an accurate feel. The least reliable way to find out what to expect is to go by a course map and descriptions from other riders. This is especially true for the climbs. You have to see them to know for sure what cluster to use. Someone will say, "Oh, the hills aren't too bad. All you need is a 19." Maybe that's true, but during the race is not the time to find out he was talking in terms of his 39x19 and you have a 42. In this case you really need a 21.

Know the weather forecast

What will the weather be? Knowing the forecast is as important as knowing the course. Not just what weather is expected for the start, but what it will be 1,000 meters up in the hills and at the finish line four hours later. A warm sun might be shining as the race begins, but that's no guarantee you won't be riding in a cold rain before you are done, particularly on a course that has significant elevation changes. Be ready for every eventuality. Have what you need for racing in hot, cold, and wet weather.

Your whole team has to be prepared. The support people must be at the top of the climb to give you and your teammates newspaper to stuff up the front of the jersey, or a jacket and cap if it is raining. All possible weather-related problems must be thought out by the coach before the race.

Study the course, especially the finish

Familiarity with the finishing stretch can make the difference between winning and losing. Check it out. There must be no surprises in the last couple of kilometers. This is no problem in most circuit races because you ride through the start/finish area several times. But not always—sometimes the course is redirected at the end of the last lap. Find out. Know what position you need to be in at a certain corner, road sign, house, or other landmark. Don't think you can rely on meters-to-go signs or marks on the road. While you are looking for them is when you will miss somebody's jump. To plan your best tactics you must know if the final meters are uphill, downhill, right after a turn, around a park, on a velodrome, etc.

If you aren't in a well-organized team that has a coach and assistants you will have to prepare your own equipment, clothing, and race food. Do this one or two days before the event, depending on your travel schedule. Whenever possible arrive two days early, then spend the day before the race resting, checking your equipment, loosening up on the course, buying your fresh fruit, etc. All of this is part of tactics—things that help you to be comfortable and totally prepared to race your best. If you haven't brought suspenders and it turns rainy, how are you going to hold up your wet, heavy shorts? Even the type of clothing material is a tactical decision.

3-rider team is best

Each team member must decide what he will try to do based on whether he is working for somebody or somebody is working for him. A team must be careful not to make its tactics too complicated. I think three riders is the ideal team size in a one-day road race or criterium. Three can usually work together easier and accomplish more than a bigger team. Also, it is simpler to split the prizes, which always has the potential of being a very sore point. With just three riders it is more likely that each one will take home enough to make teamwork worthwhile.

Let's look into some road racing tactics. First it must be said that an entire book could be written just about tactics. In fact, it could be a multivolume set. (I've al-

Part of tactics is making sure there will be someone at the top of the climb to give you a warm jersey for the cold, wet descent.

ready written one of the installments, my 100-page master's thesis on how cycling tactics are affected by meteorological conditions — that is, the role of weather.) There are so many variables that it is impossible to cover them all, so what I will do is touch on several basic ones that shape a rider's fortunes. This will help you understand road racing better. It will help you avoid mistakes and get more out of your ability. As your cycling career continues, experience will teach you many of the fine points. These depend so much on your own special blend of strengths, weaknesses, intelligence and personality that they can only be learned on the road.

(Note: The remainder of this chapter is primarily theory and example. Information about how to train for road races and peak for a major event was used to illustrate the yearly training plan. Please refer to Chapter 3.)

THE ECHELON

The most important tactic in road racing is the formation of the echelon when a crosswind starts. At this writing we don't see the single or double echelon used much in the U.S., but I expect this to change as riders keep gaining experience overseas and bringing it back home. I have been pushing for use of the double echelon since I came to American cycling. I've lectured to riders, I've had them practice, and still only a few have developed the correct technique.

The most common mistake I see is a rider who insists on taking a long pull. All this does is tire him out and either cause a gap to open or the speed to decrease. As we will see, the idea in a double echelon is always to be on a wheel either in the line that is moving into the cross wind or in the line that is returning. As soon as the lead or point position is reached it is time to get off. In a sense nobody ever pulls. This constant rotation results in a speed much higher than an individual can maintain against the wind alone, but it is done without anyone making a 100% effort. Except for one brief moment each rider always has shelter.

Reach the front and pull off immediately

In Europe where it is often windy and the teams are strong, the front echelon is what decides a road race. Out of those who make it will come the winner. In Poland and Germany there are strong winds at least half the time. In Holland it is incredibly windy. More to the west in Belgium and France there is almost no wind at all. It's the same in Italy. Riders who are used to wind look forward to it, they want it. For riders who aren't used to it, it's terrible.

A crosswind always presents a danger—or an opportunity—because it will cause an immediate selection. After a few kilometers there may be 10 echelons. No matter how strong you are, if you are not in the first echelon the game may very well be over. The riders who make it know that the race is on the line. They know that if they can establish a break now they are likely to stay away to the end. They know it's time to put the pedal to the metal. Sometimes in a strong crosswind a gap of just 10 meters is as good as 10 km. Nobody will be able to cross it. A rider who tries must ride at his maximum, which takes 30-40% more effort than those in the echelon must use to go nearly top speed. He will blow up very quickly.

An echelon should form spontaneously when the front riders sense a crosswind. Everyone is always looking for the best shelter. If the wind is coming from the left, each rider will feel a better draft to the right of the rider he is following. Immediately there will be a staggered paceline, an echelon, that stretches across the road. Perhaps 6-8 riders can fit in a single line, but it is more common for there to be two lines that include about 12-15 riders. This is the double echelon. The number that can fit depends on the width of the road and everyone's technical ability. As few as six riders can work a double echelon if they have the skill.

Big advantage for first echelon

Echelon size

When strong riders begin echeloning at the front, watch out—a breakaway may be imminent. Here the pressure is applied by the Soviet team, led by 1980 Olympic Champion Sergei Soukhoroutchenkov.

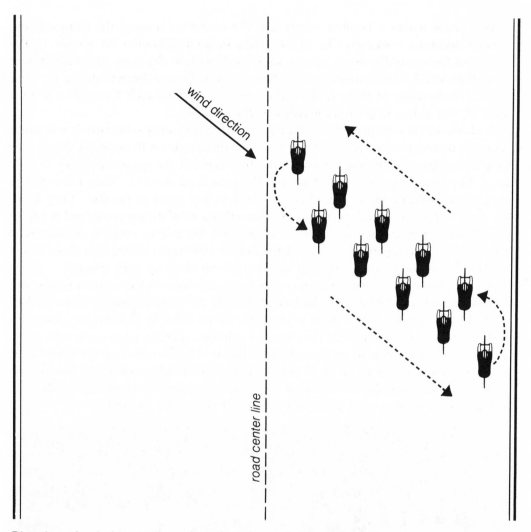

Direction of echelon rotation when there is a wind from the left.

When the double echelon forms, what happens to the rest of the field? Riders who don't get into the rotation string along the right side of the road (wind from left). They feel the brunt of the wind as they try to move up and squeeze in at the tail end of the echelon. Some actually lean far to the right to try for a little shelter — their bike is on the road but their body is off the edge. This is the critical point of the race. The echelon is made of strong riders because they are the ones who always ride at the front. Their speed increases as they begin trading pace into the wind. Each one gets good shelter and wastes no time in moving off the point position. Very soon there is a split — those who must fight the wind as they fight for a place in the echelon are dropped. A breakaway is the result.

How the breakaway forms

The only chance for those left behind is to quickly form a second echelon and take up the chase. They must not waste their energy with impossible individual attempts. The second echelon's chances are not great since so many strong riders are together up the road. Within the group will be various levels of ability, energy and ambition. This means it is often hard to form a smooth, strong chase. The better riders must do all they can to get the echelon organized. They must encourage the

Chasers' response

weaker riders to give a maximum effort: "C'mon guys. Let's catch them or die trying. We have nothing to lose. Let's go!"

The idea is to work hard, stay reasonably close, and hope something happens to slow down the leaders. Perhaps there is a forest ahead and the wind will be blocked, or a change in course direction will alter the wind and negate the front echelon's speed advantage. Maybe there will be punctures, a crash, or fighting among those riders. The chase must work at 105% to keep itself in position to benefit. The biggest hindrance may be the presence of riders who are intent on blocking for teammates in the front echelon. We'll soon see some ways to deal with them.

Joining the echelon

As the echelon is forming you must do everything you can to get in and stay in. Since it can be difficult to reenter the rotation if you drop all the way back to where riders are fighting for a place, look for a chance to move up into the front line before reaching the end. When a rider near you tries to do the same, move a little and let him in. It is important to make friends. Next time maybe he will open a space for you.

"Ticket puncher"

Sometimes a strong, experienced rider with very good bike-handling ability will station himself at the tail end of the developing echelon to "guard the gate." We call him the personnel officer or the ticket puncher. He decides who will be allowed to join the rotation. Usually his interest is in keeping out certain opposing riders so that his team captain, who is in the echelon, will have a better chance to win.

How to avoid a blocker

If the ticket puncher doesn't want a particular rider in, he will block that rider with his elbows and his bicycle. Faced with this aggression and the wind and the speed, it won't be long before the unwanted rider drops off. It's very tough to overcome these obstacles. The rider's best tactic may be to avoid the blocker altogether by moving way over in the road and trying to break into the middle of the echelon. I've even seen riders go all the way up to the point position in order to get a place. It's very hard to do this against the wind, but it will show everyone you mean business. Assert yourself. When you are strong let your legs do the talking. Other riders will respect this.

How to reduce the size of echelon

There is a tactic to reduce the number of riders in the echelon. When you want to get rid of some competition, squeeze over into the middle of the lane when you reach the point position. Then stay there. The others will start yelling. They will try to keep the echelon behind you, but there will only be room for about half of them. This works even better when one of your teammates is in position to guard the gate. He can let in your team's allies and try to keep out the main opponents. After about 2-3 km the selection will be made. Those who are left can then settle down to work and resume using the whole lane.

A strong team can accomplish the same thing if it has three or four members in the echelon. They all move to the front, squeeze over to halfway in the lane, and trade pace among themselves like a team time trial. Nobody else is allowed in. After several minutes of very high speed the riders who were forced to ride along the side of the road without shelter will be gone.

How to slow down an echelon

If you make the front echelon but your team captain doesn't, it is your job to slow the echelon down so it can be caught. There are various ways to do this but the goal is the same: disrupt the smooth rotation. Do it by pulling through too slow

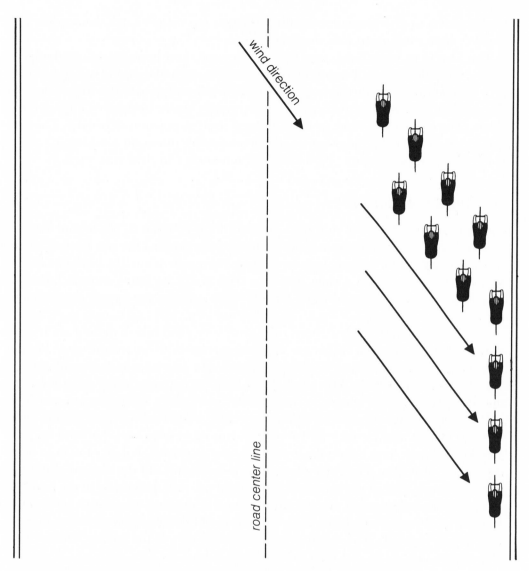

Technique of squeezing over in the lane to force riders out of echelon.

or too fast, or by sitting on the front. This invites verbal and physical abuse, so watch out. You might find yourself getting knocked down. You must show the others you are tough or you won't last long.

Be ready for an echelon to form in point-to-point races that have hot spot sprints in towns along the way. When riders go for these prizes the speed really increases. The field becomes one long line. Gaps begin to open. The riders who sprint usually sit up when they cross the line, which creates a perfect opportunity for others to attack. Soon the edge of town is reached and shelter from the buildings is lost. Or the course makes a turn. The result is a crosswind that lets the front riders go into echelon. I've seen this happen many times, and they just ride away. When you come to a town you must be close to the front whether you are interested in the hot spot or not. It is the only way to be safe.

Think ahead

Study the course so you know the location of every turn. A good coach will go over the map with his riders at breakfast. During the race analyze how each upcoming turn will affect wind direction, and position yourself accordingly. If you have a headwind now but in 2 km there is an intersection with a turn to the right, you know that it will produce a left crosswind. An echelon may develop. Move to the front and be ready.

CLIMBING

In climbing, as in every aspect of tactics, you must know who you are—what your strengths and weaknesses are. Then you must figure out where the course will play to your strong points and where it will accentuate your weak ones. Next, who is your competition?

Let's say the race is 160 km long and it has a 10 km climb. This will be the crucial aspect for you because your endurance and sprint are good but you aren't real strong on hills. In the field, however, are two guys who can go up as good as anybody in the country, Alexi Grewal and Andy Hampsten. You figure you can stay with them on other parts of the course, but how can you manage not to be hopelessly behind by the top of the hill?

Try to be as fresh as possible when the climbing starts. Until it does, ride quietly in the pack. Drink and eat for energy, but don't take any solid food during the 30 minutes before the hill. Prepare yourself mentally to make a strong effort. Expect to hurt, but believe that the pain will be worth it. If you can reach the finish line with the first group your sprint can get you a high placing.

Ride the front at your own best pace

Going into the climb, don't wait for riders like Grewal and Hampsten to begin dictating the pace. Don't hang back where a crash or bunch of slower riders can take you off the back right away. Instead, go to the front and ride at a speed that is good for you. Sometimes the road becomes narrower on a climb and this contributes to the riders' tendency to go into single file. Be ready for this. Don't get caught 25 riders back. There will be little you can do when the line stretches out and gaps start opening.

It is always better to be on the front and try to stay there than it is to try to catch up from behind. The reason is obvious: The lead riders can go along steadily at a speed 3 k.p.h. slower than anyone who is trying to catch them. But if you are not a super climber how long can you expect to stay with those who are?

The answer often depends on your acting ability. Maybe you are already climbing at your maximum pace. If you had to go even 1 k.p.h. faster you couldn't handle it. The good climbers could attack you at any time and leave you far behind during the second half of the hill. But they aren't likely to do it if they look over at your face and see no strain. They will say to themselves, "He still looks good. Let's wait

Don't show the strain

until he weakens before we jump." Little do they know that you are already cooked. The smile they see is a smile of pain. The longer you can make them think that you are having no trouble, the closer to the top they will take you. When the attack finally does come (and it almost certainly will) you won't lose as much time. Your chances of catching them on the descent are improved.

There is a lot of psychology in a tactic like this. If you can keep your act together imagine what might begin to go through the climbers' minds when their legs start burning and they still perceive you as strong. They will think, "I must be having

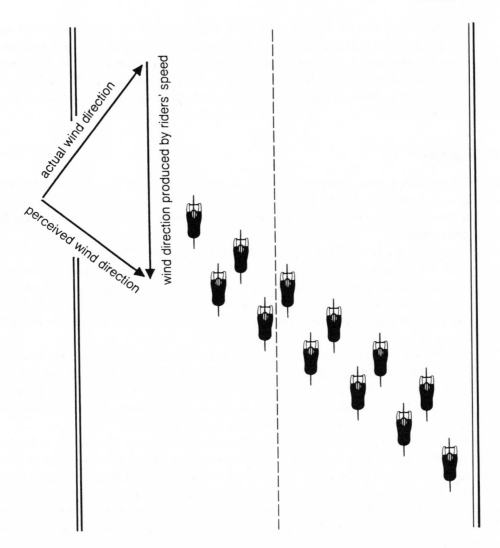

This diagram shows how the direction and speed of the riders changes the direction of the wind. In this case it is correct to echelon even though roadside trees, flags and the smoke from chimneys all indicate that there is a tailwind.

a bad day if that guy is keeping up so easily . . . there must be something wrong with me . . . I wonder what he took?" If you can trap them into this psychological game their doubts may be so great that they never will suspect you can be dropped.

Perhaps the best tactic of all is to stay right on the front, to lead on the climb. Ride at the maximum pace you can maintain to the top. Often this will be fast enough to keep everybody behind you for a while. When the pace you set is just 1-2 k.p.h. slower than the good climbers would go, they will be satisfied to let you lead much longer, especially if you appear to be fresh. When they do begin to pull alongside and go ahead, challenge them. Retake the lead and then ease back to your own best speed. Impose your pace as long as you can. In this way you will stay with them much closer to the top.

But what happens if your tricks don't work? What if the climbers are feeling as good as you are trying to act and they say, "Later"? First rule: Don't jump when

Stay in the lead

they jump. Many times the first attack is only to provoke you into blowing up. Let them have their 50 meters. Just keep your steady speed, keep working, and you may even gradually catch back up. If you do you know what's next — another attack. This time you probably will be off for good, but maintain your pace. As other riders in your group begin to go ahead, take a look to see who is still behind. When you are the last one before a big gap to the next group, do everything you can to stay in contact. By this time you should be near the top and you can risk blowing up. If you do slide backwards alone you won't lose a lot of ground. There will be some riders right in front of you to catch on the descent.

It all boils down to is this: Don't let other riders dictate to you. Know what you can handle and go at that pace. Sometimes a rider will pass you, move in front, and then start riding slower than you were going. Don't let him influence you — pass him right back. There is no disadvantage to being in the lead on a climb. The draft at 22 k.p.h. is not enough to help anyone, so ride in front where your speed can be exactly what you want it to be.

If you are a strong climber it is just as important to be near the front at the beginning of the hill. Don't think, "Oh I'm good, so I have plenty of time to move up later." Maybe, but that's not too smart. You will use a lot more energy chasing down the leaders than if you start going up with them. In any road race, and especially in a stage race, it is important to save energy whenever possible. Every single extra effort adds up and makes a difference by the end.

DESCENDING

Do you descend well? Then give people a hard time. Often a good climber, especially a young one, will not have as much talent going down the hill. Push. Check

When descending there is no need to stay glued to a wheel. Leave a gap for safety.

him out. Go fast and see what happens. Maybe he is chicken, maybe his technique is bad. Don't take a crazy risk but find out what he can do. Sometimes a rider who makes the break going up the hill will drop out of it going down.

You must not be the last rider in your group on the descent, but you also must not be the first if you don't know the road. Be second or third, not 15th where there is a much greater chance of being taken out by a crash.

When you know the descent or when there is a pace motorcycle right in front it's okay to lead. But it's even better to have a rabbit out there so you can play the fox. If you know he is familiar with the road use his knowledge to your advantage. Stay right with him. Have confidence that you can match everything he does. You are both human, you have a bike as good, your brakes are fine, your wheels are straight, your glue is tight. There's no way he can drop you. Put your wheels right where his just went, and stay about 10 meters behind. This gap is for safety, in case the worst happens and he goes into a turn too fast to make it. Then you have the split second you need to change your line and get through safely, or at least to lay your bike down and not follow him off the road. You have the benefit of seeing his mistake.

Follow an experienced rider

It is not correct to keep a low, streamlined position on a descent. Don't put your hands on the drops of the handlebars, put them on the brake lever hoods. This lets you sit up higher so you can see better and breathe easier to recover from the climb. It also gives you more bike control. Braking is no problem from over the top of the levers if you have normal hand strength. Also by sitting up tall you can let the wind on your chest help slow you down. Many riders descend on the drops, but if you use the hoods you will find it is the better position.

Hands on hoods, not drops

Another tip: Wear eye protection to keep out bugs, dust and the hard wind that makes your eyes water. If you suddenly can't see while going 80 k.p.h. through curves, it's a big problem. Keep sunglasses or goggles in a rear pocket and put them on just over the top of the climb.

Wear eye protection

Use a big gear going downhill, of course, but not always the biggest. It depends on your speed. You must be able to accelerate on not-so-steep sections. Your snap will probably be better if you aren't in top gear. Also, shift to a lower gear when there are sharp bends that make you slow down. Then you can turn quick pedal r.p.m. to get back to speed coming out.

Shifting gears

Always keep your legs moving even if you have spun out your biggest gear. Don't just hold them still in the cool wind. Revolving them slowly helps maintain blood circulation, which reduces the chance of sudden muscle tightness and cramping.

When a descent requires hard braking use both brakes simultaneously. If you apply only the rear brake it is easy to lock the wheel and skid to the outside of the curve. Your weight is on the front wheel so the front brake is much more effective, but using it without the rear can make the bike difficult to handle. At times you must apply the front brake harder, at times the rear brake harder. Make the adjustment based on how the bike is reacting. This ability comes with experience.

Braking

Some people say to alternately brake and release, brake and release to avoid overheating the rims and melting the glue. But I don't think this is a concern if the glue job is good and if you don't make the mistake of keeping the brakes on lightly all the time. Let the wheels roll free until you come to the turn, then brake as necessary. Resume pedaling when you are halfway through or as soon as you can. By putting power to the rear wheel even when the brakes are still on you will have more command of the bike. Try it and see. It helps you put the bike exactly where you want it.

The concept is the same as cornering a car. When you use the car's brakes into and through a turn, you feel unstable and you lose a lot of speed. But when you shift to a lower gear, apply the brakes lightly to correct the speed, and then accelerate around and out of the turn, it is much smoother, quicker and safer. It is a positive feeling.

TACTICS IN A GROUP

After a climb and descent the peloton probably will be broken into several groups. Some splits develop up the hill, and then the descent causes a further selection as riders go down at different speeds.

If you arrive on the flatter road in the front group decide what is good for you tactically. Maybe it's best to try to organize the riders and make the break succeed, maybe it's just the opposite. If you are in the second group and there is no teammate up front to protect, organize the echelon very quickly and chase hard. Don't give the break a chance to start increasing its lead.

When you've made the front group and you like the looks of it — that is, you think you can win against this opposition — try to inspire the others: "C'mon guys, we have a chance. Work together. Let's go!" Take good, strong pulls to show them you mean what you say, but don't overdo it. You mustn't deplete your own energy or blow off riders and cause the paceline to become ragged. Think about yourself. This is not a team time trial where you have to die on every pull.

On the other hand, do everything possible to slow down the break if you don't have a chance of outsprinting several of the riders, or if your team captain is chasing. In the latter case always keep an eye out behind. When you see him coming, and especially if he is alone, it may be best to drop out of the group and help pace him into contact. It depends on your strength. The ideal tactic is to go back, let the captain get on your wheel, and motor him up. Or at least trade strong pulls with him. But more than once I have seen a rider drop back and not have the strength to help the captain's effort long enough. Soon he is barely able to hold the captain's wheel or he gets dropped — the captain can't wait for him. If you don't have the necessary strength you will help the most by staying in the break and blocking as best you can.

Inspire others for your benefit

How to pace a rider into contact

Blocking

Blocking is a tactic used to disrupt a group and slow it down. There are several ways to block. One is to reach the point of the echelon and then squeeze over to halfway in the lane, as described above. This interrupts the smooth rotation of the riders, it makes them work harder, and it makes them mad. They start thinking about you instead of making maximum progress.

Another tactic is to slow down slightly when you are in second position. When the lead rider pulls through, a gap will open and he'll be sitting out there all by himself, doing nothing to help the break gain time. Don't slow down too much or the others will go right around. Reduce speed by 1-2 k.p.h., not 5 k.p.h., to keep them behind you as long as possible. After you've done what you can to foul things up, don't go all the way back to the last position. Squeeze into third or fourth place, move up, and do your tactic all over again. What you can get away with depends on how good you are and how inexperienced or timid the others are.

Sometimes a talented rider with enough determination can block even good riders who know exactly what he's trying to do. There was an excellent example of this in the final stage of the 1983 Coors Classic. Dale Stetina, in third place on general classification, got into an early break with more than a dozen very powerful East Europeans and Americans. It was a classic case of an echelon forming instantly in a crosswind and immediately riding away from the field. In fact, it was probably the most typically European road race ever seen in the U.S. It showed how a perfectly flat stage can have a major effect on GC. Take away the wind and that stage might have ended with a huge field sprint. With the wind it was a textbook illustration of the power of the echelon.

Stetina was in position to move into first place if he could gain 4:56 on the race leader, who had missed the echelon along with a number of other good riders, including Stetina's teammate, Alexi Grewal. Using the blocking tactics I've just described, Grewal worked against the chase's progress for almost 150 km and Stetina got more than enough time for the victory. After the race, Grewal told *Velo-news* what he had to endure at the front of the chase. "I was really getting beat up. Guys were elbowing me and hitting me all the time, especially the Swiss pros. That made me mad and then I really started getting into it. After a while they sort of gave in and were letting me move in anywhere I wanted."

What can be done to thwart a blocker besides the rough stuff? First, as soon as you see what he's up to, pass him. Immediately. When you are in second position and he tries to squeeze the echelon to the center of the road, go right underneath him and take it to the full lane again. This is a critical point because he and you are trying to use opposite tactics. It is when illegal activities can easily take place — bad language, elbows, and even punches.

You must be tough. You must repulse elbows with elbows of your own, but don't fight when you don't need to. Be fair, but don't be chicken. Sometimes you might need to lock your brakes in front of the blocker, not to make him crash but to let him know you are a dangerous guy to fool with.

If you bothered me when I was racing I would hit you with my rear wheel — bang it right into your front wheel and knock you down if you weren't a good bike handler. I would say, "You want to play? What kind of game do you want? I'm ready for anything. C'mon!" To get respect a rider must show he is strong. But, of course, this is exactly what the opponent is trying to do, too. The one who has strength and ability and *consistency* will get his way.

Always remember that there will be several riders in the group who have no real interest in going either faster or slower. If you are generally fair and use tough tactics only when an opponent uses them against you, you might swing the neutral riders to your side. If they decide to help you, your job will be much easier.

Counteracting a blocker

Conserving energy

Let's now assume you are an independent rider. You have no teammates to help or to help you, and you are in an eight-man break. Everybody is stronger than you, or at least equal. About 40 km remain. You figure that if the break is caught by the field your chances won't improve, so there is no good reason to try to slow things down. That would just waste energy, as would pitching in with pulls. After all, you'd only be helping the break take you to a certain defeat. What should be your tactic?

First, don't clean your face. Don't wipe away the salt, sweat and spit. Look like you are tired. Stay on the last position and get your bottle out. When the other riders come back after their turns at the front, tell them, "Go in, go in. I have to drink and eat now." Do this as long as you can get away with it, and as many times. When you do reenter the paceline, do it behind the biggest rider so you get the best draft.

At the front, pull only a couple of strokes. Don't give them any indication of what you can really do. Look bad, get as much rest as you can, and wait until the time is right. If you make the mistake of using your limited energy to pull through and look strong at this point in the race, you will be a marked rider at the finish. Your chance of springing a surprise in the final kilometers will be gone. By lying back it will be you who identifies the strong men.

Looking at this tactic from the opposite perspective, how does the break get rid of a guy who is having a free ride? First, tell him, "Work!" If he won't, then you and the others must take turns dropping him off the back. Here's how: When he is last in line and on your wheel, begin slowing down so a gap opens between the two of you and the group. When it has grown to 20-30 meters, move over and tell him, "Go!" If he doesn't wait that long and he goes around you, get on his wheel and let him take you back up. If he goes now, do the same. If he won't go, then you should switch suddenly across the road and jump hard. Don't let him get on your wheel. If he manages to make it back, the next rider immediately does the same tactic. Either the freeloader will blow up from the chasing and drop off for good, or he will begin doing his share of the work to stop the persecution.

Dealing with a sprinter

What should you do when one member of the break is a very good sprinter? You know that if everything goes along as is, he will have little problem beating you and the others. Maybe your strong points are endurance and power, but there isn't much distance left and no hills at all. What can you do about him?

First, understand the situation from his point of view. He is fast and smart and he doesn't much care if it is a one-on-one sprint or a group sprint, although the latter might make winning even easier — he can sit in, get a free ride, then take advantage of the other riders' moves to launch himself to the line. His tactic will be to join in every serious attempt to attack the break, but otherwise he will cheat everyone by doing just as little work as he can.

If there are riders who will work with you against the sprinter, save the tactics against him until the last 10 km. Of course if the chance presents itself sooner, take it. But your first concern must be to stay ahead of the chase. If you enter the final 10 km with a lead of two minutes or more, you are safe. You can then begin trying to give the sprinter a hard time. The goal is to reduce his authority at the end. Do this by tiring him, by making him give up hope for victory, or by dropping him when you (and possibly your allies) make an attack in the final minutes. By then it will be to everyone's advantage to work against him — if the sprinter is tired or gone, each remaining rider has a much better chance to win.

When there is a crosswind use it against him. Whether you are alone or with several other willing riders, stay close to the edge of the road (wind from left) or the centerline (wind from right) so he can't sit in the draft. Make him have to work to stay in contact. If you pull very hard for a kilometer and leave only enough room for your cohorts to echelon behind you, and then each of them does the same, a lot of kick will be taken out of the sprinter's legs.

If the wind is not a factor and it's just you and the sprinter together, or the other riders with you aren't anything to worry about, use your endurance to defeat him. When you are at the back and he can't see you, jump hard and go flying by. After he chases you down, go again at your next opportunity. Use your stamina now so he won't have much of a sprint later. Make him tired. Perhaps he will even decide to let you go and settle for "winning" second place against the rest of the break. Help him give up by discouraging him from sticking tightly to your wheel. Don't do anything illegal, but keep reminding him that following you around could be dangerous to his health.

The sprinter may decide that his best tactic is to let you go, then pursuade the others to chase. Even though he will have to work with them it won't be as hard as trying alone to counter your moves. If they can catch you he will still have enough left for the sprint. However, if you have good power and endurance you should be a good time trialist. Nobody should catch you if they spot you a lead inside the last 10 km.

I've seen many races won by a rider who breaks away alone and holds off 50 riders who are just 150-200 meters behind. I've done it several times myself because I was good in time trialing. The key is to go at your own best pace and don't worry about what's happening behind you. When you want to check them do it under your arm instead of over your shoulder so they don't think you are getting desperate. Sometimes you will see them going very fast, sometimes very slow. Everyone always wants someone else to set the pace; everyone thinks he can be the one to make a successful solo attack. That is the nature of the game, that is the gamble and the challenge. When you are time trialing toward the line you must be good and you must be lucky.

And it helps to have friends. For a classic example go back to Greg Demgen's victory in the 1982 National Road Championship. He was off the front alone with just 112 of the 182 km completed. Despite often being in sight of the chasers the rest of the way, he wasn't caught. It was an excellent ride, he was lucky, and he had valuable help. His teammates stayed in the chase group to protect him, even though several of them also had the talent to win.

Wayne Stetina was the only opposing rider who really chased Demgen hard and who had the strength to possibly succeed. If there had been three of him on the attack I don't believe Demgen would have won. It's not always a matter of the leader being physically overtaken; there is the mental resignation that often comes when he sees that the chase has cut deeply into his lead. If Stetina and others had been allowed to get even 10 seconds closer, perhaps Demgen would have decided to sit up and get caught. Maybe he would have figured it was better to try another move later or lead out one of his faster-finishing teammates.

Remember Jacques Boyer at the end of the 1982 Professional World Road Championship? He gave us a perfect example of how a rider with good endurance can try to beat the sprinters to the punch late in a race. His solo break was a smart move. It was a reasonable risk and he came close to making it succeed. He took the challenge. If the others had not chased him in time, he would have won.

Giuseppe Saronni was as smart as he was fast in the 1982 World Championship. He glued up to Greg LeMond to catch Jacques Boyer, then he jumped past LeMond to take a clear victory. Was this a bad move on LeMond's part? Not when it paid off with the Silver Medal.

Boyer was good enough to be the champion, but he wasn't quite lucky enough. And he had no U.S. team behind him, which may have been the decisive factor. He later argued about Greg LeMond's tactics in the chase group, but when had Boyer ever worked for LeMond? What motive did LeMond have to help Boyer? In this race each one was working for himself, for money, for his next contract. Le-Mond had to push hard when he did or else he would have finished not only behind Giuseppe Saronni, he would have been beaten by Sean Kelly and maybe others, too. LeMond has been criticized for towing Saronni up to Boyer and putting Saronni in perfect position to win, but we must always remember that Greg ended up in second place. It is not stupid to chase and finish second. It is stupid to chase and finish worse than you would have if you hadn't made the effort.

Sprint tactics

It is so easy to win the sprint at the end of a road race. With 500 meters to go, move into third position. At 300, be second. At 200, attack. When you have the speed nobody will beat you.

Well, it's easy to say, but not quite as easy to do. There is a lot that goes on when a group approaches the finish line, and team tactics often are crucial. Without help even a great sprinter may not get into position to win. And even if he has team-mates they might not give him their best effort if they don't have confidence in him. It is a delicate balance.

Each team member must feel it is 100% good for him to sacrifice his own chance in order to set up his sprinter. That is why Saronni was in position to win the 1982 Worlds—all the Italians were working for him late in the race. And, come to think of it, that's why Freddy Maertens won in 1981. Not because the Belgians were working for him, but because the Italians were working for Saronni. Maertens saw it developing and he glued up to Saronni at the end, getting a perfect leadout. It was a tactical mistake by the Italians to let this happen, but Maertens was a smart and very fast rider. Anybody who gives a guy like that the chance to be World Champion will have to fight to the death to keep him out of there. It's a war. But it wasn't up to Saronni himself to keep Maertens off his wheel, it was up to Saronni's teammates to use tactics like those I've been describing. Saronni can't get involved or he might fall, and then he'd have no chance at all.

1981 Worlds

No two sprints are exactly the same, even if they are contested by the same riders. Maertens may beat Saronni today, but next week it will be the reverse. There are so many variables that go into determining the outcome—supporting riders, team strategy, motivation, nerves, energy, luck, etc.—that it's virtually impossible to correctly predict the first five riders in any bunch sprint. If they rerode the final kilometer of the 1982 Worlds 10 times, there would be 10 different results. Saronni certainly would not be first in each one.

What could LeMond have done differently to win that race? This is a good lesson for every rider because it is basic to all attacking, whether it is done to try for victory or to bridge from one group to another. Basically, LeMond's jump was not strong enough to prevent other riders—primarily Saronni—from quickly gluing up. One

LeMond's error

Freddy Maertens won the 1981 World Championship because he picked the right wheel to be on in the sprint. Maertens saw the Italians leading out Saronni, right, so he got on Saronni's wheel and used him for his own leadout. It worked perfectly.

reason was LeMond's location—he was at the front so Saronni and everyone else could easily see him go. Greg would have had a better chance if he accelerated from farther back and took those on the front by surprise. When a strong rider can do this and get a gap of five meters before the others respond, they will have a very tough time catching him. When they don't have his draft they must work just as hard.

Saronni made no mistakes and that's why he won. He knew he had second place locked up—he would win the field sprint if Boyer stayed away. But if he tried to attack to catch Boyer, and fast riders like Kelly got on his wheel, it was possible he would not win a medal at all. So Saronni sat tight and gambled that someone else would go after Boyer before it was too late. He was smart enough to figure it would be LeMond, perhaps because he knew of the rivalry between the two Americans. When LeMond did attack, you could actually see the smile on Saronni's face.

LeMond's World Championship

As smart as Saronni was in 1982, that's how smart Greg LeMond was in 1983. He gave us an incredible show at the World Professional Championship in Switzerland. I was so happy to be there and watch him do everything perfectly to earn that victory.

LeMond became visible at the front after the halfway point. He knew that nothing important would happen in the first 100 km—it never does in pro races because they are so long (this one was 270 km). At midrace a dozen riders moved off the front and LeMond was right there. He saw potential danger because Phil Anderson was involved, but it was too early. LeMond pulled through but didn't work hard, and the group was caught after about 25 km.

Next, seven riders escaped and this time LeMond was not with them. The gap reached three minutes before the field began its chase. All seven riders were from different nations, so no team was interested in trying to block. LeMond was a beneficiary —it meant he did not have to exert himself to close the gap. He let the work be done by the Italians, who seemed intent on getting Saronni into position for another championship. In a way, the 1982 table had been turned.

With less than 40 km to go, six of the seven riders were caught. A Swiss remained out front, but his lead was shrinking. Now LeMond made his move. He attacked and only two riders, an Italian and a Spaniard, were able to go with him. The field had just completed the long chase and LeMond caught it off guard. It was the classic bridge. He jumped away instantly and powered right into contact. Then he kept the pressure on. He pushed hard because he was feeling good and the end was close. He believed he could succeed. He also was lucky, because he got some unintentional but valuable help from the Italian team. It went to the front of the field to block because the Italian in the break, Argentin, was a strong sprinter. His team figured he would beat the other three at the finish.

Again LeMond did the right thing. He kept the pace hard on the hills to take the speed out of Argentin and the others. He was glad for their help on the descents and flats, but he didn't want them conserving any energy. He knew they would get no help from his draft on the climbs, so he willingly set a fast pace. They had to ride very hard to stay with him. The tactic worked well.

Maybe too well, I thought, when first the Swiss and then the Italian lost contact. I feared it was too early to drop Argentin because it would make the Italians stop blocking. The door would open for a strong chase by the field. This made me very

These pictures show the key elements to Greg LeMond's 1983 World Championship. First, LeMond declined to drop Ruperez on the climbs so the Spaniard could share the work on the descent and flats. Second, LeMond made a determined, all-out effort once he decided to go it alone. Third, his tactics paid off with a victory by more than one minute.

nervous. But LeMond sensed that keeping Argentin would cost him too much time. There came the point when he felt it was better to gamble his strength against the response of the field. He took the challenge.

Now it was LeMond and the Spaniard. Behind them the Italians knew the game was over and several of them abandoned. The chases began, but they failed to pose a serious threat. The field was almost a minute and a half behind — too far back if LeMond could maintain a strong pace to the finish. Again he was very smart.

He knew he could drop the Spaniard, Ruperez, if he attacked him on the climbs, but he also knew that Ruperez was still strong enough to help him make time on the descents and flats. So LeMond waited until the final 15 km lap had started. Then he pulled away from Ruperez on a hill, using only as much energy as necessary. From there it was a time trial to the finish line. LeMond was wonderful! He did not lose a second during the lap and he arrived more than one minute ahead of the next rider. It was one of the largest winning margins in recent World Championships. LeMond left nothing to chance. In 1982 he finished second to a sprinter; in 1983 he made sure the sprinters were nowhere close.

When LeMond was in the U.S. program we taught him these tactics. That is not bragging because they are the same tactics we teach all our riders, and the same that this book is teaching to you. Tactics are always the same, whether they are used in your local road race or the World Championship. What LeMond has done with the basic knowledge we gave him is develop the strength to use it to maximum advantage. He has also studied the pros he races against. He knows who they are, their strong points and weak points. This is why he could afford to ease up for Ruperez's sake and coax the Spaniard to contribute as much as possible to their break. LeMond knew that Ruperez was no threat to beat him for the title.

I am so pleased to have worked with LeMond. With his victory he paid me back for all the time I ever spent with him. You cannot believe how happy I was. I remember back in 1977 when we first got together. Greg was a boy who was crazy for cycling. He loved it. Even then he had dedicated his life to bicycle racing, to winning. He had the primary quality of Merckx and the other great riders: Winning was more important than the prize, cycling was more important than anything. LeMond now has a lovely wife and they have begun a family, but I suspect that at this time in his life cycling is still No. 1. It is the attitude a rider must have to become a World Champion, to be the best in the world. I love a rider like that.

Field sprinting

Some road sprinters, like Saronni and Kelly, use a sudden, high-speed burst close to the line to get off a wheel and fly past the remaining opposition. Others have the ability to reach the same top speed but they can't get there as quickly. Usually they are the victims of the first type. Does this sound familiar? What can you do to win against a guy with jack rabbit acceleration?

How to deal with the "jack rabbits"

When a group enters the final kilometer its tendency is to slow down. The sprinters begin looking for the wheels they want, and everyone tries to collect his thoughts and energy. This is perfect for the sprinters because the slower they go and the closer they get, the more unanswerable their acceleration will be. Your best tactic, therefore, is to take their acceleration away from them.

Begin with about 300-400 meters to go, or even 500 if the pace is really slow. Take the front at good speed, but not too near your maximum. Then go a little faster every 50 meters. The sprinters on your wheel will start saying to themselves, "This is fast. I have to wait before I go around." You go faster and they wait longer. Reach your top speed with 150 meters to go. Now they must make their move because the line is so close. But when they swing out of your draft their jump will be almost nothing—they are going too fast to accelerate. If you are strong enough you can hold off everyone; if not, you will still get a high placing. When there is a crosswind

This photo sequence from a sprint in the Tour de France shows what can happen when a rider "closes the gate" too late. Without a chance to get by or back out, Frenchman Michel Laurent caught his wheel in the barricade. His hard fall resulted in a broken wrist, but he was later awarded the stage victory. The judges decided that the other rider, Henk Lubberding of Holland, had dangerously moved over on Laurent.

and you force them to try to pass on the windward side, you will beat them for sure.

Always use the wind. If it is coming from the left and a rider is on your wheel, ride along the very right side of the road against the crowd or curb so he can't get your draft. On the other hand, if you have a gap on the next rider, ride along the left side so the crowd or buildings will give you shelter.

Use the wind

Another wind-related tactic is to open the gate for the rider behind you and then close it on him. Let's say the wind is coming from the left. You are leading out the sprint along the right side of the road to deny the draft, but you feel like the guy on your wheel may have enough strength to jump by and beat you. Keep the speed a little below your maximum and give him some room between yourself and the curb with about 200 meters to go. He won't believe his luck—a chance to pass you on the sheltered side. What could be easier? When he takes the bait, move slightly back toward the curb. Now he's trapped. He can't get past you on the right and it's too late to back out and go around on the left. This will probably foul up anyone on his wheel, too. They'll flinch and slow down when he does. If this works perfectly you'll win. If he doesn't bite he'll still have to pass on the wind side. If he can beat you doing that, he deserves it.

Open the gate, close the gate

The main danger in this tactic is causing a crash or being disqualified under USCF rule 1L6: "No rider may make an abrupt motion so as to interfere with the forward progress of another rider, either intentionally or by accident. . . ." Note the word "abrupt." It is the judge's decision. You must close the gate gently and do it just as the rider's front wheel moves between your rear wheel and the curb. Don't wait until he is almost even with you. You don't want any contact, you just want to make it impossible for him to pass. The slight movement necessary is nothing compared to the wild switching in many bunch sprints. An intelligent official will not see it as illegal but as a valid tactic on your part.

Leadouts

When good teams are involved in a bunch sprint the leadout strategies will decide the top finishers. One or more team members will sacrifice their own chances by taking their sprinter to the front, then accelerating to a high speed with him in tow. At 100-150 meters to go he will jump and quickly reach his own maximum speed. It's hard to overcome such teamwork if you are riding alone. You must be smart and identify a rider who is likely to be given a leadout. If you can get on his wheel you may be able to use *him* to give *you* a leadout. That's what Maertens did to Saronni in the 1981 Worlds. Even if you can't get past him he will still take you to a top placing.

Team "train"

A team's dream is to arrive at the final kilometers with four or five of its riders in the lead group. When they go to the front and make their train nobody will be able to pass. The field will change from a bunch of riders to a long, suffering line. This can begin from as far as 5 km out if the team has the numbers and the horsepower. When the speed winds up to 55-65 k.p.h. with that much distance remaining, what can anybody do? Each teammate takes a super pull, one after the other until the last man, the sprinter, is hurled toward the line. Each man kills himself to put one teammate in position to win. When this is done right it's beautiful to see . . . and virtually unstoppable.

Try to stay among the front six riders in the final kilometers. As the sprint begins winding up, expect attacks along both sides. Jump left and jump right to take a better wheel at every opportunity, but never lead. Keep your eyes open, see what is developing. Watch out for an elbow when the guy you are following pulls off. Beware of someone closing the gate when you try to pass along the curb. When you move you must be quick. You must be tough, not chicken. You must be a gambler. I love to see the last kilometer when 50 good riders are still together. The movement is incredible, like a super ballet on the road. Attack left, attack right, attack this way, attack that way . . . what a dance!

Remember, in a sprint you can have only one tactic. You can't change your mind in the middle of it and try something different. If you do you will lose for sure. When there is a tailwind the sprint will be longer than against a headwind, but how long is *your* sprint? When you know that your jump is good for 150 meters and nobody can beat you in that distance, you must wait until then before making your move. Do what you do best. When the others allow you this opportunity, they won't beat you very often.

OVERCOMING BAD LUCK

Throughout this book I mention the need for luck. Sometimes the luck you have, however, will be the wrong kind. Let's look at the team and individual tactics to use when there is a puncture, mechanical problem or crash that results in a rider losing contact with the field.

Punctures

Flat tires are common in road races because the courses aren't swept clean, as they often are for criteriums. It has been proved many times that it's possible to come back from more than one puncture and win the race, so it is important to accept flat tires as part of the game and not give up when you get one. It's a great advantage to have teammates or friends who will help you get back into the fight with a minimum of lost time and effort.

When it is the captain who flats, some teammates should go to the front to try to slow the field and the others should go to the back. Usually the next best rider is one who heads forward. If the captain is not able to make it back, then the No. 2 man must be in position to take over for the team. When the support vehicle is not in sight, one of the team workers should stop and give the captain a wheel. It is far better for a worker to be the one who falls behind and chases, not the man who can possibly win the race.

If the captain has a softening tire instead of a sudden flat, the team should do its best not to let on what's happening. The captain should ease back slowly and inconspicuously to get into position for a wheel change. When his teammates see this happening they should move to the locations just mentioned. All communiction is done with glances and slight gestures, not with words. When other teams realize what is happening they might attack.

How the team responds

Wheel changes

A wheel change can be a minor inconvenience or a major setback. A lot depends on how well you and team support work in concert. Here are some tips for smooth and quick wheel changes.

As soon as the tire or wheel fails, use the standard hand signal to let the support vehicle know what you need. Left hand up means a front wheel, right hand up means a rear wheel. This corresponds to the hand used to shift the front and rear derailleur. Your signal also warns other riders that you are having trouble so they can get by safely. If the support is far down the road and it will be a minute or two before it arrives, keep pedaling even though the tire may be entirely flat. It is better to ruin a rim than to lose time just standing beside the road.

How to signal for a new wheel

Before stopping for a rear wheel shift onto the smallest cog. This moves the derailleur all the way over so the mechanic will be able to put in the new wheel quickly and the gear system will remain in alignment. Stop the bike, get off, open the brake, then pull the bad wheel out of the frame. When the mechanic arrives hold the bike steady while he installs the wheel, then remount and put your feet back in the pedals as he pushes you off. This should be a very efficient operation, and it will be if two things happen: (1) The team practices rear wheel changes; (2) The team uses identical equipment. Every wheel must be interchangeable from bike to bike. There must be no variation in freewheel spacing, no incompatibility of chains and cogs. Otherwise chain skip and shifting problems will result.

Rear wheel change

Front wheel change

When the front wheel fails, shift into a midsize cog before stopping. You need a gear you can turn when you start the chase. Take out one foot (not both) to stand on, then reach forward to open the brake and throw out the wheel. Hold up the front end of the bike as the mechanic installs the new wheel. Insert your foot and tighten the strap during the push off.

Regaining the field

Use draft from the caravan

Use the draft from the support caravan to get back up to the field. You can't just sit on your own team vehicle and let it tow you into contact, but it is not illegal to work your way from car to car as long as you don't dwell behind each one for more than a few seconds. The technique is to go fast between one car and the next, then pause on the bumper for maybe 100 meters to breathe deep and recover. This may result in a warning from the commissaire, but almost never a penalty.

Team technique

When teammates drop back for their captain they are the ones who do the pulling between cars. The captain sits on to save strength. The crucial point comes when they must bridge from the caravan to the field. Most commissaires keep this gap at 100-150 meters, so it can be tough to cross when there is a headwind or crosswind. The captain must do whatever is necessary to make it. He must take the initiative even if it means hurting his teammates. There can be no pussyfooting. Once the last caravan vehicle has been passed, it is imperative to get back into the shelter of the field as fast as possible. If his teammates can't help him any longer the captain must go it alone. He can hope they will be able to stay on his wheel, but he can't ride less intensely for their sake. His only goal is to return to the front. A break may form at any second. It's all the more likely when the other teams realize he is missing.

Crashes

A crash causes different problems than a puncture. Usually it means a significantly longer delay. Perhaps both wheels will have to be replaced, or even the entire bike (which costs an extra moment to adjust the saddle). When you go down with other riders it takes a while to get everything untangled, and then there is the confusion of several support vehicles and people all on the scene at once. Finally, there is the problem of personal injury. It may take you a few minutes to feel capable of riding again.

Reach the caravan quickly

When you crash and are behind even the caravan, you must take it upon yourself to lead the chase. Your chance of getting back into the race begins with getting back among the vehicles. If you are with teammates or other riders who are strong and can contribute, fine — trade pace with them. If not, you have to pull most of the way. There really isn't a choice. If you don't make it back you are a loser.

Beware of drivers' tactics

Upon catching the caravan you may find that drivers from opposing teams are letting long gaps open to the next vehicle. This means longer periods without shelter as you try to move up, but it won't defeat you if you've done your interval training. It is time for a hard jump and fast pace from one car to the next, not steady riding at less than maximum effort. When you reach the final two vehicles slow down slightly for some extra recovery before the big effort back to the field. Once you pass the commissaire's car it is do or die.

In this scene from the Giro d'Italia, rider No. 142 has punctured and his teammate has stopped to give him a wheel. This is an example of how a lower placed rider or domestique can help his team's better rider succeed. While No. 149 stands waiting for the replacement wheel, No. 142 can be making his way back to the peloton and into contention.

Capitalizing on another rider's problem

Now let's suppose the situation is reversed. You are safely in the front of the field and a strong opponent is stopped by a flat or other problem. What should be your tactic?

Raise the speed. This will be helped by your teammates and by members of some other teams. It will be opposed by the stricken rider's teammates and possibly their allies. But if you can succeed in either creating a break or dropping a few riders, you will make it much more difficult for your opponent to get back into contention.

The reason is simple: The commissaire's car, which leads the caravan and may not be passed by any other vehicle without permission, will stay behind a small group dropped by the field. Only when the gap becomes very large will the commissaire allow team vehicles, one by one, to pass his car and the group to go back up behind the field. He will wait until he feels certain that no vehicle going ahead will be close enough to the group to give it a helpful draft. This means trouble for your opponent. He will get caravan help to catch the dropped group, but very little caravan help to catch the field.

How the commissaire directs vehicles

So whether your efforts help a group go off the front or off the back, it increases the distance the opposing rider must cover after he passes the caravan. Since that is some of the toughest ground there is, especially when an unfavorable wind is blowing, he may be too tired to be a threat even if he makes it back.

RACE FOOD

What to eat and drink during a road race depends on its length, on the temperature, and on what your experience has shown you need. One basic rule is to eat more when it is rainy and cold than when it is sunny and hot. The food energy helps maintain body temperature.

I am not in agreement with physiologists who say you should not eat meat during a race. It is argued that meat will stay in the stomach for hours and not be of any benefit. Research has been done to prove this, but it has been done on regular people, not on highly trained endurance cyclists during competition. If the studies had been done on such athletes I think the physiologists would have found different answers.

It is especially important to eat meat during a stage race, as I discuss in Chapter 8. I've seen riders eat chicken legs and slabs of ham. This is fine and it works. When you are racing day after day it is better for digestion when you have something besides glucose and sweet foods in your stomach.

For a long one-day road race meat is up to the individual. Meat isn't absolutely necessary, but if you like it and the weather isn't extremely hot, by all means eat it. In very hot temperatures fruit is the best choice because it is wet and easy to swallow. Meat becomes unappetizing in the heat.

When the race is around 160 km carry food with you or pack a musette to pick up in the feed zone. In Europe feeds are permitted anywhere from the 80 km mark all the way to 10 km from the finish, but in the U.S. feeding is often limited to one short stretch in the middle of the race. I hope we will change to the European method because it is better for the riders. The U.S. requires riders to start with full pockets and three bottles. This feels heavy and it makes it hard to get what you want out of the pockets. If it is raining the food can be ruined before it is time to eat it.

For safety always begin the race with some food. Carry the minimum that you can complete the race on in case something happens to make you miss your feed. For example, there could be a car problem that causes your feeder not to arrive.

You must eat during a road race, especially when it is cold. Food energy is necessary for maintaining body temperature.

Or a crash in the feed zone that makes you miss your hand-up. Hot weather simplifies food choice because you should eat only fruit and drink glucose mixture. But when it is cooler or wet I recommend sandwiches in addition to fruit.

Sandwiches? What kind—peanut butter and jelly, or hamburger? No, a special type used by professional cyclists and good amateurs. These are sandwiches that can be eaten in about three bites. To make one use two small pieces of crispy bread, like toast. Touch one side of each piece very quickly to a saucer of white dinner wine. This adds flavor, helps digestion, and it will slowly seep through to make the bread soft by the time you eat it. If you start with soft bread it will become like putty.

How to make race sandwiches

On one wine-dipped side spread butter and a soft cheese like Brie or cream cheese. Use what tastes good to you. Then put on some jam or marmalade, and top with the second piece of wine-dipped bread. Make another sandwich the same way, only substitute a piece of sweet ham for the jam. Depending on the length of the race and how cold it is, you may want to take two sandwiches of each type. Wrap them separately in foil.

Eat solid food periodically during the first half of the race when the pace is relatively slow and steady. This food will have time to digest and supply energy for the final hour. Later when the pace increases and attacks must be answered, it is hard to put down anything but glucose tablets and mixture. In the final 30-45 minutes forget solid food altogether. Anything you eat then will not have time to be converted into energy before the finish. Instead, take only glucose mixture or go to your atom bottle of strong coffee with glucose *(see below)*.

Eating schedule

Liquids

When road races are long in the heat of summer, fluid replacement becomes very important. Make your mixture of glucose, vitamin C, minerals, and tea (cold)—or whatever formula you develop through experimentation—and drink one third of a bottle about 30 minutes before the start. Save the rest for after the race. Never get off the bike and start drinking water like a duck. Clean your mouth, wash your face, and sip from the bottle of mixture. You may be very thirsty but you must have self-control. Your body needs what that bottle has in it more than it needs a lot of plain water. Too often I've heard the sound of water sloshing when riders walk by. That's bad because when you fill up on liquid you lose your appetite and don't want to eat a proper meal.

Drink sparingly after race

Start the race with a bottle of glucose mixture in one cage and a bottle of plain water in the other. Put a second glucose bottle in your jersey pocket if there isn't a feed until the midway point in the race. Make sure your feeder will give you a glucose bottle at that time, and possibly more water. Water is necessary in a hot-weather race. It can be used to clean the mouth, but it is even more valuable as a spray for your neck, head and face. This is very refreshing. Use an insulating bottle cover to keep the water cool and effective. All bottles should go into your cages straight from an ice chest on the starting line.

Carry water for spraying

Begin drinking glucose mixture soon after the start. Take a sip every 10-12 minutes. You must steadily replenish the fluid that's being lost through sweating. Put a glucose tablet in your mouth and let it dissolve slowly. When it's gone put in another, and do this throughout the race. You must keep the sugar in your blood very high

Importance of sugar

all the time. Energy comes first from the glycogen stored in muscles and then from glycogen in the liver. Liver glycogen is replaced through the physiology of the stomach, which makes it important for the stomach to be supplied with sugars.

Some of the energy replacement drinks like Pripps Pluss and Excel are fine—they contain sugars and some minerals—but I don't think they are quite enough for most riders. You can put together something that gives you more benefits, perhaps by using one of these commercial drinks and adding to it. But no matter what the drink, it is still necessary to eat tablets of glucose, dextrose or fructose. Use the type you like—some athletes prefer fructose because it is fruit sugar and they feel it works better—and carry a lot of it. It's always better to have more tablets than you need rather than one too few. It all comes down to training your system—your stomach, liver, and muscles—to take the sugar you give them and give you back energy.

In the days before a race make sure to get plenty of vitamins, especially B-complex. This shouldn't mean a big change because your general nutrition should be rich in vitamins and minerals. On the evening before a race take a multivitamin tablet and a B-complex tablet with one full bottle of glucose mixture about 30 minutes before going to bed. In the morning your urine will be dark with the excess. This is normal. It means your body has taken in everything it needs.

Take vitamins, glucose before bed

Race Menu

Putting it all together, here is what to eat during a road race of about 160 km or longer when it is not extremely hot:

- Glucose mixture (at least two bottles)
- A supply of glucose tablets (or fructose or dextrose)
- Fresh and dried fruit
- One or two cheese sandwiches with jam
- One or two cheese sandwiches with ham

This is the correct order in which to eat the solid food:

1. Glucose tablets (one in mouth continually)
2. Ham sandwiches
3. Jam sandwiches
4. Fruit

The eating order is important because it gives each food time to digest and provide energy as the race goes on. If you eat the sandwiches too late they will still be sitting in your stomach in the final sprint. You must also know the terrain. Never eat right before a hard climb because your blood will go to the stomach for digestion when it is needed by muscles. Instead, stop eating 30 minutes before the hill and only drink glucose.

Atom bottle

For the end of the race I recommend a small bottle—the atom bottle—containing strong coffee, coffee with glucose, or even coffee with glucose and rum. I prefer the second formula. Use espresso coffee and experiment with the strength during training races. It will open your eyes and give you a good heart reaction, especially if you follow a good athlete's diet and do not have coffee regularly.

Drink down the atom bottle with about 10 km to go if you are in contention for a victory. If you have missed the break don't use it just to finish 15th, for instance, instead of 18th. Give it to your body only when it can make a meaningful difference. There is no danger of this caffeine causing a positive result in a dope test. It is not nearly a large enough quantity.

If your stomach cannot handle coffee you can get somewhat of a boost by drinking Coke late in the race. It has caffeine (not as much as coffee) and sugar. Before you put Coke in a water bottle shake it very well to get rid of all its bubbles. You can't be burping and sprinting at the same time.

Pre- and post-race meals

At least two hours before the race, finish eating a good size meal with a variety of foods you enjoy. What to eat depends on what you are accustomed to having before all long-distance training and racing. Accentuate the carbohydrates, but include protein and fats. This meal should satisfy you and make you confident. Do not experiment with foods new to you—save that for training rides.

Following the race, drink a moderate amount of glucose mixture, then go get your shower and massage. Only after you have cleaned up and calmed down should you eat solid food. Have a normal meal of foods that you like. There is no need for anything special or additional. You may not feel like eating, but once you begin your appetite will come. You must eat because your body needs the nutrients. Make the atmosphere as quiet and relaxing as possible. A coach who uses this meal to talk about the race and scold riders for their mistakes is making a big one himself. It will only upset everyone's digestion.

Feed zones

Before leaving this topic it is important to say a few words about the correct way to feed a rider during the race. Support people must know how to hand a bottle to a moving rider, and a rider must know how to take it. When the bottle is dropped there is no second chance. Usually feed zones are on uphills, so riders are going slow and hand-ups aren't too difficult. But even at 45-50 k.p.h. there shouldn't be a problem.

To give a bottle, the feeder grasps it by the very top and runs straight along the side of the road. He holds the bottle back toward the rider, then swings his arm forward just as the rider comes up. The rider, as he reaches out to take the bottle, swings his arm backward. The result is that the rider's hand speed is virtually the same as the feeder's. The rider does not make hard contact with the bottle so it is easy for him to grasp it. This coordination is not as difficult as it might sound, especially when the rider is going relatively slow, but it helps to practice.

How to hand up a bottle

It is a similar procedure to give a musette. The feeder runs along the road with his arm out and his hand spread wide so there is a space between the straps. When the rider is moving slow he reaches out and grabs the strap with his hand. Then he sits up and puts the strap over his head and across one shoulder. If he is moving fast he catches the musette by sticking his arm through the strap so it runs right

How to hand up a musette

Even when moving fast in a big gear, it should be easy to take a bottle. Here Tom Prehn uses the correct technique—he has swung his arm back as the feeder has swung the bottle forward. Note that the feeder is properly dressed in a team jersey.

up onto his shoulder. After he puts the supplies in his pockets and bottle cages he tosses the musette aside. Again, a little practice can pay off in the race situation.

The feeder must always wear clothing that can be identified from long distance by his riders. Normally this means he should wear a team jersey. That's one of the U.S. team's big advantages in international competition. Our star-spangled jersey makes it very easy for the riders to spot the support people, and vice versa.

RACE CLOTHING

Since road races take place in all types of temperature and weather conditions, the proper clothing depends entirely on what is expected for the particular day. Body comfort and protection, not aerodynamics, are the most important considerations when you'll be on the bike for four hours or more.

Jersey

Whatever type of material you choose (or your club supplies), the jersey must fit comfortably and have three large, accessible pockets in the back for carrying food and bottles. Correct fit is very important. When a jersey is too small or tight it is difficult to get into the pockets. When it is too large the pockets hang down over the saddle when there is weight in them. They may catch air like a parachute when they are empty.

On a cold, wet day wear a long-sleeve wool jersey with a wool, wool/cotton blend, or polypropylene long-sleeve undershirt. Between these garments put one piece of plastic to cover your chest and another piece to cover your back. An easy way to do this is by slitting the sides of a plastic garbage bag (so air can circulate) and cutting a hole in the closed end for your head to go through. If the rain stops during the race or you start getting too hot, it's easy to reach up and pull out the plastic. I also recommend wearing a bandana to keep a cold wind off your throat and neck. It, too, can easily be removed at any time. By the way, a plastic bag can protect your feet as well as your torso. First put on a sock, then a small bag, then the shoe.

Use plastic for protection in cold, wet weather

When it's only chilly, forget the plastic and wear a short-sleeve wool jersey. Choose a long- or short-sleeve undershirt, depending on what the temperature is expected to do. On warmer days wear a thin wool undershirt and race in a lightweight wool, cotton, synthetic or blended jersey. Use what feels best to you. (Even in hot weather you should wear an undershirt when you race. It helps reduce road burn in a crash.) Stay away from dark-colored jerseys in the summer because they will make you hotter by absorbing the sun's rays.

Always wear an undershirt

Long wool tights are always a good idea when training in even slightly cool weather, but they should not be worn in a race. The only exception might be when it is extremely cold. The problem with tights is that they still create air resistance by making your legs bigger with rough material. Also, legs work so hard in a race that long tights may cause you to become overheated. It is much better to wear shorts and

Don't wear long tights

The feeder should hold the musette straps apart so the rider can either grab one or put his arm through the middle.

use hot cream. If it is also raining, cover your skin with Vaseline after the cream is applied. It is certainly a mistake to race in tights in the wet. The material will become heavy with water and make your legs feel cold.

Shorts

Many different styles of shorts are now available, but not all are well designed. Some have a synthetic chamois, which is better than nothing but not as good as quality soft leather. A padded chamois will improve comfort *if* it is properly designed. If not, it will give you lots of trouble. Also, for shorts to be comfortable they must stay in the right place. The legs must be long enough to prevent them from bunching up in the crotch. Unless the shorts have a bib top, wear suspenders to keep them up. Suspenders are essential on a rainy day.

Synthetics are best for racing

Various materials are being used to make shorts, including wool, cotton, Lycra, and other synthetics and blends. Lately the trend has been away from natural fibers to the shiny, lightweight, nonabsorbent aerodynamic materials. This makes sense to me. The traditional fabric, wool, now has become suitable only for training in cool weather. It is not seen in races any more since the synthetics and natural/synthetic blends have become available. Pure synthetics feel colder on the skin than natural materials, but this doesn't matter when you are working hard in a race. Lycra, for example, is lighter than wool or cotton, it won't soak up the rain, and it is much slipperier in the wind.

The most important point about shorts is this: They must feel good on you. In general, it is best to buy shorts made by one of the major clothing companies. They have the proven designs and quality. Try the different materials. Try a bib top and padded chamois. Find out what gives you comfort and reduces the risk of abrasions from the saddle. You must pay more for quality shorts, but it is money well spent. Shorts are not the place to economize.

AERODYNAMIC EQUIPMENT

I like equipment that helps a rider in the fight against air resistance, even for road racing. Some people say that aerodynamics is only a fad and a marketing trick, but they don't know what they are talking about. Tests have been done to show the difference between equipment that is and is not aerodynamic. The benefits are real. I'm not the only one who believes it — in many countries they are developing aerodynamic equipment. It is necessary because competition at the international level is so close, especially in the timed events on both the road and track. Every single fraction of a second can make a difference. It can mean winning a medal or not.

Aerodynamic equipment can pay off in road races for the same reason: It helps you go faster. We give riders aerodynamic wheels, for example, and ask them how they feel. The answer is always the same: "Incredible. That's nice!" They can tell the difference and it's better. There is no question about it.

Not for bad roads, stage races

My advice is to use all of the aerodynamic equipment you can. Go for a frame with streamlined tubes, race on V-section rims, use components that are designed to reduce air resistance. This equipment is good for everything with two exceptions: roads that are extremely rough, and stage races. Whenever conditions aren't so demanding that durability is the No. 1 priority, lightweight aerodynamic equipment will help your performance.

(Supplementary information about equipment and clothing for road racing may be found in Chapters 8 and 9.)

Criterium

Criteriums are America's most common bike race. They are fun to ride, they have glamor, and they have big prizes. This tempts some riders to specialize. My strong advice is to resist the temptation. I'll say again right now what you will read in almost every chapter of this book: You must not try to be a "criterium rider" or any other type of specialist at the expense of your development in all types of racing. You must prepare yourself to be a good on a bicycle. When you are a zero climber I don't care how fast you are—you are not a good cyclist at all.

If your strongest point is speed but your climbing and endurance are not so good, then it's fine to make criteriums your short-term goal. Perhaps you will want to plan your year around a top performance in the National Criterium Championship. But while you are doing this, you must also be training for and competing in road races and short stage races that will improve your weak points. This will pay off in the long run. It is wrong to just keep doing what you are good at and ignore everything else. By the same token, criterium racing is the ideal remedy if you have good power, good endurance, but no speed. Criteriums will make you faster.

If you want to improve your ability in criteriums there's one sure way to do it: Ride a lot of criteriums. Even better, make them points races full of sprints. The ideal program is to supplement weekend criterium racing with Tuesday workouts that give you even more short-course experience. These can be club training criteriums, or mass-start events at the track such as points races, miss-and-outs, and scratch races. It's not wrong to put this kind of emphasis on criterium racing for 4-6 weeks if there is a major criterium you want to peak for. And it's not wrong to regularly compete in criteriums throughout the season. Just don't let your training and racing program get out of balance with them.

PEAKING FOR A MAJOR RACE

Let's assume that one of the red-letter races on your yearly planning chart is the National Criterium Championship. How do you sharpen your speed and peak for it?

1. Cut your endurance, which means long-distance riding.
2. Cut your power work, which means climbing.

You are preparing for a short race—criteriums are always 100 km or less, never 160 km like a road race. You cannot be your fastest for a short race when your endurance is good for long ones. And you cannot be your fastest when you are spend-

Criteriums bring cycling to town, where there are glamorous prizes, cheering spectators, newspaper photographers, and fun courses. Enjoy criteriums, but don't race so many that you neglect your development in the other road events.

ing a lot time in the hills. For these reasons the big criteriums should be scheduled relatively early in the season. They should come before the major one-day road races and stage races. I was so happy in 1983 when the USCF National Championship Committee decided to move the Criterium Nationals from late in the season to late in May. This was perfect. In late May nobody has great endurance or super power. Riders are still developing, so it is the ideal time to be racing criteriums.

The peaking program depends on the strength and talent of the individual rider. For example, in April of 1983 three of the best U.S. amateur criterium riders—Davis Phinney, Jeff Bradley and Ron Kiefel—went to Europe for a month of short stage races. They returned three weeks before the USCF National Criterium Championship and cut back to one-day road races, criteriums, and some track. That's a super preparation. Phinney then won the Nationals, and one week later he also took the U.S. Pro Criterium Championship against a field that included about 50 European professionals.

Begin with 3 weeks
to go

Begin the peaking process with three weeks to go. If you can ride a basically flat stage race with 4-5 stages, that's perfect. Stay away from anything longer or hillier. If there is no stage race, ride in flat races on Saturday and Sunday, then do two days of hard motorpaced intervals to simulate racing. This will deplete your body so it can rebound with peak amounts of energy and strength, as I discuss in Chapter 3.

After this very hard work, ride short and easy for two days to recover. Then resume the standard weekly training schedule, but with several important alterations:

How to alter the
weekly schedule

1. Reduce the length of Wednesday long rides to 100 km maximum.
2. Stop road racing and enter only criteriums and mass-start track events.
3. Avoid hills—all training and racing must be on basically flat roads.
4. Emphasize Tuesday speed work.
5. Reshape Thursday intervals from the decreasing or climbing type to the criterium type.

Criterium intervals have efforts of 200-300 meters and, as usual, there is recovery only to a heart rate of 110-120 b.p.m. before the next jump. A sequence of criterium intervals might go this way (in meters):

$$200 - 250 - 300 - 300 - 300 - 250 - 250 - 200$$

Do as many as 10 efforts if you can handle it. After the sequence has been completed, recover fully and make one last sprint of 150-250 meters.

During the final two weeks your training distance should fall to 70-80% of normal. The Wednesday reduction will account for much of this. One week before the championship (let's say it will be on a Sunday), work very hard for two days. Don't ride a short stage race, just compete in a long criterium and follow it with another, or go motorpacing the second day for at least 100 km with some intervals and sprints. Then recover with easy rides for a couple of days, and resume the reduced-distance weekly schedule during the days that remain. Make sure you begin to feel super fresh for the race. Do the Thursday intervals at about 70% of normal effort. Have a steady, comfortable ride on Friday and test the race equipment. Do a short ride with some warm-up jumps on Saturday. Then you are ready.

As soon as the big criterium has passed, you must change your training schedule

Criterium racing give you valuable training for bike handling. It teaches you how to ride fast with confidence just centimeters from other cyclists. This is Thurlow Rogers, left, and Doug Shapiro.

or you'll lose your endurance. Start riding long distance again on Wednesdays, and resume weekend road racing. Get back into the hills to keep your power.

Sharpening up

Perhaps you'd like to do well in several big-money Sunday criteriums during the season, but you don't want to drastically change your schedule for them. Let's see how to alter training slightly during the week before these races so you go to the line feeling fast and fresh.

Monday   Short and easy, as usual

Tuesday   Speed work, as usual

Wednesday   Steady ride of 80 km maximum

Thursday   Criterium intervals

Friday   Two hours steady, as usual

Saturday   Short ride with two jumps to test bike

So, it is only on Wednesday and Thursday that the normal schedule is changed. The long midweek ride is shortened considerably because you only need to maintain endurance, not increase it. It is best to conserve energy on Wednesday so you can do a good, hard interval session Thursday. Switch to criterium intervals, as described above, and cover 50-60 km during the workout.

CORNERING

One thing that sets criteriums apart from the other road events is all the corners. You must be good at taking them fast. The techniques I'll describe work equally well whenever you come to sharp turns in a road race or time trial.

The first rule is to have your tires glued on very well. The second is to go through each corner at *full speed*. Good riders can do this. It is especially necessary early in a criterium when you are trying to get to the front of a large field. Most riders slow down when approaching a corner. If you keep your speed you can pass eight or ten at a time.

It's a good idea to let riders know you are overtaking them. But don't yell "Left!" or "Right!" because someone might not understand and he'll move over right in front of you (he might even do it on purpose). Instead, yell "Hey!" or "Watch it!" and riders will tend to keep their line since they're not sure exactly where you are. Give each one enough room to continue through the turn on the line he has taken and there won't be any problems. When you are good you can pass riders anywhere in a corner—going into it, in the middle of it, or leaving it.

Always allow a margin for error. Don't ride two centimeters behind a wheel in a corner, ride half a meter behind. Whenever you can, give yourself an out to the left or right if the rider in front brakes suddenly. Try never to overlap a wheel, espe-

Keep your speed

Warn others that you are passing

Don't overlap wheels

Even if only one tire is poorly glued the result will be the same.

cially on the rider's outside. If he skids or crashes he will slide out and take you with him. Situations like this are hard to avoid when you're in the middle of the pack. There is so little self-determination. Your speed and your line (and your chance of staying off the ground) are mainly decided by the riders surrounding you. That's why it is best to get up front, and why it's worth the effort it takes to keep a position among the first 10 riders.

Good criterium riders sometimes give people a hard time in corners. When you are behind one be cautious about trying to make a pass. He will block you. It is not illegal, but it can be dangerous if you don't anticipate it. On the other hand, if you have good cornering skills it can be you who imposes his will. You can make the defensive and offensive moves. For example, if several average riders in front of you are slowing down to take the corner with an inside-to-outside line, dive underneath them from outside to inside. You will pass them so fast and leave the turn with a good gap. Of course, you must first be certain that nobody is coming up on *your* inside. To be good in criteriums you have to sense where other riders are. You can see them in front of you and beside you, but you must also know when they are right behind you. Your ears must work like rearview mirrors.

Always remember that for a good bike handler, a narrow 90-degree corner is nothing. But in the early laps there may be danger from less-skilled riders who try to stay on the front. Even the better riders tend to use this period for warming up and getting a feel for the turns. Sometimes they make errors, too. Be careful. Ride on

Stay on the front to avoid crashes and speed changes

the very front if you need to. Keep the speed high and soon the cream will rise.

Besides crashes, a big problem for riders in the middle and rear of the field is the constantly changing speed. They have to slow down to funnel into each corner, then sprint hard to catch back up to the leaders. This creates an endless series of intervals—slow down, jump, slow down, jump. . . . It makes the race much harder. Riders at the front, on the other hand, can retain virtually all of their speed through the corners. They don't have four (or more) energy-killing intervals each lap.

You must stay near the front in a criterium. How can you be a factor if you are still braking for a turn while the leaders are sprinting back up the course?

Handling techniques

Criteriums help you develop confidence in big fields. They teach you that when other riders bump your elbows and shoulders it won't necessarily make you fall down. Contact can cause crashes, of course, and a good number of riders hit the pavement each season. The best way to avoid falling is to ride relaxed. Keep your elbows bent and loose, not locked and tense. Then when a rider bumps you it won't automatically make you jerk the handlebars and go off line.

Pedal while braking
for extra control

Ride with your hands on the lever hoods. In a criterium you don't need to brake hard and slow down suddenly, you need fine adjustments in speed. You can make them very well from over the top of the levers. This position also lets you sit up higher to breathe easier and see the course better. Stretch and relax a little when you stop pedaling during the approach to each turn.

Ride with hands on
hoods

If you must brake for a corner do it before you start leaning in. If you misjudge and are still going too fast it's best to resume pedaling while you continue to apply the brakes. This makes the bike more stable. Try it and you will feel the extra control. Of course, after a certain point there is the danger of striking the road with the inside pedal. This isn't good, but it isn't too serious. It shouldn't make you crash. When I was riding, my pedals were half gone (particularly the left one) from hitting the pavement. But I never fell because of it. During a criterium in the 1983 Coors Classic, Thomas Barth, the East German who has won the Peace Race, hit a pedal so hard it lifted his bike right off the ground. But he didn't crash or cause a problem for the guys behind him. A good rider can handle this situation.

I know of only one rider who could pedal all the way through any corner, no matter how sharp it was or how fast he was going. If he was in the break on the last lap, forget it—no way could you beat him. He would keep pedaling when you had to coast, and he would be gone. Stanislaw Szozda was his name. He was a top performer for Poland in the Peace Races and World Championships of the early 1970s, and he was a world-class kamikaze in a criterium. I'll try to describe his cornering technique because if you can learn how to do it you will be very tough to deal with. I'll admit that this is easier to understand when you can actually see it done.

Szozda used his arms much like a track rider making a standing start—straight and firm. Each time his inside pedal went down he would prevent it from striking the ground by pushing the bike to the opposite side. That's not easy to do while still turning. He stood all the way through corners and when he came out he looked like a pursuiter leaving the line. He would continue to use his arms, this time to increase the force against the pedals. He practiced and practiced his technique, and I saw the benefits often. He would go into a turn with another rider and come out with a 20-meter lead. When the finish line came just after a corner not even Szurkowski, who had more speed, could beat him. Szozda used to say that his legs couldn't beat Szurkowski so he would use his arms and legs together. It worked.

Szozda's cornering technique

For all the rest of us, the critical part of a corner is the first half. If your speed and line are correct going in, then everything will take care of itself. Have a balanced

Keep your elbows loose, not locked, so that when somebody bumps you it won't make you jerk the handlebars and lose control.

Jeff Pierce, shown lapping the field, illustrates several points about successful criterium racing. Because he has escaped alone, he can choose his own line and continue pedaling deep into the corners. He can ride relaxed on the hoods to breathe easily. He never has to brake.

Keep a balanced position

position on the bike with normal weight distribution. There's no benefit to trying anything unusual. Be in the middle of the saddle, not out on the tip or way back on the tail. Stop pedaling as you dive sharply into the turn. Use your inside knee for balance. Just as soon as you feel you've passed the critical point, move forward on the bike, stand up, and accelerate.

Using corners to advantage

If you intend to attack be the first rider in your group to reach the corner. This will let you take the best line at maximum speed. If you know that the others tend to be timid and slow in turns, you can count on an instant gap. If the group is large and it contains some good riders, help create a split by going in fast and accelerating hard coming out. The weaker, less-skilled riders will be dropped if several consecutive corners are taken this way.

Break doesn't have to brake

A breakaway group always has an edge because its riders never have to touch their brakes. On the other hand, only those right at the front of the field have this advantage. To the break's way of thinking, then, the more corners the course has, the better. The one time this isn't true is when several break members have relatively poor cornering skills. This will cause gaps to open between riders after turns, reducing the break's efficiency and tiring the ones who have to continually catch back up.

Those who do corner well will ultimately benefit from this situation if it doesn't cause the break to be caught. There will be less competition for them in the sprint.

Teamwork

Teamwork can easily decide the outcome of a criterium. Riders who have a team-mate in the break only have to slow the field a little to help him stay away. As you'd expect, corners are where team tactics are most effective since straightaways give opposing riders room to make counter moves.

The speed of the field can be controlled quite effectively by just a couple of riders who go to the front before the corners, take an outside-to-inside line, and brake. There is some danger in this game, of course. It makes everybody behind hit their brakes because there's nowhere they can go. Some might get mad and start shouting or even throw a punch. Others will try to get past and form a chase. If they succeed, the blockers must join in, sit on, then start getting in the way in corners again.

How to block in corners

When a good group breaks away, the race may very well be over for the rest of the field. These riders can draft to save energy while still going at maximum speed.

TACTICS

The best tactics to use depend on your answers to these two basic questions:

1. Are you racing for a team, or for yourself?
2. Is the winner decided by the finish line, or by points?

If the winner will be the first rider to cross the line on the final lap, a criterium is very similar to a road race. So tactics are very similar. Stay among the first 10-15 riders at all times. (If the field is big and the road is wide, it is okay to occasionally be 35-40 riders back.) Don't ride in the center of the pack where it is dangerous, ride near the side. If the wind is coming from the left be on the right side, and vice versa. Make no hard efforts for the first half unless it's necessary to keep yourself *Relax during first half* in contention. Spin a light gear, watch carefully, sit in, and stay comfortable. Spray *of race* your head, drink some glucose mixture, eat a little food. By the middle of the race you should be almost as fresh as at the start.

When a strong team is in the field, it is usually safe to assume that it will try to protect its leader by keeping the early pace fairly fast. This discourages other riders from trying to break away—when nobody breaks, nobody has to chase. Meanwhile, weak and unskilled riders will be dropped off the back and out of the way.

If a strong break does go early you must join in and then ride economically. It is not your job to pull hard and inspire the effort. Take a couple of pedal strokes each turn at the front, then get off. Why ride this way? Because you know what is coming later. In the second half the speed will go up and aggressive moves might start coming one after the other. Any one of them could turn out to be decisive. *Use strength in* This is when you must use the strength you've been saving. You must stay right *second half* at the front, respond to moves, and begin making your own. You can't let a group ride off without you. Solo attacks are another matter—usually they are not a big threat, but it depends on the rider. When a good time trialist goes, watch out.

Don't hesitate to attack by yourself when you sense the right moment. Perhaps there is a crash. Maybe a couple of the top contenders have dropped back from the front for a moment. Decisions must be instant, and commitment must be total. Maybe only two or three chasers will catch you. Now you can work together to stay away. Since everyone's odds are improved, an alliance is intelligent.

Dealing with stronger riders

Perhaps you've joined a large group that got away with half a dozen laps to go. You look around to size up your 10 companions and, uh oh, there's a Davis Phinney and a Steve Bauer. Trouble—these guys can eat you alive in a sprint. There's no sense in thinking about a last-lap victory strategy. If you are going to have any chance at all you've got to try something before then.

There is one thing on your side: the element of surprise. Usually in a situation like this, the two strong men will mark each other. The pace of the whole group will be dictated by what they do. When it gets down to about three laps to go, the action may quiet considerably as the riders begin resting and plotting for the finish. That's perfect for the super sprinters, but not for you. So drift to the back of the group and wait for a good moment, then jump hard. Go flying past as if the finish were just around the next corner instead of two laps later. What will happen? The

Phinney will watch the Bauer, and the Bauer will watch the Phinney. They know they can catch you, but they also know that whoever leads the chase is going to wind up getting beat by the other. If neither one has teammates in the group to pull them up, and if you are good at cornering and time trialing, you just might steal the race.

Last-lap strategy

One reason it's worth the effort to get away with a small group becomes very clear at the finish. It's much easier to sprint against a few riders than against a big field. I don't care how good you are — a field sprint is always dangerous and unpredictable.

As the finish draws near, start your computer working. Which direction is the wind blowing? How soon is the line after the final corner? Who is the strongest man in the group? What is his tactic likely to be? What is your best talent to use against him?

When you know the strong man is not as good as you in the corners, attack him with 300 meters to go.

When there is a long straightaway to the line and your jump is good, control him as long as possible. The shorter the sprint, the better your chance.

When he has a good, long sprint get on his wheel. Push him to reach maximum speed as early as possible, wait until the last moment, then try to kick past. If you fail, second place isn't too bad a result. Stick tight — don't let him open a bike-length gap on you or you won't have any chance at all.

When there is a headwind never lead out the sprint. When there is no wind and your jump is the best in the group (and you are not big), you can win from the front. Control the speed, then go when there are 150-200 meters left. Your draft won't help anyone. But don't try it with 300 meters to go or you will lose for sure. That's too far to hold maximum speed.

Field sprinting

A field sprint is a whole different game. It's very hard to win without help. Riders won't wait until a couple hundred meters to go — they will start attacking with a kilometer to go. It gets so fast! It's too much for a rider to handle alone. Someone must lead you to the front and close to the line to put you in position to make your jump for victory. Ideally, this will be a teammate or two who has practiced with you and knows exactly what to do. But what if you are riding alone? Then you must be smart and glue up to one of the best sprinters. Fight for his wheel because other riders will want it, too. Hope that he will tow you right up to the line, but if you see the chance to get onto an even better wheel, take it.

Leadout is essential

When riders are tough and nobody gives in, there will be a crash. Sometimes a rider will knock you down even though it means he too will fall. He wants to teach you a lesson so that next time he has a better chance to win. Next time you'll remember you can't play with him. When riders get to know each other on these terms, reputation and intimidation become important forces in a criterium.

Who wins? The best rider *if* he is also the luckiest rider. You've got to be in the right place at the right time. It's not rare for a strong rider with a super leadout to be beaten because someone was glued up to him. He jumps and thinks he's won, then a guy comes off his wheel to squeeze past in the final meters. In many field

Luck can make the difference

Davis Phinney will win this sprint over Steve Bauer and Hugh Walton, but he isn't doing it all by himself. Phinney's leadout man on the 7-Eleven team, Ron Kiefel, has successfully put him into position to use his speed. Without such teamwork, even a super sprinter like Phinney will find it very difficult to win.

sprints the very best sprinter does not win. When there are other riders almost as good, luck becomes more decisive than skill. So work for your luck. Be as rested as you can, be in the best position you can, and jump as hard as you can. Often you will lose, but you will still place very well. And sometimes you will win.

Example

It wasn't a criterium, but there was a race in 1983 that ended with a very good example of sprint strategy. It was the women's World Road Championship and it saw four riders—Marianne Berglund, Rebecca Twigg, Maria Canins, Mandy Jones— come to the final kilometer together. Twigg had made a couple of unsuccessfull uphill attacks and now they were riding slow, but their minds were working fast. Berglund and Twigg were the best sprinters in the group, but Canins had shown super strength throughout the race.

All these women had raced against each other before. But in this event Berglund was the one who used her knowledge of the others perfectly. Earlier she sat on Canins every time Twigg attacked, letting the Italian tow her back into contact. Now it was time for Berglund the take her fate into her own hands and use the strength she had been conserving.

With 500 meters remaining, Berglund marked only Twigg. With 250 to go Twigg attacked, and Berglund was right on her wheel. Canins and Jones were dropped. Now it was a two-up sprint, just like on the track. But how many track riders can lead out a 250-meter sprint and still win? Not many, and neither could Twigg. In a situation like this it is necessary for the lead rider to wait as long as possible before jumping. The closer to the finish, the better. Twigg's premature sprint gave Berglund plenty of time to glue up. Berglund then made her winning jump with perfect timing just 50 meters from the line, giving Twigg no chance for a response. It was flawless strategy by Berglund, and that's why she became the world champion.

Twigg vs. Berglund

Marianne Berglund's triumph over Rebecca Twigg in the 1983 World Championship showed what happens when a smart sprinter is allowed to play her hand.

Twigg learned a lot from this. Even a world pursuit champion (which she was in 1982) can't go hard from the front with 250 meters left when there is a well-rested sprinter around. On the other hand, maybe Twigg would have been successful if she'd started her move with 500 meters to go, but *not* at full speed. That's the way a sprinter can be controlled. Get closer, ride faster . . . closer, faster . . . closer, *faster.* When 50 meters remain it is the critical point and the sprinter must try to pass. But when she swings out into the wind she will already be going almost full speed. Then there is the chance to hold her off at the line.

It's a game. It's exciting. That's why this is such a great sport. When a bunch of good riders comes to the finish you never know who will win. If a rider comes first in more than 10% of the national races he enters, you know he is more than just very good — he is also very lucky. A little mistake, a little bad luck, and there is no way to win against good competition.

Nitz's tactic

Cycling is an individual sport all right, but the results are not based only on the individual. Leonard Nitz, for example, is a rider who plays the game of sitting at the back of the field. Sometimes he wins criteriums because of this tactic, sometimes it is the reason he loses. Everything depends on what other riders do. If the field splits or there is a breakaway, he loses his chance to win. On the other hand, he might reach the final laps both very fresh and still in contention. The other top riders tend to forget about him. They're at the front watching each other. He sits, sits, sits and saves energy while they use it. When he is lucky he gets the chance to use his energy when it counts the most.

POINTS RACE

If you are serious about winning a points race, never go for the first sprint. Your physiology isn't ready, and every hotshot local rider in the field will be trying to impress his friends. Don't let any break form without you, but don't get yourself into the heat of the action until the sprint worth double points at midrace.

Save energy during first half of race

Why not try for first-half sprints? First, they will take a lot out of you. At the beginning of the race everybody is strong. Even average riders can give you a very hard time. But those who go hard from the gun will be dead later, and your chances will be better. Don't skip any easy points—glue up to a rider if he will tow you along for a point or two—but don't go after them aggressively. Simply use the first half to warm up well for a full effort the second half. That's when you must be able to sprint at your best and respond to serious breakaway attempts or make your own. Second, if you succeed in getting early points you will be a marked rider for the rest of the race. Don't let people know how good you are. It will only make it more difficult to win.

Contest every other sprint in second half

Be at the front for the midrace sprint and then stay there. Watch to see who is looking good and which riders are working together. Which teams are fighting it out? From this point on, contest every second sprint, not every single one. If the sprints come every five laps, you can't go for all of them without risking your recovery. By going for every other one you will be able to give one a full effort and not blow up.

Stay away from the heavy action between aggressive riders and teams. Ride on the other side of the road. If you get mixed up with them you will call attention to yourself and be forced to waste energy. When I was in points races, sometimes a rider would come up to me after the finish and say, *"You* won? When did you get any points? I almost never saw you in this race." That's exactly the idea. Don't show off. If you can win a points sprint by half a bike length don't win it by 20 meters. All that does is waste energy and make it harder to win points again—everybody begins to watch you because you look so strong. It's much better to get your points quietly, then disappear to 15th or 20th place for the next several laps. Relax, drink some glucose mixture, spray your face, feel comfortable. If on the next points sprint three guys open a gap, let them go. It's not worth an effort just for fourth-place points. You must be smart.

After midrace all the good riders will be hot and ready for action. Now you must be careful not to miss a breakaway. It is certain that attempts will be made. When they go, glue up. In a points race it is a disaster to be left behind. No matter how many points you have, you cannot win if a group gets away and laps the field. Be especially wary of an attack right after a sprint. As some riders sit up past the line, others will continue going hard or they will come flying by from the rear of the field. You must *always* be ready to respond.

When you make the break you can collect points much easier. Now there is a small group to sprint against instead of the whole front of the field. There are times, however, when it is best to ride defensively in the break. If you are the leader on points and several close challengers are with you, don't work. Let them keep the pace high if they want to while you use your energy for the sprints. Another tactic is to block so the break is caught. Instead of trying to deal with these riders alone in the remaining sprints, let other riders get involved again. The good riders in the field will be fresher than the break's riders, so your close challengers aren't likely to get the big points.

It is impossible to cover all the possibilities in a points race. For example, some-

Here's a lesson for everyone. In a sprint, save the victory salute until after the finish line.

times it works best *not* to try for the double points at midrace. If everyone else seems to be keying on it, too, then go for the sprint just before it and the one just after it. If you do well in them you've accomplished the same goal—foundation points for the second half of the race. Generally, however, you will do very well if you go into a points race with this plan:

General plan

1. In the first half of the race, don't miss a break and go only for easy points.
2. Go for the double points sprint at midrace.
3. Go for every second points sprint from the middle to the end of the race.

This was exactly the strategy on the track when Leonard Nitz won a silver medal in the 1981 World Championship Points Race. On the other hand, at the 1983 Pan American Games the U.S. plan was for John Beckman to go with every single break. An Argentinian charged off almost from the gun, Beckman did his job, and even before the halfway sprint they had lapped the field. The result: Beckman won the gold medal. It was our other rider, Brent Emery, who had the speed for this event, but the break went much too early for a second-half strategy to work. Like in all of cycling it is good to be good, but it is also good to be lucky.

Know your point total

At championship points races I always have an assistant to keep score just like a judge. He writes down the results of each sprint and makes a running total. Then we call out the information to our riders as they pass. They must know the situation in order to choose the best strategy. You should have a coach or friend help you in the same way. Otherwise you'll never be certain where you are placed and how many points separate you from the leaders. Often there is an announcer who gives the standings, but he can be hard to hear and he might only talk about first and second place. To race the event well you must have your personal information.

Treat primes like points

What should you do in a criterium that offers a number of primes? Exactly the same strategy as in a points race. Stay out of the way of the kamikazes for the first few primes, warm up real well, size up the competition, then begin asserting yourself after the first third of the race. Again, don't go for every prime because you'll be dead by the end—and the end is what is going to totally determine the winner. Watch out for breakaways and watch out for team tactics. When a strong criterium team is present its best riders will be given leadouts. Maybe they'll alternate from one rider to another. Try to read this strategy and get on the right wheel.

EQUIPMENT

Special criterium bike

If you are especially good in criteriums and compete in the big ones every season, it can pay off to have a special criterium bike. The frame should be super stiff for efficiency, and built with tight dimensions for responsiveness. The bottom bracket should be slightly higher than on a normal road frame for more pedal-to-ground clearance in corners. Use crank arms 2.5 mm shorter than your normal length. This also increases ground clearance, and it improves acceleration. Sprinters on the track, for example, usually have 165 mm cranks, which are the shortest most companies make. Position your saddle slightly higher than on the road bike, and lower the handlebar stem by about 3 cm. This will improve your aerodynamics.

Shift lever location

Equip the bike with a handlebar-end shift lever for the rear derailleur and a down tube shift lever for the front derailleur. I used this set-up back in the days when I was fast enough to be counted on to win prize money for my team. I know it can help you in a sprint. Here's how it works: Let's say you are in the final 50 meters and you've made a gearing mistake. The road is flat or slightly downhill and you chose 53x15 for your jump. That was fine, but now you need the 14 because you are spinning out and riders are coming alongside. If you must take your hand off the bars to reach down and make the shift, forget it—you will be passed. But with the handlebar-end lever you can get the higher gear much faster. All you have to move is the little finger of your right hand.

Why not have the front derailleur lever in the handlebars, too? One reason is that 90% of crashes on the road happen on the left side. There is more risk of damage to the lever if it is sticking out of the handlebars than if it is on the frame. Also, there is hardly ever any need to make a quick shift with the front derailleur at the end of a race. Unless there is a steep hill you will always be on the big chainring.

In most situations down tube levers allow a fast enough gear change and they give you the best shifting accuracy. For this reason most riders prefer them to handlebar-end levers. But since a bar-end lever for the rear derailleur is such an advantage in a sprint, I recommend it for all criteriums and even road races. Give it a try and you'll find that once you are accustomed to it, it works very well.

Wheels

A radially laced front wheel is not much good for anything but a flat road time trial, but some small and light riders can race criteriums on them when the surface is smooth and the prizes make it worth the risk. But a better choice is a one-cross or two-cross front wheel, especially for a big rider.

Wheels with 32 or 28 spokes are safe for everyone except heavy riders with rough technique. The lighter weight and improved aerodynamics are a real advantage over 36-spoke wheels. Tires of 195 or even 165 grams can be used on smooth courses with normal corners. Take a risk when the risk is reasonable, because it can help you win. The best tread pattern for criteriums has thin ribs in the center for efficient rolling on the straightaways, and a herringbone pattern on either side for a good grip in the corners.

Tires must not be too old or too new. The rubber on an old tire, even one that's never been used, can dry out and lose a lot of its adhesion. The result is a greater chance of skidding when you're taking a fast corner. Fresh rubber is not good, either. *Don't race on brand new tires* When a tire is brand new the tread is soft and almost sticky. It will pick up small gravel instead of kicking it away, and there will be a puncture. A tire will perform best if you use it 6-12 months after it was made. Always train on it first to (1) make sure it is not defective, and (2) wear off the shininess that makes it a little slippery. After a couple of training rides it will hold the road much better at race speed.

Inflate tires to 7.5-8 atm. for the normal criterium. Higher pressure might be faster on the straightaways, but it will give you trouble in the corners. Put in about half an atmosphere more when the pavement has bumps and potholes. This will protect the rims and help prevent a wheel failure. I do *not* agree with those who *Don't decrease air pressure for wet roads* say to reduce pressure when it is raining. To me a softer tire feels flexible, loose and more slippery, not less. It also increases rolling resistance. I even used to add a little pressure when it was wet. This worked for me and I know good riders who do it, including professionals.

If you have the choice of two tires, put the lighter one on the rear wheel. The

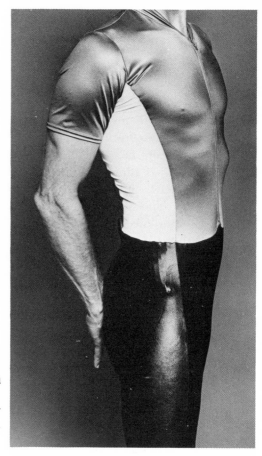

For hot-weather criterium racing, choose a skinsuit with mesh panels along the sides. Mesh improves ventilation to increase your comfort and quite possibly your performance. (Skinsuit courtesy of J.T. Actif.)

Use a lighter tire on rear wheel

rear is the engine wheel, the one that gets the power and responds to your acceleration. When it is lighter its speed can change faster. But don't forget that more of your weight is on the rear wheel. The tire must not be so light that it greatly increases the chance of a flat. Keep an eye out for wear—a rear tire never lasts as long as a front, so a lightweight tire needs to be changed often. The front wheel, being only a rolling wheel, won't be handicapped by a tire that weighs 20-30 grams more. In fact, it will give you the benefit of greater protection.

How to glue on a tire

Great wheels are worth nothing at all if a tire rolls off in a corner, so the glue job is very important. Always apply glue to the rim *and* to the base tape of the tire. Wait until both surfaces are almost dry—they should feel just a bit tacky—then mount the tire. Inflate it to about 3 atm., center it on the rim, then pump it to 7-8 atm. Let at least 24 hours pass before you ride it. If the rim is brand new, clean it with mineral spirits so the glue will adhere well, then apply two coats. Let the first one dry completely before you put on the second. It's not a bad idea to put two coats on a tire, too.

CLOTHING

A lightweight, form-fitting, one-piece suit is ideal for criteriums. Clothing manufacturers are putting a lot of thought into design and materials, making the suits more breathable and comfortable.

For hot weather I recommend a suit with a mesh panel running down each side, which improves ventilation. I also like a suit with a small internal rear pocket, although these don't seem to be on the retail market yet. You don't need to carry much in a criterium since the distance is almost never more than 100 km, but it's nice to have a place to put several glucose tablets or maybe a piece of orange or dried fruit. If there is no pocket, these things can be stored up the edge of a sleeve, behind a race number, or under a headband.

Whatever you do, don't wear a loose road-type jersey with big external rear pockets. You never need to carry that much, and the air drag is a handicap. One water bottle should be sufficient, but if you need to carry another install a second cage. Throw out each bottle when it is empty.

In hot summer conditions when riders need extra water I am strongly in favor of hand-ups during criteriums, but too often they are not permitted by race officals. Spraying from the roadside is also necessary in hot weather. It helps riders a lot if the sprayer does it properly and aims for the head. If you want to be certain of getting cooling sprays, carry a second bottle of plain water so you can douse yourself. Use an insulating cover to keep the water cold and more effective.

Always wear gloves. They keep your hands from slipping on the handlebars, and you can wipe off your face with the mesh on the back. Also, gloves protect your palms if you fall. Crashes are not too rare in criteriums, and even an easy fall can cut your hands badly. Also for your protection, wear a light undershirt. It can reduce abrasions because it provides a surface for the skinsuit to slide against.

CHAPTER 6

Individual Time Trial

There should be no such thing as a good rider who cannot time trial, but we do see it occasionally. Why? The usual reason is improper training, or improper understanding of the training techniques. Or it could be a faulty race technique: poor warm-up, poor bike control, poor gear selection, etc. Another factor is weak mentality. A rider who is strong enough to be a very good time trialist won't be good unless he believes in himself. He must concentrate on making the effort, not give in to the relentless pain that is actually proof of correct time trialing. Rarely is there a rider who lacks the inborn ability to maintain a steady state of work, which is exactly what the time trial requires—it is an event of work more than speed.

These factors and others will be discussed as we look into what it takes to excel in the individual time trial (ITT). My approach will assume that you are keying on a major event, such as the 40 km (25 mile) District or National Championship. I will agree with you if you feel that it is personally important to pinpoint such events and peak for them, but it is a mistake to do only time trials and ignore other types of racing. A real cyclist isn't one whose schedule consists of four time trials a year. Therefore, I will not lay out a season-long preparation specifically for time trialing. That would be the wrong approach to bike racing.

Time trialing ability is very important for success in mass-start racing. It is exactly what you are doing when you chase following a puncture, when you bridge from group to group, and when you solo off the front toward a victory. Often an ITT will be included in a stage race and it will have the most to say about where you place in the final general classification. Remember the 1983 Tour of America? The first five places on final GC were identical to the first five in the time trial stage. In a stage race you must be a strong time trialist just as you must have power on the climbs and speed in the sprint. Time trialing means hard work for an extended period, so it puts a premium on endurance.

The individual time trial is called the "race of truth." I agree. You can't sit on somebody's wheel, and you won't win just because everyone else met a misfortune that you were lucky to avoid. I was once in a road race where the lead group of 30 riders crashed while trying to squeeze through a narrow gate to the finish in a stadium. As we were untangling ourselves, a guy we'd dropped came through and won the race. A time trial is different. You can't expect something unusual to help you. In this sense, it is the road event most similar to track and field. You can be quite certain that you will have an unhindered chance to do your best. Your performance is up to you, and your result is an honest one.

178

The ability to time trial can frequently pay off in mass-start racing. It is exactly the skill you need to bridge from the peloton to the break.

Like luck, tactics usually are not as decisive in an ITT as they are in mass-start events. In a sense tactics are easier — there is no danger of missing the breakaway — but they require a great amount of self-knowledge. You are dealing with intense physical output and with psychology and motivation.

The key to successful time trialing is winning the fight with yourself. You must never give in to the pain by reducing your effort. Always remember that every other good rider is hurting just as much — you are not the exception. Pain is normal and it is necessary. Just look at Francesco Moser's face during his rides for the world hour record! Anyone who does not hurt is not going as fast as he can. Pain is what guarantees success. So don't think about pain as a negative thing, think about it as proof you are riding the race correctly. Let the pain build your psychology. Make motivation the dominant force. Concentrate on just one thing: steady hard work.

Welcome the pain

TRAINING FOR TIME TRIALING

As you now know, winter preparation is the same for all the road events. If you are really hungry for the ITT and want to do some specific preseason work, emphasize intervals on the ergometer or wind-load trainer during Specialization (March 1 — April 15). Do them the same way I described in Chapter 3 for self-testing or when cyclocross training is missed. That is, two nine-minute sets, each with progression to a higher gear every three minutes. A very serious time trialist can even start doing this workout once a week in December, then increase to twice a week during Cycling Conditioning (January 15 — February 28) if bad weather is canceling outside riding. As strength improves use bigger gears, but make sure pedal r.p.m. stays between 86 and 92. This is the proper range for the ITT. When you are actually racing, it is not right to slug away in the biggest gear and forget about cadence. Before long you will be traveling slower than a rider who is spinning at 90 r.p.m. in a smaller gear.

Winter preparation

Specific preparation for the 40 km District or National ITT should begin with one month to go (or even earlier if your race calendar permits). The daily training pattern remains the same, but the three midweek workouts are customized for time

How to peak for a major event

The one-hour time trial is one of cycling's most severe tests. Pain and determination was written on Francesco Moser's face when he set the new standard of 51.151 km on a track in Mexico City in January, 1984. The Italian pro was helped by the latest advances in time trial technology, most notably disk wheels that eliminate much of the air turbulence created by spokes.

trialing. Basically, the speed work and intervals of Tuesday and Thursday will have lengthier periods of exertion than during preparation for criteriums or road races. The idea is to experience the steady high work output of time trialing.

On Tuesdays, warm up well and then do hard efforts of 1-1.5 km with full recovery between each one. The distance and number of repetitions will depend on how strong you are and how good you feel. Maybe you can do only two efforts of 1 km

Tuesday workout

each before your legs give out. Fine, do what you can and improvement will come. I strongly recommend a bicycle computer for this training so you will know exactly how you are performing. The speed should not be your maximum, but it should be slightly higher than your average when competing in a flat time trial. If you ride at 40 k.p.h. in a race, do this training at 43-45 k.p.h. Stay in the same gear for each effort; when you can no longer hold your speed for the distance, you are done. If you don't have a computer, use your watch and go for 60, 90 or 120 seconds.

On Wednesdays, endurance training. You must keep your endurance, but don't overdo these rides. One hundred kilometers is plenty; if you don't feel too good, cut it to 80. No training ride should be longer than 110 km during the month before a 40 km ITT. It is not long-distance endurance that needs to be increased during this period, it is endurance of power and speed. Wednesday workout

On Thursdays, interval training. Warm up, then try for six 2 km repetitions. Gear down between efforts, spin along at 32 k.p.h., check your pulse until it drops to 110-120 b.p.m., then go again. Use the biggest gear you can turn at 90 r.p.m. for each interval and the entire workout—don't shift lower when you start getting tired. Always do the first interval with less than maximum effort to complete the warm-up and see how you are feeling. Generally, the second and third intervals will be the fastest. If you are having a good day, the fourth may be as fast or only a second or two slower. The stronger you are, the more consistent your times will be. But if the fourth interval is slow and the fifth is even slower, no more. Stop whenever two times go up, or even after one if it is a big increase like 15 seconds. If you can do only four repetitions instead of six, fine. Do what you can handle, do all you can handle. Thursday workout

When possible, do the intervals under the supervision of your coach or someone else who can time you and observe your riding position. Time trialing is very consistent work and Thursday is your primary practice for it. Pedal action should be smooth through 360 degrees. Knees should be close to the top tube. The back should be flat, with the body as aerodynamic as possible. You should look like a model. No torso movement, arms loose, hands always on the drops. Concentrate. Breathe from the diaphragm. Keep the bike on a perfectly straight line. If you ride like a snake you will be slower because it makes the course longer. To stay straight you need a relaxed, comfortable upper body. Concentrate on form

You must keep your head up to see the road, but this can be hard to do in a streamlined position. If it makes your neck muscles tight, try tilting your head slightly to one side for a while and then to the other. This should make you more comfortable and still let you see what is coming. Whatever you do, don't just put your head down and ride. A time trial is generally a very safe race, but when accidents happen then tend to be bad ones. Twice in my riding career I saw very good cyclists die in time trials. One of them hit the back corner of a truck that had stalled on the side of the highway. It was only 25 cm over the pavement, but the rider had his head down and was looking only at the white line. He died instantly with his skull split open and his spine broken in three places. I was the second rider to pass and I could see his body under the truck. Another time it was a good Junior who died when he rode into a car. I remember these terrible crashes very well and I always describe them to my riders. You are traveling fast and you never know what might happen just ahead. You can never take anything for granted. *Keep your head up.* Keep your head up

There remains some question about the best training program for the final two weeks. I recommend entering this period with a flat road race on Sunday, an easy ride on Monday, then hard interval training on Tuesday and Wednesday. Or, if you still feel tired Tuesday, ride easy that day and do the intervals on Wednesday and Thursday. You must be fresh for the hard work. If you feel real strong on the second day of intervals, you may want to add a third. It depends on your condition, recovery, motivation and, beginning the second time around, the results you got with this program.

Special intervals

The interval workouts must be on flat roads. Warm up with motorpacing and gradually increase to big gears and high r.p.m. Then alternate intervals with the motorcycle (or car) and without it. When behind, go for about 6 km; when in front, 2-3 km. Follow the basic procedure for time trial intervals just discussed, and do as many repetitions as you can until performance drops off. Monitor yourself with a bike computer, your watch, or (best of all) do this training under the supervision of your coach. As always, concentrate on perfect time trialing form.

Reduce distance in last week

When this training is finished you will be tired. Go easy for the next several days and enter just one race on the weekend. A criterium is best because it is short and fast. It won't wear you out. Then go back to the normal training program for the final week, but cut total distance by about 30%. Tuesday should have just a couple of hard efforts, not five or six. The same goes for Thursday. Two days before the race, go out easy for about two hours and check your equipment. One day before, ride for an hour and put in one or two efforts of 400-500 meters at racing speed. Then you are ready.

Training races

Several short efforts are ideal

Your bike club may have a weekly time trial of about 15 km, and you may think that riding it is perfect training for the 40 km event. It isn't. Instead of one 15 km time trial, you will do much better if you spend that time riding five 3 km time trials in the same manner as Thursday intervals. Why? It's simple. When you do one 15 km effort you don't learn very much. You have one start and one turnaround. But if you do five shorter time trials you have five starts, five accelerations, five efforts to maintain r.p.m., and five turnarounds. You have five chances to practice your technique. Also, you can ride 3 km at a faster speed than 15 km, which makes the workout harder and more beneficial. You can do repetitions in different gears to see how they affect your acceleration, speed, comfort, breathing, etc. One time you can concentrate on turning a big gear, the next time on breathing deeply from the diaphragm, and the next time on a strict aerodynamic position. All this will teach you many things about time trialing. What gives you results and what does not? Do these wheels make you faster than those wheels? The clock will give you answers in black and white.

My advice to clubs, assuming they want to help their riders the most, is to replace single long time trials with several short ones. I know the East Europeans do their time trial training like this, and they are the fastest amateurs in the world. Nobody needs to train 15 km hard to be able to race 40 km hard. Intervals of 2 or 3 km are plenty. I never rode anything longer for time trial training and neither did other top Polish riders of my era, including Tadeusz Mytnik. He was fantastic. He could ride 40 km faster than *anyone*. He trained with fast intervals like I've described, not by plugging away at race pace for long periods.

What this also means is that it isn't necessary (or even desirable) to ride 40 km time trials in order to get good at 40 km time trials. For one thing, too many time trials can hurt your psychology. The ITT is a very tough event. You don't want to do too many of them. So instead of racing in another time trial during the week or two before the District or National Championship, it's much better to go to a criterium or flat road race. Either event will make you ride faster than a time trial, and yet they are not as hard on you mentally or physically.

Don't overdo ITT racing

Early morning events

One frequent problem with time trials is an early morning start. There is an advantage — the weather is usually calm — but most riders find it hard to do maximum work so soon after sleeping.

If your big race will start at 7 or 8 a.m., use the preceding week to accustom yourself to riding at this time. Generally, the body needs a minimum of two hours to wake up, so get out of bed at 5 a.m. for training. This is not too early — if you get up later you will still be asleep on the bike. Have your glass of water with honey and lemon, eat a light breakfast of fruit or a hardboiled egg with toast, do your stretching, then go training. On race day, follow the same procedure with the possible exception of having just glucose mixture and skipping the solid food. Most riders find it necessary to eat at least four hours before an intense effort like time trialing, but this isn't practical if it's an early morning event.

Acclimate your system

When your start isn't until midmorning or later, eat the food you are in the habit of having, but be sensible. If you are used to a farmer's breakfast, eat one or two pieces of bacon instead of five. You must satisfy your stomach, but a big meal before a hard one-hour effort is more likely to be harmful than helpful. Some riders are too nervous to eat solid food and prefer fruit juice. What's right is what works for you. Once at the race site, sip from your glucose mixture and then drink down one third of the bottle about 20 minutes before you go to the line.

Prerace meal

Racing techniques

A successful time trial begins with a super warm-up. You must be ready to make an intense effort right from the first pedal stroke. Find out exactly what time you have to be at the start, then begin warming up with one hour to go. Wear a watch so you will be certain of the time remaining.

If the air is cool, wear a full training suit. You must keep your body very warm. In hot weather the legs can be left uncovered but use the jacket. Underneath, wear an undershirt and wool jersey. Prevent the top of your skinsuit from getting wet with sweat by rolling it down around your waist.

Start the warm-up by riding easily for 15 minutes. Use your training wheels, not the super wheels you have for the race. Spin, change your hand position, stand up a little, get loose. Next do several progressively harder intervals. Jump and go fast for about 1 km, then turn and ride back easy. Raise the temperature of your body and begin to sweat.

How to warm up

With about 20 minutes to go, stop at your car. Put on your racing wheels. Remove the warm-up clothes, wash your face and neck, towel off, and pull up the skinsuit top. Tighten your shoe laces. Apply the cream and oil to your legs and arms (it's much better to have someone do this for you). Rinse out your mouth. Drink from your glucose bottle. Then go out again for five minutes and do a couple more jumps to test the wheels. Stay on the bike hot and ready to go until it's time to take your place in the start order. No surprises—that's what you are trying to accomplish. Everything must be scheduled. This will help reduce your anxiety.

The start

As you ride up to the start area, shift into the gear you wish to leave the line in. This should never be your biggest gear or your smallest. If, for example, you have a six-speed setup with a 53-tooth chainring and a 13-18 cluster, you should not start in the 18. The extreme chain angle is not efficient and it is unsafe — it could cause skipping or even derailment. In this case, the 17 is a better choice. How do you know for sure which gear to use? From your experiences in training and previous races.

The effort

Get off the saddle for the start and stay off until you have the gear turning briskly. Then sit down and begin shifting toward your primary gear. Do not get off the saddle again except after sharp turns that slow you down, after the turnaround, and when you come to short, steep hills. It is wrong to stand up for any other reason. I have watched and ridden with many great time trialists and all of them stayed in the saddle as much as possible. It is necessary for maintaining pedal r.p.m.

Similarly, it is a mistake to finish with an out-of-saddle sprint. The finish of a 40 km time trial does not come in the last 100 meters but in the last 10 km. Gradually pick up your speed with 5 km to go, 4 to go, 3 to go, 2 to go, 1 to go . . . then die on the line. Use every last bit of energy during the final minutes, not the final seconds. The main reason why you don't stand up and sprint should be because you can't stand up and sprint—everything in your body has gone into the distance.

If the warm-up has been thorough, the race won't seem real tough in the early minutes, but it will become so as you maintain the effort. Speed may change a little because of hills and wind, but the effort must be consistently high. On a flat course during a calm day, a good time trialist's 5 km splits will be almost identical.

Pedal r.p.m.

Pedal r.p.m. should stay between 86 and 92. A slight hill may make you drop to 82, but I never saw a good time trialist go below 80. You must shift down before your cadence gets that slow. But unlike r.p.m., it is not possible to tell you exactly which gears to use. Gears depend on your strength, riding technique, the weather conditions, course terrain, and what experience has taught you. You must know everything before the race and install the ideal gear range.

Overtaking a rider

When overtaking another rider, do it with conviction. Pick up your speed. Go by him in a manner that tells him he cannot stay with you. If you pass slowly, it invites him to try to ride alongside, which does happen even though it may be technically illegal. It is better to get rid of him quickly so your concentration can return completely to your own effort. Then it becomes his responsibility, not yours, to ride in a manner that does not violate USCF rule 2E9: "No rider shall take pace behind another rider closer than 25 meters (80 feet) ahead, or 2 meters (7 feet) to the side. A rider who is observed taking pace shall receive a time penalty." The penalty chart ranges from 1 to 99 seconds, depending on the speed of the riders and distance of the illegal pacing. Of course, until you get past the rider it is you who must stay well to one side or risk being penalized.

Most turnarounds are 180-degree left-hand turns marked by a pylon in the center of the road. When you get within 100 meters begin to ease your pedaling. Take this moment to stretch your body and collect yourself. Put your hands up on the brake lever hoods, a position that facilitates breathing and gives better control through

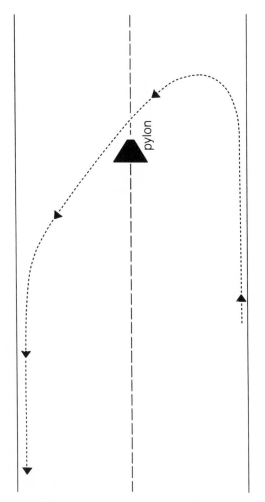

TURNAROUND TECHNIQUE

This is the fastest way to make the turnaround. It allows you to resume pedaling sooner than turning in a symmetrical curve.

the turn. Drink your small flask of coffee and glucose if you've carried one. Shift into the proper cog for accelerating. Normally this will be one tooth smaller than you used at the start because you've been turning the big gears. Move to the far right edge of the road. Stop pedaling with the inside (left) pedal up. Brake as necessary.

Roll slightly past the pylon, then point your left knee toward it. This adjusts your center of gravity to help you make a sharp, tight turn. As the diagram shows, the proper method is to cut back past the pylon on as straight a line as possible. This is better than a symetrical curve because it shortens the distance and allows you to resume pedaling sooner. It takes good balance and good position on the bike to turn this way, but it will save you time. Work on it in training. Now stand to accelerate, then sit and shift toward your primary gear, just as at the start.

On a straight-road course never ride along the very edge. It is dangerous there because of cracks, gravel and broken glass. Use either the strip of road where the right-hand wheels of cars travel, or the strip in the middle of the lane between the wheels. The choice depends on where the pavement is smoothest and cleanest. Try

Making the
turnaround

to ride or drive the course on the eve of the race to inspect the surface, memorize the location of hazards, and develop a plan for where you will place your bike.

When there are curves, cut through them to create the shortest line. This is a perfectly legitimate tactic and it is used by intelligent riders. You are allowed to ride anywhere in the right lane from the edge to center line, motor traffic permitting. By thinking ahead and keeping your path as straight as possible you will save yourself some distance, which means time. Of course, be careful anytime the optimum line takes you to the road's edge. If the pavement is rough or dirty, relax the line a little. It is much better to lose a fraction of a second than to lose the air in a tire.

Most time trial courses are flat, but not all. During a stage race ITT, for example, you may find undulating terrain. The question always arises: Is it better to stay seated on hills or stand up?

On a course that has long, gradual hills, always shift down and remain in the saddle. Don't stand and attempt to maintain the flat-road gear. That approach is futile. Use the derailleur to keep pedal r.p.m. in the efficient range. Shift, move to the rear of the saddle, and go up to the brake lever hoods to help make breathing a little easier.

For short, steep hills it can be efficient to get off the saddle and sprint over without a gear change. However, if you find yourself standing for more than a few seconds it is a mistake. You can't maintain pedal r.p.m. very long when out of the saddle. You will soon lose both speed and energy. Never let yourself get into a situation where cadence bogs down and you are forced to sit in the middle of a hill and shift to a lower gear. An incredible amount of momentum will be lost.

Dealing with weather

Weather can have a huge effect on time trial results. This is especially true when there is a big field, such as in a stage race. When you have 100 riders and they start at one-minute intervals, the weather can change totally between the first man's start and the last man's finish. Anything can happen as a weather front approaches. I've seen a rider go out in dead calm air, then turn and have a gusty tailwind to blow him back down the course. He just flies! I've also seen a rider fight a headwind all the way out, and then turn around precisely when the wind does. He just dies! Luck is so important.

On windy days a low, aerodynamic riding position is a must. A headwind demands extremely hard work, of course, but try to use just as much effort with a tailwind. Many riders tend to sit up and relax a little when the wind is at their back. It's a natural temptation because it seems that speed can be just as great with a more comfortable effort. But unless a tailwind is blowing at 40 k.p.h. or more it only reduces the air resistance, it doesn't eliminate it. Only if you keep pedaling with full effort will a tailwind really help lower your time.

In crosswinds take advantage of whatever shelter the course provides. If the wind is coming from your right and there are fences, hedges, trees, houses, etc. lining the road, stay as close to them as safety allows. It is the same tactic used by the breakaway in a criterium when there is a wall of spectators.

When it is raining, coat your legs with heavy oil or Vaseline to keep out the water. If it is also cold, first rub on a warming cream such as Musclor 2, then apply Vaseline. Vaseline works better than oil to prevent cream from being washed away.

Greg LeMond displays beautiful cornering form in the prologue time trial of the 1984 Tour de France. Note his bike's streamlined tubes and V-section rims.

Stage race time trialing

A stage race time trial, unlike a championship event, doesn't give you the opportunity for peak preparation. It will come somewhere among several days of long road races, or at the very beginning as the prologue. Often it will be quite short (less than 10 km) but occasionally even longer than 40 km. The course may be hilly or perhaps straight uphill. It may be a circuit or point-to-point course instead of out and back. But despite these possible variations, one thing is consistent: The time trial is a crucial stage for gaining places in the general classification.

The general preparation is made by working on time trialing technique in training and by occasionally competing in an ITT. Remember, a good bike rider is good for every event.

When you have time trialing ability and the ITT stage is drawing near, start planning for an excellent ride. Get fresh by riding conservatively in the preceding day or two. Stay tucked in the front third of the field. Conserve strength. Don't do any work that you can avoid. No hard pulling, no solo moves. Most top contenders will be using the same strategy. Don't worry if several lower-placed riders take advantage of the situation by breaking away. Give them their couple of minutes. This won't hurt you, but you must guard against better-placed riders joining them. Here is where good teammates can be a big help.

A strong time trialist may center his entire race strategy on the ITT stage. When the day comes he will push to the maximum. If he is good, and lucky, he can even take No. 1 GC because of his single stage performance. We saw it happen at the 1983 Tour of America when Bert Oosterbosch, the former world pursuit champion, finished in the field during three stages but won the 15 km time trial by 30 seconds. It was more than enough to give him the overall victory. He took maximum advantage of his strong point in an event that suited it perfectly, and he defeated several riders who had more complete talent. If even one of the other stages had required some climbing, the final GC might very well have had a different look.

On the other hand, if time trialing is not your strong point you must limit the damage that is likely to result from the stage. Do this by being aggressive on the other days. Always be looking for an opportunity to make time, then capitalize. Build all the cushion you can. On the day of the time trial, give it your best effort. Every second you save can make a difference.

Some stage races double the challenge by having a time trial up a hill. A good climber won't win this stage unless he is also a good time trialist. It takes both abilities because it is not like a normal climb with a group of riders. It is not a case of riding slow the first half and fast the second. There is no jump, jump, jump to attack and drop opponents. Instead, the objective is to make a strong, consistent effort all the way up. In this respect it is just like a flat time trial. Many times a thin, light climber who is good in an uphill TT will be almost as strong in a flat TT. It takes the same physical and mental power. Alexi Grewal and Andy Hampsten are two riders who have this dual talent.

You don't have to worry about an aerodynamic position at climbing speeds, of course, but as in all time trialing you must pay attention to smoothness, efficiency and rhythm. There is no single riding technique I can tell you to use — it depends on the climbing style you've developed in all of your training and racing. The objective is simply to get from the bottom to the top as fast as you can. Whatever helps that happen is right; whatever doesn't is wrong.

Secrets for better performance

Now would you like a couple of secrets for better time trialing? There are special techniques for pedaling and breathing that few riders know about. Both can be used in other types of racing, but they pay off best in the steady, near-maximum effort of the ITT. I am sure these techniques will improve your performance if you can learn to do them subconsciously.

First, a way to give each leg about six minutes of rest during a 40 km time trial — and gain speed rather than lose it. Does this sound crazy? You'll see that it isn't. To understand the concept, please look at the palm of your hand. Notice that it is nice and pink with blood. Now make a hard fist for five seconds. Open it and see what's happened—the blood has been squeezed out and the palm is white. But soon it becomes pink again.

Something similar occurs inside your legs when you are pedaling hard. Muscle tenseness restricts the flow of blood, which in turn reduces the amount of nutrients and oxygen that blood provides. The result is diminished work capacity. When you are pedaling hard and fast through 360 degrees, there is really no time when leg muscles are relaxed enough to permit a greater blood supply.

So once the time trial has begun and you are up to speed, here's the secret: Let your right leg come around one time with no exertion against the pedal. Five strokes later, do the same with the left leg. Five more strokes and relax the right again, then the left again, and so on through the entire time trial. Thus, each leg is not pushing during one stroke in every 10, or 10% of the time. If you ride 40 km in 60 minutes, that means each leg is getting 10% of 60, or approximately *six minutes* of rest. That's a lot. Meanwhile, no speed is lost. In fact, speed should increase because you are letting your leg muscles recover and receive more blood. They stay fresher and stronger.

How to rest your legs during the race

This works, believe me. Some of the best riders in the world have trained themselves to do it. You will never know they are pedaling this way when you ride behind them, but they are. Jacques Anquetil told me he did it. I used this technique, and so did many top riders in Poland, including Nowicki and Mytnik, the man who was known as the Polish Locomotive. For several years nobody in the world could beat Mytnik in a time trial. During the Peace Race and Tour de l'Avenir, people never asked who would win the ITT stages, only who would be second to him. He had an incredible ability to sustain a high speed.

In an uphill time trial the correct technique is whatever gets you to the finish line in the least amount of time. This is Steve Bauer, applying all his body weight to the pedals.

Former world pursuit champion Bert Oosterbosch is shown aboard another version of an advanced time trial bike. Note the small front wheel, the brake behind the fork crown, and the extended seat tube.

In Poland I saw a test in the physiology lab that relates to this pedaling technique. Using a spring-loaded device like the trigger of a gun, a person squeezed it with his index finger until fatigue was so great he just couldn't do it any more. This took about five minutes. Then he did absolutely nothing for 10 minutes before squeezing it again. This time he lasted three minutes. After complete recovery he repeated the test. But this time he spent the 10-minute rest period by pulling easily on the trigger with almost all resistance removed. He didn't just sit there doing nothing. Then when he did the second set he easily exceeded three minutes. This shows that muscle recovery is aided by easy motion even more than it is by total rest. In terms of the pedaling technique, it explains why each leg's soft stroke every 10 revolutions really can result in improved performance.

It is not easy to pedal this way. You must train yourself to make it automatic. You cannot have it on your mind in a time trial because there are other things that need your concentration. It may take 20 training rides, or 50 or 100. If you work on it, it will come.

Related to this pedaling is the second trick, which deals with breathing. Together, breathing and pedaling set the rhythm of a time trial. Some riders synchronize their breathing by exhaling on each soft pedal stroke. Usually this requires resting a leg on every third revolution instead of every fifth.

How to breathe more efficiently

No matter what breathing pattern is natural for you, the correct technique is to inhale air slowly through the mouth and nose together, then exhale it sharply through the mouth only. There is no big secret to that, but do you know how to do it in a way that prevents your mouth from going dry? A dry mouth is very bothersome in a time trial — remember, you have no water bottle — and it can ruin your concentration. But it's not hard to prevent. Again, the technique must be practiced until it becomes totally natural. Try it right now. Let your jaw drop slightly open and jut it forward a bit. Move the tip of your tongue up behind your bottom row of teeth. Already you will notice extra saliva flowing. By breathing with your mouth in this position you will never dry out again. I guarantee it.

EQUIPMENT

Because the ITT is a race judged solely by time, your equipment must be as efficient, as light and as aerodynamic as you can make it. The seconds you save can (and often will) make a difference in your final placing.

For an important event on a flat or slightly undulating course, make these modifications to your road bike:

Modifications to
road bike

- Take off the front derailleur, its cable and shift lever, and the small chainring. Low gears aren't needed, so why carry the weight?
- Remove the water bottle cage, pump brackets, etc.
- Like a tour rider coming to an ITT stage, lower the handlebar stem about 3 cm. This automatically creates a lower, more aerodynamic riding position.
- Clean all the grease out of the hubs and remove one ball bearing from each side. Lubricate with light oil.
- Use a three-speed freewheel. That's all you need for a flat time trial, so save weight by removing the other cogs and improve the chain efficiency as well. Install the cog that is correct for your start and turnaround, and the two sizes you need for riding at speed. Center them by using spacers in place of other cogs. Some freewheel systems, like the Shimano Freehub, make this very easy to do. Our riders in international team time trials use a three-speed gear system whenever the course is suitable.
- Install a longer chain. It should actually hang limp in the highest gears. This tells you there is no tension on the chain from the derailleur pulleys, so it can travel more efficiently.

If you doubt the last point prove it to yourself with the bike on your workstand. Put on a long chain, shift to high gear, spin the crank smoothly to high r.p.m., then let go of the pedal. The chainring will keep turning for several revolutions, driven only by the slight force from the freewheel. There is very little resistance against the chain. But if the chain is shorter so that it does not droop, the chainring will stop turning immediately. The freewheel cannot overcome the tension on the chain caused by the derailleur. This may seem a small point but, believe me, the extra efficiency pays off during the 5,000 or so crank revolutions of a 40 km time trial. For the same basic reason, climbers will lengthen their chain so it hangs limp when they are using the small chainring.

The one problem with a single chainring and long chain is an increased danger of accidental derailment. Since there is no front derailleur, it's possible for the chain to bounce off on bumps or during rear gear changes. For safety, use a chainholder. These are not available commercially but you can easily fabricate one out of an old front derailleur. The cheap black plastic Simplex derailleur is perfect (and many shops have a box full of old ones because they are not very perfect for anything else). Cut down the cage until a thin horseshoe remains. Position it low over the chain just where it feeds onto the chainring. If the chain bounces it won't fall off. Many time trialists do not use the precaution of a chainholder, but it is worth having if it does its job even once. All of the U.S. team's custom Raleigh TTT bikes have a reinforced hole tapped in the seat tube to accept a very trim chainholder. It is made of a thin threaded rod with an inverted U brazed on at the end.

Wheels and tires

At this time the best wheels for time trialing are built with aerodynamic V-section rims and bladed spokes. This rim design has become widely available, but only the East Germans are currently making a really light model (about 200 grams) with internal spoke nipples. And they are the source of the best blades to lace up these rims with. The problem for us in the U.S. is how to get hold of these products. It's been almost impossible, but the USCF has managed to obtain enough of the spokes to build wheels for the Worlds, Pan Ams and Olympics. The more common eliptical spokes are not nearly as thin as the German blades, but they still have an advantage over standard round spokes.

Wheel construction depends on a time trialist's weight and riding style. If you are 150 pounds or less and are fairly smooth on the bike, I recommend 24-hole small-flange hubs. Lace the front wheel radially; lace the rear radially on the left side and one-cross on the right. These patterns reduce turbulence to the minimum. Other than the rider's body, rotating wheels are the biggest contributors to air resistance.

A rougher or slightly heavier rider should use a 28-spoke wheel on the rear, 24 on the front (same spoking patterns as above). A rider weighing 175 pounds or more should use a 28-spoke wheel on each end. I don't believe any rider needs 32-spoke wheels for time trialing, especially if V-section rims are used. They are significantly stronger than conventional rims. (Note: Loctite or a similar compound should always be used on the spoke threads and in the nipples when the wheel is laced radially or one-cross. This will prevent the nipples from vibrating loose.)

Tires should be as light and narrow as practical. Whether to use silk or cotton is partly determined by the weather—silk tires should not be ridden in the wet. In general, silk tires have less rolling resistance than cotton tires, but this is offset by a quality cotton tire's ability to safely take more pressure. I think most riders will do very well on a 190-220 gram cotton tire pumped to 8.5-9.5 atm (125-140 p.s.i.). A mat or rib tread has less rolling resistance than a mixed tread.

Some national team riders have used 130-gram silk tires in time trials on fairly rough asphalt with absolutely no problems. Superlight tires are the way to maximize rolling efficiency. It's somewhat of a gamble, but it's an acceptable one as long as the decision is made intelligently. For example, at the 1978 Junior Worlds in Washington, DC, all my assistant coaches told me, "Eddie, 165-gram tires are too light for the team time trial. The road is not good enough for them." I said, "Possibly, but I think they are fine." Since I like to sleep well at night, I had an alternate on the team test the tires by riding the full 70 km course on the spare set of wheels.

Then we inspected them very carefully. The tires and rims were still perfect. So we used the 165-gram tires, filled with helium to 130-145 p.s.i., and we won the bronze medal. (Helium saves about 10 grams per tire.) I saw other teams using 195-gram, even 220-gram tires. Our choice gave us a very important advantage. You, too, should do everything within reason to gain an edge. Wheels and tires are the place to start.

No matter what else you do, keep your head up. Francesco Moser shows both excellent time trialing form and one of the most advanced TT bikes yet seen. Note the disk wheels, special frame, and the single chainring with the front derailleur acting as a chainholder. The photo is from the 1984 Giro d'Italia, which Moser won in large part because of his performance in the time trial stages.

Special bikes

Frame design

If the ITT is a big event for you, it is a good idea to own a special time trial bike. These have been seen in international 100 km team events since the late 1970s and now they are becoming available from various manufacturers and custom framebuilders. You know the design — short head tube, sloping top tube, custom-made upturned handlebars, aerodynamic tubing. If you order a frame like this, I recommend that the seat tube length be identical to your road racing frame (or as identical as possible given the steeper angles). I also recommend that the frame be made for standard-size wheels (so-called 27-inch) rather than 26- or 24-inch. Right now this is my preference because high-quality 27-inch rims and tires are much more available. In the future this may change. If quality components for 26- and 24-inch wheels do come on the market they will be the better choice. A smaller rim is a stronger rim, so fewer spokes are necessary. Weight is saved and air turbulence is reduced.

Equipment designers are hard at work, and testing and evaluation is constantly being done. Who knows what the future holds? In 1983 the Raleigh bikes we used to win the 100 km team time trial at the Pan American Games were undreamed of just a couple of years before. They had a 24-inch front wheel, 27-inch rear. This

Jacques Anquetil, a great pro road racer and time trialist of the late 1950s and '60s, told me he used the leg-resting pedaling technique that I describe in this chapter.

makes sense aerodynamically because it decreases frontal area and puts the riders closer together for a better draft. The pursuit team rode Raleighs that were even more radical — they had two 24-inch wheels. All these bikes featured another way to reduce air resistance; narrow forward alignment made possible by hubs only 6 cm wide in front and 9 cm wide in rear. But as advanced as these bikes were, they will be obsolete by the time of the 1984 Olympics. Our TTT bikes for Los Angeles are likely to have featherweight aluminum frames and brakes concealed inside the rear stays and top of the fork. All you will see is the pads. Instead of brake levers there may be a twist grip built into the handlebars similar to the throttle on a motorcycle. The wheels could be just as revolutionary.

I believe we have only begun to see a wave of innovation that is coming in spokes, lacing patterns, hub design, rims, and tires. In 1983, for example, the French company Roval began marketing a pair of super wheels for around $250. They are built with sealed bearing hubs and V-section rims. The spokes have concealed nipples and a hammerhead that fits into the top of the hub flange. The front wheel is laced radially with 16 spokes; the rear has eight radial spokes on the left side, 16 one-cross spokes on the freewheel side. Tests have shown these wheels to be very efficient and actual competition has proved their strength. Some riders are even using them in road races, such as Alexi Grewal at the Coors Classic.

Innovative wheels

When you order a time trial frame, make sure it will accommodate the recent advances in aerodynamics:

- Front brake behind the fork
- Rear brake behind the bottom bracket
- Shift lever on top of the down tube
- All cables inside the frame tubes

Frame features

As for components, use

- Sealed bearing hubs, which eliminate concern about adjustment and lubrication
- Roval or custom-built aerodynamic wheels
- Small, lightweight brake levers like the Modolo Kronos or Orion
- A narrow seat post and a light, streamlined saddle
- Smooth plastic handlebar tape only on the hand position when racing
- Aerodynamic pedals or, even better, the Cinelli or Contak pedals that eliminate toe clips and straps
- A sleek, lightweight derailleur
- A narrow bottle and cage when a time trial is long enough to require liquids

Components

In sum, everything that can be aerodynamic must be aerodynamic. It is important to ride such a bike often. You must get used to the handling characteristics.

Crank arm length and chainring size

No matter what type of bike you time trial on, keep the same saddle height as on your regular road bike, but use crank arms that are 2.5 mm longer and a chainring that is one tooth larger. If you normally ride with 170 mm cranks go to 172.5; if you use a 53 chainring put on a 54. You will find that the longer cranks let you turn the 54 as if it were a 53. The physics of using a longer lever arm means more power but also more time for the movement. That is, pedal r.p.m. can be fewer and road speed will remain the same. Or pedal r.p.m. can stay the same and road speed will increase. This is a good deal in a time trial. The effort is steady—you aren't concerned with sprint-type accelerations that make longer cranks a drawback.

The chart, which is based on a study done in the Soviet Union, illustrates the point very well. It tells us that for a given gear ratio and pedaling cadence, it takes less power to maintain road speed as crank arm length increases. While it is based on 5 mm increments, there is also a benefit in going up by 2.5 mm. Why not go all the way from, say, 170 mm to 175 mm or even longer? Because a change that big would very likely upset your muscles and pedal action. You would have to train a lot with the long arms to become efficient with them. This isn't the case, however, for an increase of 2.5 mm. If you use your road bike for time trialing, install the arms and bigger chainring when you set it up for the race. Take at least one ride to make sure everything is working perfectly, then recheck all fixing bolts for tightness.

CRANK-LENGTH

To Maintain Speed of: 62 k.p.h.				To Maintain Speed of: 51.5 k.p.h.			
Gear ratio	Pedal revolutions @ 1 min. @ 1 sec.	Crank length (mm)	Power (force on pedal in kilograms)	Gear ratio	Pedal revolutions @ 1 min. @ 1 sec.	Crank length (mm)	Power (Force on pedal in kilograms)
50 × 14 (96.4 in.)	135 / 2.26	165 170 175	43.67 42.38 41.18	46 × 14 (88.7 in.)	122.1 / 2.03	165 170 175	29.66 28.79 27.98
58 × 16 (97.9 in.)	133.5 / 2.22	165 170 175	44.35 43.04 41.81	54 × 16 (91.1 in.)	119.5 / 1.99	165 170 175	30.38 29.49 28.65
52 × 14 (100.3 in.)	130.4 / 2.17	165 170 175	44.82 43.50 42.26	48 × 14 (92.6 in.)	117.1 / 1.95	165 170 175	30.89 29.98 29.13
60 × 16 (101.3 in.)	128.8 / 2.15	165 170 175	45.30 43.87 42.57	56 × 16 (94.5 in.)	114.6 / 1.91	165 170 175	31.56 30.63 29.76

SOURCE: Poland's Academy of Physical Education and Federation of Sport, Cycling, 1977.

Aerodynamic clothing

As important as aerodynamic equipment is, wind tunnel tests have shown that it is the shape of the rider, not the bike, that creates the most air resistance. There is little that can be done about the design of the human body, but quite a lot about how well the wind moves past it.

A skinsuit is a must for time trialing. The more rubberized the material, the better. When the material itself can't breathe, there must be a mesh panel down each side of the torso to let body heat out. Tests have shown a greater aerodynamic advantage to a one-piece suit with built-in hood, long sleeves with built-in mittens, and even long tights. The USCF is looking closely at this, but it worries me that the East Germans aren't using full body coverings—there's no doubt they have tested them like we have. One problem may be not enough ventilation; another is the legality of such suits in the eyes of the UCI. At any rate, a full suit isn't as practical for a road time trial as it is for short events on the track.

For the ITT you will be sufficiently aerodynamic and air-cooled if you shave your arms and legs, oil them, and wear a short-sleeve skinsuit. A criterium-type suit with an inside rear pocket isn't necessary since you don't need to carry food or fluid. The exception is for a lengthy event when you might want to have a small flask of strong coffee and glucose. Some riders always carry a glucose tablet (more of a psychological aid than anything else), but this doesn't require a pocket — it can easily be stored just under the edge of a sleeve.

A streamlined hardshell helmet is essential. Wind tunnel tests have proved the benefit. The best design has no air holes or scoops and is tapered to fill in the gap between the head and back.

Don't wear cycling gloves because the mesh backs catch more air than smooth skin. Shine your shoes and cover the laces with tape, or wear lightweight, tight-fitting shoe covers. These are widely seen in international competition but still might not be sold commercially when you read this. However, I believe that before very much longer we will see specialty items for time trialing and criterium racing in many pro bike shops. Keep abreast of developments and use the items as soon as they become available.

Team Time Trials

During my racing career the 100-kilometer team time trial was my strongest point. I was always the best or second best rider among the four. By the time I finished competing, I had been a member of a winning team 19 times.

In 1962 I rode on the first team in the world to break 2 hours and 15 minutes. We did 2:14:10 in Poland's National Championship. This time is no big deal now, but it was fantastic then. The team that had won the previous year finished five minutes behind us. The commissaires couldn't believe it—we had gone faster than Italy's gold medal team in the Olympics two years before. They said it was incredible, impossible. They even remeasured the course. I remember we were riding bikes with steel cranks and the road was not flat but rolling. Before my career was over, my team got down to 2:07. That was about 20 years ago and it is still a very respectable time.

At this writing, the U.S. doesn't have a 2-man team time trial as a District or National Championship race. As late as 1979 there was not even the 4-man 100 km event. Now that we do have it, I am pushing for the 2-man. It is only logical. This country is big but cycling still is not. Clubs are not very strong. Getting two riders together is much easier than getting four together. In other parts of the world the 2-man TTT is popular and it's included in the National Championship program. The standard distance is 50 km, or half the length of the 4-man TTT. At the end of this chapter I will include a brief discussion of the 2-man event, both because it is excellent preparation for the 4-man and because I hope it will soon be a race Americans are riding.

By the way, in many countries the individual time trial is not 40 km (25 miles) as in the U.S. but 25 km. So the progression is sensible: 25 km for one rider, 50 km for two riders, 100 km for four riders. In addition, national time trial championships are scheduled so that riders can naturally build from one event to the next. The individual time trial will be in early May, the 2-man in late May, and the 4-man about three weeks after that. This gives riders time for specific preparation. Unfortunately, the U.S. National Championship program is not so rational. We have the individual time trial, 4-man time trial, and the road race all scheduled in one week. This is plainly a mistake because it does not allow riders time for the special training and rest they need to race at their best in each event. And since the traditional Nationals dates are too close to the Worlds, the riders cannot achieve their potential there, either. It is a shame that our policy makers don't understand this.

They actually prevent top American performances by their allegiance to an unenlightened way of doing things.

But I am off the point. Let's look at the riding techniques for the team time trials, how to train, and how to do your best on race day.

CHARACTERISTICS OF THE TEAM TIME TRIALIST

The 4-man time trial is the major team event in road racing. Seniors race 100 km and have the opportunity to compete in the World Championships, Pan American Games and Olympics, as well as the Nationals. The Junior distance is 70 km, but it wasn't until the National Sports Festival in 1983 that U.S. Juniors had a TTT besides the Worlds.

There is a special set of requirements for team time trialists:

- They must be fast.
- They must be smart.
- They must have quick recovery.
- They must have good ability in the individual time trial.
- They must have excellent bike-handling technique so the effect of the draft is maximized.

The last point cannot be emphasized enough. A rider who has all the physical ingredients except the skill to ride one inch behind a wheel cannot be on a time trial team. There was a perfect example of this in 1979 at our selection camp for the Junior Worlds. The national 25-mile champion that year was John Patterson, a big, fast, powerful guy who looked like a super prospect for the 70 km team. But he had very bad technique around other riders, not because he was chicken but because he always trained alone and lacked the experience. He wanted to stay one meter behind a wheel. The result was a big increase in the amount of energy he had to use. He worked on this problem and did improve, but not enough to make the team. The end came when we paired him with Greg LeMond in 2-man time trialing. They were the two strongest riders, but LeMond dropped him in the first 8 km because Patterson did not draft correctly. He was taking much more wind on his body. Patterson was very upset when he wasn't picked for the team, but what could we do? In many other respects he was a fine rider, and he went on to race professionally.

Generally, the best TTT riders are huge—tall and with large muscles. We are dealing here with big gears and flat roads. It is an advantage to be powerfully built. Ideally, all four riders will look like they came from the same mold. They will have identical heights and weights. Of course, it is the rare coach who is so fortunate, and many times the team will include riders of various physiques. After all, actual selection is made by performance, not by size. For example, take our "spider," Andy Hampsten. He is long and skinny, but he is an excellent team time trialist and he has two medals from the Junior Worlds to show for it. He is fast and he is also a nice guy—he wants to work very hard for the team. This is another essential trait. Team time trialists must be nice persons. They must be ready at any time to help their teammates. The last several seconds during each pull are very painful, so each rider must be willing to continually face this severe discomfort for one reason: to help his teammates succeed. This must be the primary motivation.

Importance of holding a wheel

Sacrifice for the team

What does it take to make an excellent 100-kilometer time trial team? The Soviet Union's 1983 world champions displayed several key ingredients: streamlined helmets, skinsuits and shoe covers; aerodynamic bicycles; four superbly fit, evenly sized riders; and the technical skill to ride at full speed for two hours just centimeters apart.

Like Hampsten, Alexi Grewal is a fine climber and stage racer who could also be a very good team time trialist. What's held him back is his own uncertainty—he doesn't believe in himself for this event. It was the same for Davis Phinney, but he overcame his doubts. At the 1980 Olympic Trials I put him in the TTT selection program. He didn't want it. He hated it. He told me, "It's not for me." I said, "Davis, you are not right. You are a fast man, you have good recovery, you are a big man. The team time trial will be very good for you." Three years later we were in Venezuela at the Pan American Games and Phinney led the team to a new U.S. and Pan Am record of 2:03:20. In that race he took pulls of 45 seconds, sometimes one minute. He was incredible! We remembered what he had told me in 1980 and how much things had changed. "Now I love this," he said. In fact, Phinney has become the king of 100 km riders in the U.S. I'm sure he could ride for any team in the world, including the Soviet Union.

Self-knowledge is essential

You cannot be a good team time trialist without a strong mentality for the event. You must know exactly what you are capable of doing on each pull and throughout the race. You must never allow even one second of slowdown before you let your teammates come through. That means 90% effort on each pull, not 100%, because it takes some energy to make a smooth change and then get back onto the paceline. You have to constantly concentrate on how much is left in your muscles. It's like driving a car. How full is the tank? When it's down to a quarter you can't drive 130 k.p.h. or you won't make it to the next gas station. When your energy is getting low you must realize it and cut your pulls from 20 seconds to 15 or even 10. If you are bullheaded and keep trying to do 20 seconds, you will soon be able to do nothing.

You may be the strongest rider among the four, but if you insist on showing it you are no good for the TTT. All you will do is kill your teammates. Instead, you must use your strength in such a way that by the last 10 km you are as tired as they are. This is done by:

1. driving up the speed during each pull, but not so much that it hurts the others; or
2. lengthening each pull to give the others more rest; or
3. a combination of the two.

For example, each time you pull increase the speed by 1-2 k.p.h. and the duration to 35 seconds. Your teammates will be able to handle this pace, and the extra recovery time will help them. Don't jump up the speed by 5 k.p.h. and pull the usual

The U.S. gold medal ride in the 1983 Pan Am Games was a tribute to advanced technology, very good preparation, and the leadership of Davis Phinney. He has become one of the world's best 100-kilometer riders.

20 seconds. You'll kill them. It takes great intelligence to do it right, as well as a lot of practice with the team. How long to pull? How fast? When the strongest rider uses his strength correctly, it takes a very experienced eye to see which of the four he is.

On the other hand, the weaker riders on the team must accept their limitations and not try to match the strong men pull for pull. Generally, the team's pace in the first half of the race is dictated by what the weakest rider can handle — it does no good to blow him off with 75 km still to go. (In the 4-man TTT, time is taken on the third rider to cross the line, so only three have to finish.) Often the weakest man will pull for only 8-10 seconds each time, which is sufficient to allow the rider who has just swung off to get back in the line — there must never be two riders out of the paceline at once. By taking short pulls, the weakest rider can contribute to the maximum of his ability.

After about 50 km, the pace is increased to what the third strongest rider can handle. The fourth rider may not be able to pull through any more, but he should stay with the team by hanging on the end of the paceline and letting the others enter in front of him. This is for insurance. He will be available if one of the other three goes out with a mechanical or physical problem.

With 25 km to go, the pace is increased to what the second strongest rider can handle. Now it is the third rider who must shorten his pulls or begin sitting at the end of the line. The fourth rider will probably be dropped, which is a bad situation, but it is almost unavoidable when going for a maximum team performance. It is the price that must be paid when the riders have unequal strength. It is a situation most likely to be found on teams that do not have a broad base of good riders to select from.

On the best teams, all four riders will be closely matched and they will finish together, dead. Each one will use every last ounce of his strength. During various parts of the race, a rider will slightly lengthen or shorten his pulls, depending on how he is feeling. His objective is to contribute as much as possible to maximum speed and do it right down to the final meters. Success comes only when all four riders have this kind of self-knowledge and dedication to the team.

RACING TECHNIQUES

Here is an absolute rule for any type of team time trialing: The bikes must have the same size chainrings and clusters. It is essential for the riders to be in harmony and feel the same rhythm. It requires the identical gear in order to pedal at the identical r.p.m. The movement of the team must be like the movement of one rider.

A team can save one minute in 100 km by using the correct technique for trading the lead position. This is important because it is almost always the case that riders, particularly inexperienced ones, do not realize when they are slowing down at the front. However, the second rider can easily feel it. When he does, he should automatically start going around. If he waits until the front rider pulls off, distance, speed and time will be lost. You will understand how much in a moment.

In a 4-man TTT each pull should last 15-20 seconds. This is ideal. It means that 200-250 meters will be covered during each rider's turn at the front. In a 2-man event the pulls are longer, about 30-35 seconds. This is necessary to give a rider sufficient time behind the wheel before he is on the front again. There is only one man to ride behind, and it normally takes 7-10 seconds to line back up after a pull.

Why don't 100 km riders pull longer? Simple. If they do, if everyone on the team pulls for 30 seconds, they will go slower than a team whose riders are pulling for 15 seconds. It is easier to recover after 15 seconds of maximum speed than it is after 30 seconds. Pulling longer means pulling slower. The exception is when one or two team members are clearly stronger than the others. This was the case with Davis Phinney at the 1983 Pan Ams, and with Roy Knickman on the 70 km team at the 1982 and '83 Junior Worlds. No Junior in the country was at Knickman's level. We had him pull for 30-35 seconds right from the beginning while the others did the normal 15 seconds. This is the right way to get the most from a superior rider's strength and not kill him before the end of the race. The wrong way is to put him on the front for pulls of 45 or 50 seconds every time. This makes him use almost 100% of his strength on each pull. Soon he will be unable to recover in the 45 seconds before he is back on the front. A rider must push hard for the benefit of team speed, but he must also retain the energy necessary to hold a straight line at the front, change positions smoothly, and not let a gap open before getting back in the draft.

The ability to accurately gauge lengths of pulls comes with experience. Some American riders tell me they count pedal strokes, but I think if you do that for two hours you will go crazy. The clock must be in your head and in your legs. Once it's time for the lead rider to finish his turn, the second rider anticipates by moving over a few centimeters opposite the pull-off side. Should the leader remain on front several seconds longer, the second rider will still have a good draft. When he sees the leader edge over, the second rider starts moving forward. It is when his front wheel reaches the front wheel of the leader that the leader decreases speed and drops back. *He must not slow down before then.* It is the second rider's duty not to jump up the speed as he moves into the lead. It is both necessary and natural to go a little faster through the draft as the pass is made, but there should never be an acceleration of 3-4 k.p.h.

How important is it to change the lead correctly? Most riders (and some coaches) think the proper technique is for the lead rider to swing off, slow down, and let the other three ride through. But what is the actual result of this? Think about it. It means that during each change the team *loses one full bike length.* That's equal to 2.5 meters. If there are four pulls each kilometer, that's ten meters lost. During 100 km it adds up to 1,000 meters, which is worth about 1 minute and 20 seconds. That's a huge amount of time in a team time trial. In the Moscow Olympics, for example, the Soviets won the TTT by 32 seconds over East Germany, which beat Czechoslovakia by 0.7 seconds. Precious time will be protected if the lead rider maintains race speed until the second rider draws alongside. Then the distance lost during each change will be reduced to the minimum, to perhaps half a meter. About 8 meters will be preserved each kilometer, or 800 meters during the 100 km. That's worth a minute.

When teammates pass each other they should be so close that their elbows touch. This is normal and it doesn't make good riders uncomfortable. The closer the riders, the better the draft — this means side-to-side closeness as well as front to back. As the former leader drops back alongside the last man in line, his speed should not be so slow that he has to jump to catch back on. Instead, when his front tire is at the last rider's rear axle he should be going almost the same speed. Then it takes very little effort to slide over and rejoin the paceline.

Want to make it even easier? Here's a way to save a couple of pedal strokes each time you move back onto a wheel. The very best riders do it, but it takes a good

How to change the
lead

Correct technique
saves time

deal of practice. Just as your front wheel drops back past the last rider's rear axle, stop pedaling briefly, stand, and pull the bike back between your legs. Make your slight turn in behind the rider and put your bike forward again as you sit down. There you are, right on his wheel, all in one smooth, easy motion with a little stretch for your body, too. The technique is similar to throwing your bike at the finish line in a sprint, only it begins with pulling the bike backwards.

TEAM SELECTION

In most clubs there is usually no question about who the 100 km team time trialists will be. They are the strongest riders, or at least good riders who have the time to train together and develop their technique. Often the team is decided many months in advance of the National Championship. It is different at the national level, however. I will describe the USCF's selection process for major international events like the Worlds and Olympics. This system can be applied by clubs fortunate enough to have a pool of potential 100 km riders to choose from.

The trials begin 4-6 weeks before the event. The procedure goes like this:

1. Individual time trialing
2. 2-man team time trialing
3. Long team selection (8-16 riders)
4. 4-man team time trialing
5. Short team selection (5-6 riders)
6. Training camp
7. Final selection of 4-man team

At the same time, riders are being selected for the individual road race. That team is composed of members of the long team and it may include one or more of the TTT riders.

The individual time trial reveals each rider's endurance and power. Seniors race 10 km twice or 20 km once. It depends on whether we are looking primarily for speed (10 km) or for endurance (20 km) in the particular group we are working with. For example, if the riders have just finished a stage race we know their endurance is good, so we give them a couple of short time trials to test their speed. (The Junior distances are 7 km and 15 km.)

Next, riders pick partners for 2-man time trialing, or the coaches make the pairings. Either way is okay as long as the paired riders had comparable times in the ITT. The coaches always have the final say. The length of this time trial is 35-40 km for Seniors (25-30 km for Juniors). Just one may be ridden if time for the selection is short, but two will paint a better picture. A second race gives riders the chance to eliminate mistakes that may have hurt their performance in the first one.

A coach follows each 2-man team to study both riders. He fills in a performance chart, which includes this information:

1. Time duration of each pull
2. Change in team speed caused by each pull
3. Bike-handling technique and teamwork

It works best when someone drives for the coach so he is free to use the stopwatch and take notes; otherwise he should talk into a tape recorder. Basically, the coach

The selection of a 4-man team includes 2-man time trialing. Here I'm about to start two more riders during a USCF training camp.

watches for how each rider's pulls affect the team. For example, he writes down +1 if Rider A's pull results in an increase of 1 k.p.h. A -1 says the opposite happened. A +4 means the pulling rider is going to kill his partner. That is too big an increase. The coach stays close behind the riders so he can sense their slight changes in speed. He must be smart and realize the natural fluctuations caused by terrain and wind direction.

Based on the numbers and their own impressions, the coaches put together at least two 4-man teams, maybe three or four. Collectively, these riders are called the long team. As few as eight riders may be included, or as many as 16. Generally, the No. 1 4-man team is composed of the best performers from the best 2-man teams. Sometimes both members of the fastest 2-man team will make it, sometimes just the better of those two riders. It depends on what the performance chart shows.

The 4-man teams race for a distance of 80-90 km. We don't go the full 100 km because a shorter distance can be ridden faster. This contributes to the riders' preparation for the upcoming championship—we are not just selecting, we are developing. A coach follows each team and once again records the lengths of each rider's pulls and any changes in speed that result.

Now the coaching staff sits down and evaluates the 4-man performance charts and each rider's technique, teamwork and mentality. The two best riders on the win-

4-man time trial

ning team automatically get a place on the championship team. The coaches pick at least three riders (four is best) to compete for the remaining two places.

There is now one month to go. All riders on the short team train together under a coach's supervision. Perhaps in two weeks one rider is cut, leaving the minimum of five. Sometimes it is not decided until two or three days before the event who has won the fourth and final place. Or, the trials may produce such clear-cut results that the four starters and the alternates are determined with four weeks still to go. (A late change is always possible because of an injury, illness, or discipline problem.) The coach must be honest with the riders and tell them where they stand as soon as he has decided. If he is uncertain about the fourth starter, he should go to the three who have already made the team and ask their opinion. It is important to find out who they respect and have confidence in. A coach must always talk with his best riders. They are on the bike, he isn't. They may have a definite feeling about who is right for the team. On the other hand, the coach must be aware of selfish motives, such as club affiliation, that may color the opinions he hears.

This selection system (and a similar one we have for the team pursuit) is not used anywhere else in the world as far as I know. It certainly was not used in the U.S. before I came in 1977. In my first six years, our team time trialists won a total of six medals in the Junior Worlds and Pan Am Games. But despite this success there have been difficulties for me. Some people in the USCF and the U.S. Olympic Committee would like team selection based entirely on times so it is completely cut and dried. I can understand their point of view, but unfortunately they know very little about team time trialing. A rider's technique and mentality are not always reflected in numbers.

Paceline order

After the 4-man team is selected, the paceline usually is ordered in size from the smallest rider to the largest. In this way each rider gets a relatively good draft from the teammate immediately in front. Once established, the rider order is kept during all team training.

Sometimes, however, it is not best to go strictly by size. An example is when there are two small riders and two large ones. If the small ones are together, the speed is likely to decrease during their consecutive pulls, then increase when the two big guys go through. This is not good for the rhythm of the team. In this case it would be better to arrange the riders as small-large-small-large. For the same reason, if all riders are about equal size but two are stronger than the others, the strong ones must be separated.

Rollers can be used to help each team member get accustomed to riding very close to the man he follows in the paceline. This is also helpful when the riders have not had much TTT experience. Four sets of rollers are set up one behind the other so the wheels of the bikes are just 2-3 centimeters apart. This makes the eye used to seeing a moving wheel right in front. There is no need to spend a lot of time doing this exercise, but it can be a good way to use a rainy day. It also works for team pursuiters.

Frequently one of the riders takes the role of team captain. The coach can designate him, or he will emerge naturally based on an edge in experience or strength. It is essential that this person have the respect of his teammates. He will if he shows a degree of superiority on the road — everyone respects strong legs. But he must also be intelligent and have an expert's knowledge of team time trialing. The captain acts as a coach within the team during training, and he is the one rider with authority to speak up about something during competition.

Team training

The team (including alternates) should train as a unit *each day* during its month-long preparation for a major competition. This is the ideal. The weekly schedule is the standard one:

Monday   Easy ride

Tuesday   Speed work

Wednesday   Long ride

Thursday   Interval training

Friday   Easy ride

On weekends the team should race together and try to break away together. Team-mates must spend their time on the bike together. It is how they get to know each other's bike-handling quirks and habits. It is the way they become totally confident riding one inch apart.

Tuesday speed work is done with a coach, who uses a car or motorcycle. After a good warm-up, the riders accelerate smoothly in their paceline until reaching *maximum* speed, then each rider pulls through for 15-20 seconds (about 250 meters). The coach does the timing from behind and uses the horn to order each lead change. As soon as all riders have had a turn, the coach passes and lets them get in the draft. They ride steadily until full recovery, then go again. The number of efforts depends on how the riders feel. If they are still tired from weekend racing, perhaps they'll go only twice. If they feel fresh, perhaps six times.

Tuesday speed work

Thursday interval training also uses motorpacing. But this time the coach leads some of the hard efforts in addition to providing shelter for recovery. Interval workouts are described below in the discussions of peaking and remedial training.

Three weeks before the big event, we have the team do a race simulation of not more than 80 km. This is a good, hard workout, and we include the No. 1 alternate so we can see all five men ride together.

Peaking for the big event

Peaking begins with two weeks to go, or perhaps 10 days to go for experienced TTT riders who are in top condition. The first step is several days of racing, or race simulation with motorpacing. Younger and weaker riders should do two days, older and stronger riders should do three or four. It is ideal for the latter group to compete in a short stage race that promises a fast pace and does not have anything tougher than rolling hills. If this is not possible, the team should race on Saturday and

Begin with racing and/or motorpacing

Sunday—preferably a long, flat road race followed by a long, fast criterium—and then switch to motorpacing for one or two days. If those races aren't available, there should be four days of motorpacing. Motorpacing is always the best choice if there is any doubt about the races' quality and terrain. Training must be on roads closely resembling the time trial course, which normally means flat like a table.

TTT intervals

This motorpacing is done with intervals. Hard efforts are usually alternated from in front of the car to behind it, one after the other. All rest periods are taken in the draft at a minimum speed of 40 k.p.h. The time to go again is when the riders have recovered to heart rates of about 110-120 b.p.m. (If they are physically matched well enough to be on the same team, their heart rates should be quite similar.) The distance of the unpaced efforts should be 3-4 km; those ridden behind the car should be 50% longer. This is only a guideline because everything depends on what the riders can handle. The speed will be much higher behind the car than in front of it, of course, and each rider's pull will be about 30-40 seconds vs. 15-20 seconds during unpaced training and in a race.

Motorpacing improves paceline technique

Working a paceline while motorpacing is an excellent technical exercise. It is even harder to do than when racing because the speed is faster. A team that has poor technique will improve by emphasizing relatively short intervals behind a car or motorcycle. During this and similar training, it is the responsibility of the last man in line to signal the driver whether to go faster, slower or stay steady. The last rider catches the most wind, so he can judge the effort accurately. He is also the easiest one to see in motorcycle mirrors. The coach watches for a thumb up or down, or a flat hand.

If a lack of good races makes it necessary to rely entirely on motorpaced intervals, the first two sessions are ridden as a 4-man team. Total workout distance should be 100 km the first day and about 80-90 km the second day. The proper amount is that which nearly kills the riders. However, they are the ones who decide this, not the coach. They must be given the final say in the speed and number of intervals. The coach should not dictate, only suggest.

Team is split

On the third day the riders split into two 2-man teams, which go out separately for another 50-60 km of motorpacing. The interval efforts are shorter than those done by the whole team, but just as strenuous. On the fourth day each rider trains alone with the coach, doing shorter intervals yet.

Why break up the team like this? Because it is never the case that riders have equal strength. After two hard days as a full team, they are tired. So the two strong ones are paired and the two weak ones are paired. This allows all riders to continue working very hard. If they remained as a 4-man team, the stronger riders would be held back by the weaker ones. On the final day everybody is dragging, so each rider does what he can based on his own reserves of energy. It is the day that puts the pedal to the metal—absolute exhaustion by the end of training.

Why must riders train so hard less than two weeks from the big race? Please review the discussion of peaking in Chapter 3.

After two or three days of short, easy recovery riding, the team resumes the normal training schedule but reduces the distance by 20-30%. The effort remains high on Tuesday and Thursday, but the workouts are shorter. On the weekend before the event, the team should race in a long criterium.

One day before the time trial, the team loosens up by riding 1 km two or three times at maximum speed. Or it rides 2 km twice. Pace is traded just like in a race.

There must be a super effort similar to Tuesday speed work — even faster than average race speed. The pace is easy before and after each exertion, and about 50 km is covered. This is excellent for testing. It makes sure the equipment is right and the riders are right. It gives the coach one last chance to identify and replace a rider who is having a problem. If an alternate is riding better than a team member, that team member must be taken out, no question about it. There is no room for sentiment. For example, I like Thurlow Rogers but I had to replace him with Ron Kiefel on the 70 km team for the 1978 Junior Worlds. Thurlow's bike had been stolen and he just wasn't riding well on the new one, probably because his position wasn't quite the same. In addition, he was not feeling recovered from the road race three days earlier. We talked, and it was my decision to replace him. He understood and he agreed with me. It was too bad but it was necessary for the good of the team, and we won the bronze medal.

Final training session

Remedial training

It is common for a 4-man team to encounter one of these basic problems:

- Poor endurance
- Poor speed
- Poor technique

The best time to make the correction is during Thursday interval training (always the hardest training of the week). The special work should begin with a month to go and continue during the peaking process two weeks before the big event. As usual, each rider's pull should be of race duration (15-20 seconds) when riding in front of the motorcycle or car, and twice as long when riding in the draft. It is changes in the distance and intensity of the entire interval effort, not the length of individual pulls, that will remedy the team's weak point.

When speed is good but endurance is not, the workout should consist of five intervals of 10 km each. Team speed will be slower when the efforts are this long, but the distance will build endurance. A pace car is not essential. If one is used, the length of efforts in the draft should be 15 km. Alternate paced and unpaced efforts.

How to improve endurance

When endurance is good but speed is not, motorpacing is a must. Alternate hard, fast intervals of 5-6 km behind the car with 3-4 km in front. Recover in the draft at 40 k.p.h. between each effort. In general, total distance of the workout should be about 60 km, but it may be longer or shorter depending on how the riders feel. Besides sharpening speed, this fast paceline work is the best way to improve team technique.

How to improve speed and technique

Tuesday's speed work should not be more intense than normal. The number of efforts always depends on how well the riders have recovered from weekend racing. The first jump is always 1 km with each rider taking one pull. Then recovery behind the car, and go 1 km again. If the riders feel fatigue, that's plenty. If not, a couple more 1 km efforts can be done. But it is Thursday's training, not Tuesday's, that is used for working hard to correct the team's shortcoming.

The same principles hold for individual time trialists and 2-man teams. When endurance is the problem, on Thursday increase the length of each interval and the workout as a whole. When more speed is needed, do shorter but faster intervals.

RACING TECHNIQUES

The warm-up

A thorough warm-up is essential. Each team member must be ready for a total effort right from the first pedal stroke. Basically, the warm-up procedure is similar to what I outlined for the individual time trialist last chapter. It must be done on schedule, it must be done as a team, and it must be complete. If possible, motorpacing should be included. It is the best way to bring the team up to speed without creating fatigue. When it is time to assemble for the start, the riders must be hot and ready to go, but composed.

The start

The team lines up four abreast. Usually there are holders so the riders can have their feet strapped in. Their order on the starting line is just as it will be in the paceline, but whether that means from left to right or right to left depends on the direction of the crosswind. For example, if the wind is coming from the left, the leader will be on the left. He starts fast and the others come up to him, automatically forming the correct echelon. The starting gear is never the lowest or the highest; with a 12-17 straight block it is usually the 16. This is for safety. If the 17 were used, the angle on the chain could cause it to ride off the chainring (six-speed setup), or the hard acceleration could cause contact between the rear derailleur and the spokes. A 24- or 28-spoke wheel is not very stiff.

The rhythm

Once the team is up to speed, the riders should be in the identical gear and, therefore, pedaling with the identical r.p.m. This establishes the all-important rhythm. From this point on, the rest of the team changes gear only when the leader does. If the terrain or wind makes it necessary for him to shift, they follow into the same gear. This can't be done instantly and in perfect unison, of course, but it has to be done as soon as possible. Rhythm must be maintained.

The turnaround

At about 100 meters before a turnaround (normally there are several in a TTT), the riders begin to slow down and let gaps open. This gives each one a chance to relax a little, stretch, and take a drink. When they come to the pylon they should be about one meter apart—there's no sense being closer and inviting a crash. The turn back down the course is made just as diagrammed in Chapter 6. Cut back past the pylon on the straightest line possible in order to shorten the distance and resume pedaling sooner. On a strong team it doesn't matter which rider leads into the turnaround. But on a team with a range of strengths you certainly don't want one of the weaker riders in charge of setting the pace back down the course. A weak rider must get off the front during the last 100 meters even if he just got up there. An experienced team will make the adjustment during the kilometer before the turnaround, altering pull lengths to put its strong rider up front before the slowdown begins. After the turn is made, the leader must glance back to make sure the team is intact before he starts accelerating down the course.

The pass

When an opposing team is being caught, the passing team's strongest rider must be on the front. He accelerates steadily with a long, hard pull that takes his team by with a speed advantage of 3-4 k.p.h. Just as in the individual time trial, the opponent must be made to feel it is useless to try to challenge. And as in the ITT, the same USCF rules for passing apply: "No team shall take pace behind another team closer than 25 meters (80 feet) ahead, or 2 meters (7 feet) to the side" or a time penalty will be assessed. After the pass is made, the leader pulls off but the team must hold its speed to expand the gap. This is hard on the riders physically, but mentally it is a lift — an opponent has been crushed. Once the gap reaches

100 meters or so, the team can settle back to its normal race pace. It must never give a team it has passed a chance to catch back up. Doing so invites a competition that will disrupt rhythm, concentration, and the chance for a top performance.

During the last 10 km it is all by the coach's dictation, all by the horn of the team car. Each rider stays on the front until he hears it. This is when the coach kills his ... by giving them slightly shorter pulls, which has the effect of raising the speed. ... use a portable PA system to call out orders, but it is hard ... eters ahead. In the 1983 Junior Worlds in New Zealand, ... ntry ever to have radio communication with riders during ... uys in the 70 km TTT wore a special aerodynamic Bell ... cked in the fairing. I was able to give them instructions ... ted them on their split times, their progress against other ... ngths of pulls during the final kilometers. It worked very ... ze medal despite tire problems that caused three stops ... same helmets when we arrived at the track for the team ... es decided not to let us use them. The legality of radio ... cycling's world governing body, the UCI. I, for one, ... if this new technology is approved.

... each rider must reach the front at full speed and hold ... next rider to come around. With 300 meters to go it ... osition of a double echelon. Reach the front and pull ... l the way to the finish line.

... final stretch it is often the weakest riders who can do ... the race they have been taking shorter pulls or even ... something left for the last kilometer. The team's strong ... be to the point of getting dizzy with exhaustion. He ... ind in the final 200 meters and finishes fourth. I have ... rld Championships. Three guys finish and then comes ... a pained smile cracking his face. "Why is he happy?"

MONHEGAN, MAINE

The finish

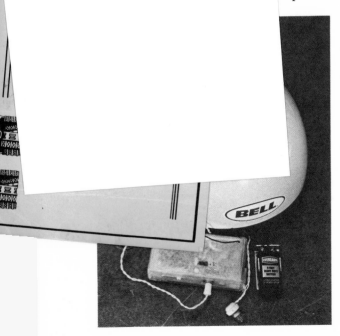

In 1983 the U.S. became the first country to use radio communication between the coach and the team time trialists. The tiny receivers were carried inside the tail of the aerodynamic helmets.

someone in the crowd will say. "Look, he couldn't even keep up." The reason he's behind is that he has ridden at his limit for 99.9 km. The reason he smiles is that he's watching his three teammates, his friends, reach the goal they have all worked so hard for.

Overcoming problems

It is called a crisis when a rider gets into trouble physically and is unable to keep up his effort for the team. What should he do? First, reduce the length of pulls. If he continues to feel bad he can cut them all the way down to the 8-10 second minimum that it takes the rider who just pulled off to get back into the paceline. What the stricken rider must never do is cause the team's speed to drop. If he simply can't contribute, he should stay in the fourth position and open gaps so his teammates can get back in. After 5-10 minutes of this, he should be ready to resume taking 8-10 second turns at the front. Perhaps he will be able to pull even longer in a few more minutes.

A good coach will know that a rider is having a crisis as soon as the rider does. The coach can see it from the support vehicle — he can see the change in the way the rider sits on the bike, in how he pedals, and in what the speedometer reads during his pulls. If the rider won't admit the crisis and he persists with slow pulls, the coach uses the horn to signal him out of the lead. The team must be trained to respond immediately—hear the horn and change the front, no matter who is setting pace. The coach must be like a fifth man in the team. He must sense the pace as if he were on a bike.

Puncture or fall

When a rider punctures or falls during the last 10 km it is best for the other three to leave him. The time lost while waiting will be more than he can help the team gain in the final minutes. In fact, if anyone but the strongest rider has to stop after the halfway point of the race, it is usually best for the others to go on. The decision is made by the coach, behind in the support vehicle. It is a gamble, because anything that slows or stops one of the remaining three riders is bound to cost the team many places in the standings, or prevent it from finishing at all. But risk is always part of sport. The coach who never takes a risk will rarely be a winner.

Normally it is best to change wheels when a puncture occurs, rather than give the rider a spare bicycle. There is usually only one back-up bike and it probably won't fit the rider properly unless he's the strong man—the bike should be set up for him. When a bike is changed we figure it costs the team 30 seconds; a wheel change is double that, especially if it is a rear.

When a rider has to stop, the others slow down, sit up, breathe, drink if they have fluids, and stay together. They increase the pace as the rider comes up, and he gets on the end of the line. After he goes through the front once and the speed is up, he moves back into his normal paceline position.

Sometimes riders talk to each other during the race about the pace, length of pulls, how they are feeling, etc. I don't like this and I don't want it to happen on my teams. When you are talking you aren't breathing. You lose energy. Deep breathing is very important for maximum performance. It is much better to communicate by making a small gesture. For example, when the front rider is finishing his pull and he moves over by 10-20 cm (let's say to the left), he can wiggle his right fingers to let the second rider know that he really is ready to give up the lead. This is a simple way to avoid hesitation and lost time. It is a good technique for Juniors or inexperienced Seniors, but it is rarely seen among the best riders. They communicate by their slight changes in bike position.

One time a yell is appropriate is when the new leader increases the speed too much. Then the second rider—we call him the driver—must shout a warning. The second rider also has the responsibility of establishing the echelon when he senses a crosswind, and he must immediately tell the leader which side to pull off. For example, if the second rider feels more draft by riding to the left of the leader's rear wheel, he will yell "Right!" and vice versa. Since the leader's concentration is on setting the pace, he often won't feel the slight changes in wind direction that are apparent to the second rider. Without notice that the pull-off side must change, there could easily be wheel contact and a crash. No yell is necessary when the pull-off side is to stay the same. If he's uncertain, the lead rider should glance back under his arm before moving over.

The leader must remember that his teammates are not always looking down the road. He must keep his head up and choose the shortest line, just like a single rider in an individual time trial. He also must remember that his bike is, in effect, four times as long as normal. When he sees the need to change the line, he must do it smoothly, never abruptly. All this was underscored in the 1982 Junior Worlds when our 70 km team had three punctures at once because the front rider led everyone right over a patch of broken glass.

Communicate with gestures

Changing the echelon

Earning the edge

As important as proper training and race tactics are, they aren't the whole story. Look at the results of the team time trial in the 1980 Olympics. After nearly two hours and three minutes of racing, East Germany beat Czechoslovakia by 0.7 seconds for the silver medal. A split second after 100 km! Was it just a matter of luck, or did East Germany somehow earn that edge?

Consider the U.S. 70 km team at the 1980 Junior Worlds. We won the silver medal by 2.6 seconds over Denmark and 2.9 seconds over Italy. Were we lucky to be second instead of fourth? I don't think so. We did things to help our riders perform at their best while other coaches didn't. For example, we didn't wait until the last day to travel from Mexico City to the race site. We did some training on the course with jumps and intervals to get familiar with the road and make sure everybody was feeling good. Our hotel was right on the course. On the eve of the race we had a big dinner and the riders ordered what they wanted. Massage was at 8 o'clock, followed by a glucose drink, vitamin B injection, and bed at 9:30. The riders were allowed to sleep in until 7:30 the next morning. Meanwhile, the Danish riders were getting up at 5 o'clock to catch the 5:30 bus for the 110 km trip to the course. I'm positive this cost them 2.6 seconds, and probably a lot more.

When you are lucky it is because you are good and you don't make mistakes. The one who makes a mistake, any kind of mistake, will lose a close competition.

Clothing, equipment, feeding

Everything I discussed in Chapter 6 for the individual time trialist applies to the TTT rider. The same aerodynamic clothing and lightweight, streamlined equiqment should be used. The good cyclist's diet should be followed. What to eat, if anything, on the morning of the race depends on previous experience and what time the team is scheduled to start.

Forget spraying and feeding in a team time trial. You might be able to eat one or two glucose tablets if you need to, but that is all. During a 4-man TTT your pull comes approximately every 700 meters. You have one minute rest and then pull, one minute rest and then pull. You have only about 15 seconds at the back, which gives you just enough time to loosen your body, nothing more. You must concentrate and stay on the wheel. You can't be sitting up or reaching around for a spray bottle, food, or anything else. The clock is running, so you can never let up. It's a much harder event than a criterium, where you can sit in the pack, spray your head, clean your face, and joke with your friends. In a criterium it is good to try to feel comfortable; in a TTT you don't dare take the time.

Glucose mixture

When faced with either dry or humid heat, each rider should carry at least half a bottle of glucose mixture in an aerodynamic bottle and cage. Or the two stronger riders will carry one full bottle apiece and the two weaker riders nothing. The bottles are shared, but it is the strong men who carry the weight. The weaker riders may have an empty cage to put the bottle in until they can hand it back, or they will use an internal pocket in the rear of their skinsuit. Sometimes they pin their number to work as a makeshift pocket.

It's important to know when you can safely carry nothing. In the 70 km TTT at the 1983 Junior Worlds, for example, the U.S. team rode with no water bottles and no cages. The temperature there in New Zealand was comfortable and the air wasn't too dry. The riders knew from their training they would not need liquids. It was interesting that all the best teams did as we did, while some of the weaker ones rode with the weight and air resistance of bottles and cages. It showed the difference between teams that think and teams that don't.

Atom bottle

You might hear some physiologists say a rider needs as many as four bottles of liquid in a 100 km race. That's nonsense. I rode many team time trials with just one bottle of glucose mixture, and I rarely drank more than half. Rather than a lot of needless liquid, you might find it useful to carry a small bottle of strong coffee and glucose to drink near the end of the race. In Poland we called it the atom bottle. I liked to have it and I would use it if I had a crisis. I recommend it to 100 km riders. It will wake you up.

Stage race TTT

A team time trial is often included in a big stage race. All of the basic information I've given about the 100 km event applies, but there will be some differences. For example, the length of the stage is normally much shorter (about 50-70 km), the team usually has more than four riders, and there is likely to be a wide variation in physical size and strength among teammates. Another difference is equipment. Sets of light wheels or tires may be available for the stage, but normally teams ride standard road bikes instead of super TT machines. However, there are two simple changes the mechanic can make to help his riders improve their performance. One Lower the stem, is to lower handlebar stems about 3 cm. This puts the riders in a better aerodynamic install longer cranks position. The other is to install crank arms that are 2.5 mm longer than each rider has been using. This improves leverage and allows riders to turn a one-tooth bigger

When a team time trial is included in a stage race, various factors must be weighed to decide the best tactic for each individual rider.

gear with no increase in effort *(see chart in Chapter 6)*. The disadvantage — slower acceleration for sprinting — is not a factor in time trialing. A team won't normally have an inventory of all the necessary crank arm lengths, so it is up to each rider to supply his own. Longer cranks should be part of every road racer's personal inventory. In fact, he should also have a pair that are 2.5 mm shorter than normal to use in criteriums. The benefit is a faster jump and more ground clearance when pedaling through corners.

A team must consider several factors when it plans strategy for a TTT stage. Does the stage count for team *and* individual general classification, or just team GC? If it is the former, everyone will have to work hard to help the team's well placed riders; if it is the latter, those riders may be wise to sit in and rest up for the remaining stages. A team with six or more riders can use a double echelon, which helps its top GC men. They can pull through without making a real hard effort, but team speed will barely be diminished.

Team strategy

2-MAN TEAM TIME TRIAL

The 2-man team time trial is a very tough event. It requires 50 km of maximum speed and a super synchronization of effort. Harmony is a must. That's why the 2-man is such good preparation for the 4-man.

2-man riders, like the individual and 4-man time trialists, follow the normal weekly training program until one month before the championship event. Then Tuesday's speed work and Thursday's interval training are based on jumps lasting 2-4 km. These are always ridden as a team.

On Tuesday, however, it might be possible to jump only 1 km twice, even though

In the 2-man team time trial, each rider must pull at his maximum for at least half a minute before changing the lead. This is Alexi Grewal.

full recovery is taken between efforts. The riders might still be tired from weekend racing. That's fine — they do what they can.

On Thursday it is a different story. They must be ready to do the maximum.

Interval training   A good workout is two intervals of four pulls each, then two intervals of three pulls each, then two intervals of two pulls each. They should do even more if they can handle it. Each pull should be of race duration (30-40 seconds) with recovery to a pulse of 110-120 b.p.m. between each interval. If one rider is stronger he should not increase the speed, he should pull a few seconds longer. The exertion must be the same from the start to the finish of each hard effort. Speed may vary because of changing wind or terrain, but the goal is to make the work consistent. This is exactly how the event is raced.

On Wednesday's long ride and Friday's two-hour easy ride, the teammates should train together. This helps each rider become totally familiar with his partner's pedaling style and bike-handling habits. They should always trade pace, never ride side by side. Every kilometer of this practice improves team technique.

The peaking process closely resembles what is done for the other time trials. About two weeks before the big event, the teammates compete together in a short stage race. If there isn't one, they enter a flat or rolling road race the first day, a criterium the second, and then add one or two days of motorpacing. If there are no suitable races at all, they do three or four days of intervals with motorpacing. Beginning with full race distance, each succeeding workout is 5-10 km shorter than the day before but no less intense. On the final day each rider goes out with the motor individually to do all he can handle. At the end they are dead. Next comes several days of recovery riding, a fast criterium on the weekend, and about 70-80% of normal training distance the final week. The Tuesday and Thursday efforts are just as hard but fewer in number. The day before the time trial, they ride easy for about two hours but put in a couple of race-like efforts lasting two or three pulls each. This wakes up the legs and tests the race equipment. Both bikes must be set up just like they will be ridden in the event.

Race strategy? You know the answer by now. The basic idea is for each rider to contribute his maximum potential. All the points about time trialing apply. Each rider must give at least 90% during the 35 seconds or so he is at the front, then the change must be made efficiently. Remember the proper technique — the lead rider pulls over but does not slow down *until* his teammate has accelerated and drawn up beside him. Then he drops back and into his teammate's draft as quickly as possible. This is necessary to maximize recovery time. Believe me, every second behind a wheel is precious when you're pulling for one half of the race.

If the course happens to have hills (not too unusual for a 2-man event) be aware of one important tactic: Never change the lead during the 50 meters before a crest. There is danger that the rider who swings off will be dropped. He is tired from pulling uphill and it's easy for a gap to open. He must push to the top before he lets his partner come through. This is very painful, but at least he'll have a downhill to help his recovery.

CHAPTER 8

Stage Race

All of the riding skills, training know-how, and racing education you have gained in the events already discussed are put to use in the stage race. It is the ultimate test of road racing ability. Almost always the winner is the best rider, especially when the event is long and it includes various types of races and terrain.

It is the goal of many cyclists to be a stage racer. For others it isn't. I want to make it clear right now that there is nothing wrong with you if your ambition is to excel in criteriums, or time trials, or one-day road races and not in stage races. Some very accomplished riders in these other events have not done well in stage races or even entered many of them. That is fine. I do not fault them.

It takes a certain set of abilities to succeed in stage racing, as we will see. If you simply do not have the right type of talent you are no less a cyclist. Is Mark Gorski inferior to Thurlow Rogers because he competes for 200 meters and Rogers competes in the 2,000 km Peace Race? Absolutely not. Both have great talent, only it is different talent. Like Gorski and many others, perhaps your successes will come in other types of events. You can still enter stage races and go for victory in stages that cater to your ability, but don't get down on yourself if you are not one of the select few who can win the general classification (GC).

There are two types of multiday road events: the stage race and the tour. The difference is duration, although there is not a universal definition. When an event lasts 2-4 days I call it an easy stage race. When it lasts 6-10 days I call it a tough stage race. A tour is a major event, usually international, that lasts from 12 days to as long as three weeks.

With this distinction in mind, a rider may compete in several stage races during one season—especially the weekend variety that has just 3-4 stages—but he should not compete in more than two tours. Also, the tours must be separated by at least two months. A tour is very hard on a rider, especially an amateur. He must be sure to have sufficient preparation and, just as important, sufficient recovery. Some professionals can handle two closely spaced tours, such as the Giro d'Italia and Tour de France, but even for strong and experienced riders it is a very difficult task.

In the U.S. there is only one race that can properly be called a tour (in 1984) and that's the Coors Classic, which has grown to about 12 stages. Actually, in its present format with so many criteriums it is far from a real tour—but I'd better not get started on that. Since the short, weekend stage race is the type of multiday event most amateur riders are likely to encounter, that's what I will emphasize it in the following discussion.

CHARACTERISTICS OF THE STAGE RACER

How can you tell when you are ready to enter your first stage race? A good way is by racing on both Saturday and Sunday. Or race on Saturday and do long-distance motorpacing on Sunday. When you feel recovered and strong on the second day, your endurance is good enough to try a three- or four-stage race. Give it a shot. Maybe you will complete it, maybe not. But if you quit you must have a valid reason, not just because you hurt—everybody hurts in a stage race. I've ridden a few tours and I never saw a rider (even the best) who wasn't looking for the end with a few stages to go. Nobody ever told me they wished the race was a couple of stages longer.

Stage racing is for you if your endurance and recovery are very good. These are the two most important attributes, followed closely by climbing strength (power). Then comes speed. Racing experience is essential, of course. Not so important is excellent technical ability. There is no requirement to always ride 2 cm from a wheel as there is in the team time trial.

Endurance and recovery

Several years in a hard program is what it takes to get sufficient endurance and strength. This means that it is all but impossible for a rider who is young in age and/or experience to compete successfully in a stage race, let alone a tour. It is why someone even as outstanding as Greg LeMond will be held out of the Tour de France until his fourth year as a professional. It is why his program has included less severe stage races each season. A rider must be fully prepared for the Tour or it will kill his body.

It is the same for an event as short as four or five days when you are early in your career. After two days you will feel so tired and so sore. The ability to recuperate comes with the development of your body. Development doesn't happen in the three weeks before the race, it happens over the course of a year or two. Considerably more time is necessary to become a tour rider. If you try to make a shortcut, if you try to ride hard stage races too soon, you will shorten your career. It is very possible to break your body and your psychology.

Physical and mental development

On the other hand, if you develop yourself as a road rider and begin stage racing only when you are really ready, it can strengthen you and advance your career. The general plan is always to ride more kilometers each new season and ride harder races. The multiday race is the hardest of all in terms of endurance. For the rider who is ready there will be a positive development; for the rider who is not, especially the younger one, there is danger.

Back in 1979 I faced a tough decision when Greg LeMond, who had just turned 18, asked to ride the Coors Classic (then known as the Red Zinger Classic). Naturally his sponsor was all in favor of it, and Greg himself wanted very much to race because it was America's biggest event. But for all of the reasons I just mentioned I was against the idea. Finally, Greg and I reached an agreement: He could race, but we would meet after every single stage to discuss how he was feeling and whether he should continue. If at any time on the road he began feeling it was too stressful, he would quit without any psychological scars. I trusted his intelligence and his ability to evaluate how his body was reacting. He trusted the wisdom of my rule that he must stop if he became deeply tired.

As it turned out, LeMond had no trouble completing the race. In fact, he finished fourth on GC and might even have won if he hadn't fallen during a breakaway in the final stage. Of course, the race was not as difficult then as it later became—there were only nine stages and not many good foreign riders—but it was a tip-off to LeMond's extraordinary talent. Later that season he won three medals, including gold in the road race, at the Junior World Championships.

In 1983 the situation happened all over again, this time with Roy Knickman. He too was 18 and asking to ride the Coors Classic. As always there was pressure from a sponsor. But by then the race had grown to be much tougher. It had 13 stages (including two two-stage days) and there were good amateur and professional riders from several European countries, plus the Colombians. Even more than before I did not think the race was appropriate for a Junior, but I relented because of Knickman's special ability and his promise, like LeMond's, to stop racing if the fatigue became great. This time, however, it never got that far. A crash shortly before the Coors Classic resulted in a head injury to Roy and he was not able to start. Personally, I was sorry for his accident but not sorry he missed the race. It is against good judgment to put any teenager, even a LeMond or a Knickman, into a two-week race against good international Seniors.

Stage race preparation

No major special preparation is necessary for a weekend event of 3-4 stages. The important thing is to race on both Saturday and Sunday during the preceding two or three weekends. Choose races with about the same length and terrain as the stages will have.

Continue the basic road race training program (*see Chapter 3*) during the weekdays between races, but make these alterations:

Alterations to weekly training program

- In the third week before the stage race, increase your training distance. Emphasize endurance.
- In the second week before the stage race, go back to normal training distances but work extra hard during Tuesday's speed work and Thursday's intervals. Emphasize speed.
- During the week of the race, reduce training distance by about 20-30% so you arrive at the event feeling very fresh and strong. Emphasize recovery. This is imperative—you can't begin a stage race when you are tired.

The longer and harder the stage race will be, the longer you must prepare for it. I like to see riders spend six weeks getting ready for the Coors Classic. The longer they train specifically for it and the longer they spend at altitude, the better they will race. Most riders don't have this luxury, however, because they must compete with their team in other events around the country. Often they don't make it to Colorado until one or two weeks before the start.

Tour preparation

Preparation for a tour starts at the beginning of your career. Each season's program must increase your strength, give you more endurance, and make you smarter. Only after this has happened and you have competed in several short stage races should you begin considering an event that lasts a full week or longer.

Once you are ready, your season's program must aim at the tour. With three months to go, all your training and racing should be designed with the tour in mind. Compete in two stage races, the second one ending between three and two weeks before the tour starts. These races should have 4-5 stages and be separated by about one month. Between them, compete in road races rather than criteriums—short, fast lap races are not what you need to get ready for a series of long road stages.

If there is no stage race that comes 2-3 weeks before the tour, it can be simulated with five days of motorpacing. This is not ideal, but it will work. Each workout must equal the length and intensity of a road race. I'm talking about 160 km, not 100. Look at the profile of the tour stages and train in similar terrain.

Actual stage racing is by far the best final preparation. For example, many of the U.S. riders got ready for the 1983 Coors Classic by riding a three-day race in Denver two weeks before. Some added at least one long, hard session of motorpacing on the fourth day. Each rider must accurately judge how tired he is getting and how many days he will need to recover. Are you a second-year Senior or a fifth-year Senior? It makes a big difference during this preparation.

After this intensive racing or race simulation, rest is essential. Go easy for a couple of days until you feel the energy returning. Total training distance should be reduced to about 80% of normal between this point and the tour. However, the efforts during Tuesday's speed work and Thursday's intervals must remain strong even though the workouts are shorter. (The best intervals are the decreasing type and the climbing type described in Chapter 3. Switch to them about two months before the tour.) On the final weekend compete in a road race each day or do long motorpacing. Forget the criteriums.

You must go into a tour fresh. If you are tired you will have no chance. Two days before the start, go out for an easy four-hour ride. One day before, do about three hours with a couple of jumps. These rides will be simple for you because you have so much endurance. Don't do them with a fast pace as if peaking for an event like the team time trial. That race goes at 50 k.p.h. while a tour averages 40 k.p.h. This is a big difference, and it means that training speed should be cut during tour preparation so that endurance-building time on the bike can increase. Remember: It is not necessary to train 160 km in order to race 160 km. Instead, on your long days train for four hours (no matter what distance this equals) when four hours will be the duration of the stages. Training pace is always slower, so it is the time on the bike, not the distance, that matters.

Some riders prefer to take it *very* easy during the week before a tour. Watch out, because it's possible to rest so much that you actually begin to lose some endurance. It's almost a matter of being too fresh. Then during the first couple of stages the body wakes up and form gets sharper. This is an acceptable approach, but I would not advise it until you have enough experience to fully understand how your body works. For your first long stage race or tour, it is best to go in rested and fresh but also 100% capable of racing at your full capacity the very first day if the situation demands it.

ELEMENTS OF SUCCESS

Nobody is a sure winner in a stage race. Too many unexpected things can happen. You may want to do well and hope to do well, but you can't start the race expecting to win. However, if you are good and you try your best and you are lucky—and somebody else isn't — you may find youself in position to win. That's what stage racing is all about. You must look for a very good situation to make your attack. Day by day, like a fox, you must watch for the possibility.

But you don't have to do it alone. Even more than in one-day road races, teamwork can decide the winner of a stage race. Of course, even the best teammates cannot help someone who does not have good tactical and technical skills. Among the necessary talents are

Personal attributes

- Climbing ability
- Strong jump to go from group to group
- Ability to hold position near front of field
- Toughness
- Intelligence
- Constant concentration

The last trait is so important. If you lose concentration for one moment it can cost you 50 positions. Then you must use considerable energy to get back up to the right place — or maybe a crash will take you out right then. You must work all the time to keep good position.

During a stage race there is no such thing as full physical recovery. This means that the intelligent, experienced rider can use his head to beat a rider who normally is stronger than he is. It happens all the time. We are dealing here with hills, distance, wind. These are what cause the selection, what break up the field. Tactics for each single stage and the race as a whole revolve around these obstacles, especially hills and wind. Some are individual tactics and some are team tactics, but often they are intertwined.

These riders have a nice view of the race but they certainly aren't in it. You must stay near the front every stage if you intend to do well in the general classification.

Again, what are tactics? Basically, everything you can do that is

1. Good for you, and/or
2. Bad for your opponents

Much depends on how good you and your team are vs. the competition. Much depends on the terrain and weather. There are many, many variables, but the line must be drawn at the point where tactics become unethical or illegal. Sure, you can help your team captain if you knock down several opposing riders. You can get rid of a guy on your wheel by swerving at the last second around a car. You can hit your brakes too hard on a descent and make other riders lose control avoiding you. But these are dirty tactics. You must not do them, but you must also make sure no one does them to you. Always give yourself a way to avoid a hazardous move by riding both several inches behind and slightly to the left or right of the wheel ahead. You will still get the draft, but there won't be contact if the rider abruptly brakes or swerves for any reason.

Tactics must be legal and ethical

Tactics are founded on your knowledge of such things as

- Where on the course it is best for you to attack
- Which teams are likely to key their attacks to the terrain, e.g., the Colombians on the climbs and the Dutch on the windy flats
- When it is safe to eat, and when it is not
- What clothing and creams to use for the day's conditions
- Where the coach will be stationed on a cold, wet day to hand up a rag with Capsolin or a rain jacket
- Where team support will give you information and hand-ups during a circuit race (why carry four water bottles when you can get a full one each lap and climb with four pounds less weight?)

You see why cycling has been called a thinking man's sport.

A very smart tactic is to make friends. Don't be a fighter from the first stage because the others will like to kill you. Be nice and maybe somebody will give you food or water when you need it. Maybe they will spare you from a dirty tactic. Like in life, you never know who might be the person you need help from most, so it's much better to have a hundred friends than one enemy. This is true even for the coaches. When I know my own riders are safe, sometimes I will stop and change a wheel for someone on another team. Perhaps his coach will do the same for one of my riders tomorrow.

Make friends

On the other hand, don't be nice to bad people. Answer their aggression by being tough in return. Don't be dirty, but don't do them any favors. Help those who deserve it if it will also help (or at least not hurt) yourself and your team.

Strategy

In a long stage race or tour, a smart rider who is going for a high place on GC will be almost invisible during the first few stages. He will ride easily in the field and do only what is necessary to avoid being left out of a move that could be important. If a break of 10 forms with several good riders, for example, he must go with it but he must not pull through — a couple of strokes at the front, then off. Instead of working hard he must think about staying comfortable and fresh, about eating

Conserve energy early

and drinking, about conserving energy. He mustn't go for the leader's jersey at this time. It's too soon. The race becomes much more difficult once he puts it on. Then he has to protect it, he has to chase everybody because everybody is interested in getting away without him.

When the race leader is in a break, his best tactic is not to work unless he is certain it will help his cause. He should stay safely sheltered and pull off as soon as he hits the front. This may not be liked by the other riders, but it is accepted. They know it's not up to the race leader to help the break's speed, but just to remain part of it.

In most stage races the first days are not hard in terms of aggression or terrain. The usual situation is flat courses and bunch finishes. But should an early stage be hilly, you must be ready to work hard so you don't lose time. It is on such courses that GC places are won and lost, not on the flat roads. In most cases the climbing begins midway through a stage race and so does the serious competition.

Protect yourself

Even then, the primary stage race tactic remains in force: Protect yourself and save energy. After the midway point every jump costs you something. It's like a computer account. You never recover 100%. But this is the time to start spending energy when it can pay off. Watch constantly for a good break going, or a crash that catches good riders. Try to make time whenever you have a decent chance.

Use your strong point

Next, look for opportunities to use your strong point. If it is climbing, wait for the hilly stages and then go for it. Use your potential. Or perhaps you are good in the crosswinds because you have experience in them, while some of your competition is from places without much wind. These riders won't have quite the same

When you are a first-rate climber like Greg LeMond, conserve yourself until the hilly stages. Then use your strong point to force the pace and gain valuable time. It is in the hills that general classification places are won or lost.

ability as you to fight for a place in the front echelon. They won't have the know-how to respond to changes in wind direction caused by turns in the road. Use your superior experience to drop them by attacking when a stiff crosswind starts.

It's almost impossible to break away in a direct headwind, so it's not smart to try. You will work so hard out there alone, but the riders in the field have it so easy trading pace. They will give you 150 meters and let you cook, knowing they can catch you anytime they want. So sit comfortably in the field and let others be the ones who kill themselves trying to get away. Be ready to join if the echelon forms, but don't do more than one or two strokes at the front. When you know the next 50 km will be into the wind, relax, rest and enjoy the slow pace.

Sit tight in a headwind

In a strong tailwind, watch out—you are now dealing with high speed. If you don't make the front group with the good riders you are very likely a loser. If they organize and form a double echelon they will go so fast that even with the tailwind it will be impossible for you to catch them. And there's another danger in being at the back of the field at this time: crashes. Everybody is moving so fast that a slight miscalculation can cause wheel contact and a big accident. Riders just don't have time to avoid the pileup.

Be up front in a tailwind

After the first few stages the race should be easy to size up. You will see who is working for whom, which teams are helping each other, and who is strong and who is not going well. This is a major difference between a stage race and a road race. In a one-day event you will not know all the riders or have much time to figure out the team tactics. In a multiday event you should be able to write a book about the various strategies by midrace. Once you understand the situation, and if you yourself are not a marked rider, it will be relatively easy for you to make your own attack. If you are not considered a dangerous rider, the others will not be glued to your wheel. You may succeed in winning a stage or moving up several places on GC.

Size up the competition

Team structure

How should a team be structured? What types of riders should be included? We already know that a rider who does not have super endurance and at least good power and speed will not win a stage race. The winner will come out of those who can do all things well, and do them day after day. A rider who is only a sprinter can forget it—he will never win GC. A rider who cannot climb cannot win.

It is ideal, then, for a team to be composed of good all-round riders. Unless a coach is going just for stage wins, it is not correct to select a specialist in climbing, a specialist in road sprinting, a specialist in criteriums, and a specialist in time trialing. Any success for a team like that will come at the expense of individual and team GC.

All-round talent is best

Many fast sprinters and criterium riders are not tactically smart in long road races. They don't have the experience. They don't know how to create the opportunities to really use their speed. You may have the fastest sprint in the field but it won't win you a stage unless you are in super position with 300 meters to go. That's what is necessary to make your speed worth something. What is super position? It means being behind a teammate or two who has the ability to lead you clear of the other 100 riders rushing to the line.

Without teamwork you can't win. With it maybe you can't lose. I remember an interview with Ryszard Szurkowski after one of his many victories. A reporter asked

Because hilly stages are so critical, here are two more climbing tips: First, on a switchback climb, the outside line will be easier because it is less steep. Second, use the technique of traversing if you ever encounter a climb so steep that it is too difficult in your lowest gear. Britain's Milk Race has climbs like this, and here's Evgeny Ivanov of the Soviet Union and Matt Eaton of the U.S. to show how to handle one. Traversing works because the zigzag route lessens the grade.

him how hard the race was. Szurkowski replied, "Hard? No, my team is so good. I had such an easy time that I could not lose. My whole job was to put my hands up at the finish." He told the reporter to go talk to the rest of the team, the "gray guys" in the field who were the reason for the victory. I liked to hear this because it is what makes the right atmosphere in a team. Of course, Szurkowski was certainly the best and fastest rider, that's why he was team captain. He was the one who had to go like a kamikaze in the final meters. But when the whole team is good, it really is easy for a rider like him to win.

The captain must always be polite and show appreciation to his teammates. Perhaps in a certain stage one rider accomplished very little. He did almost nothing to help, not because he didn't want to but because he was a little sick or he just had a bad day. The captain must go to him and say, "Thank you." It is so good for the rider's spirits, and tomorrow he really will do something. This is all part of the captain's role. He must understand each of his teammates and use psychology just like the coach does. Like Szurkowski, he must repay their efforts by always mentioning them by name, by making sure they get publicity, and by sharing the prizes fairly. Cycling is an individual sport, but a good team is the key to consistent results.

Captain must show appreciation

Race support

Because you have to race again tomorrow, you must take care of yourself correctly following each stage. Right after crossing the line make your way to the team car. Rinse your mouth and drink your glucose mixture. Clean your face, arms and legs. Take off your wet jersey, put on your training suit, and change out of your cleated shoes. Pedal your bike to the hotel in a small gear to stay loose, or go in the car if riding isn't practical. Take a shower right away, get your massage, and go down to dinner. Then back to your room for rest.

Personal post-race regimen

In the same way there must be organization and smoothness at the team support level. *Excellent* organization and smoothness. A stage race is as big an undertaking for the coach, mechanic and masseur as it is for a rider. Part of their job is seeing that the riders have nothing to worry about when they are off the bikes. This contributes to maximum recovery. The staff must also maintain a pleasant atmosphere— no shouting or quarrels can be permitted. For example, the stage finish is not the place to discuss a rider's mistakes. If he is upset and screaming about something, the coach should calmly say, "Please be quiet. I don't need to hear about it now. Get cleaned up and relax. Don't worry. We will talk later." The best time may be the following morning after the rider has had time to put things into perspective.

While the riders take their showers, the three support people often work together to wash the bicycles. At least this is the way it works on teams that don't have a professional mechanic and professional masseur who do only their own jobs. In amateur cycling everyone must be able to do every job well. It is a big job to service the bikes, especially when a rainy stage has made them filthy. The task is even tougher when crashes break wheels and other equipment.

After each machine has been washed with a brush and soapy water, then dried, the mechanic cleans the power train, lubricates the chain and cables, tests the gear and brake adjustments, and checks *everything* for proper tightness. While doing this he keeps an eye peeled for signs of a developing problem—a small crack in the water bottle cage or a toe clip, for example. Then he washes each wheel, checks the

Mechanic's duties

Bert Oosterbosch reaps the rewards of riding for one of Europe's top professional teams. First there is great mechanical support, as illustrated by the spare wheels and bikes atop the team car. Next is an excellent coach, Peter Post behind the wheel. Not to be discounted is the value of high-energy race food and effective medical care (note elbow). By providing such support, a team enables each of its riders to do his very best.

hub, trues the rim, and inspects the tire tread carefully. If he hasn't already talked to the rider, he finds him and asks if there was any mechanical difficulty during the stage. The mechanic must be very responsive to what riders tell him. It is his job to make their bikes operate perfectly and look terrific. In this way he has a key role in building the team's psychology.

Masseur's duties

Likewise, the masseur has a demanding and important job. He must give each of the five or six riders 30-40 minutes of massage each evening. That's at least three hours of hard work. Also, he is usually the person responsible for buying and preparing the race food, and cleaning the water bottles. In South America he must have a filter for the water and boil it before it is drunk by any member of the team. The masseur's duties often include treatment of minor illnesses and injuries, which frees the race doctor to concentrate on the most serious problems.

Following the stage the coach will help the mechanic or the masseur or both. It depends on where he can do the most good. With cooperation it is possible for all tasks to be finished by 9 p.m. Once things are under control, the coach can leave to pick up the results, represent the team at meetings, or attend official functions.

Coach's duties

The coach can never stop working because he is the organizer. He must see that all jobs are handled as efficiently as possible. He must keep the atmosphere friendly and yet demand the maximum from everyone working under him. They will not mind when they see how hard he is working too. They will mind when he takes a shower right after the stage and heads for the bar to drink with the bigshots or chase girls.

At about 10 p.m. the coach makes his rounds. Has everyone had massage? Food? Glucose? Vitamin injection? Has there been treatment for everyone who is sick or injured? Are the bicycles ready? The coach will personally check each wheel, tire, and the bike as a whole. Then and only then might he visit the bar, but just for a drink or two. Next he will sleep well, knowing that everything is ready for tomorrow. But if there is even one small problem, he will stay up to see that it is resolved.

What I am saying is that a stage race isn't just competition among riders, it is competition among *teams*, and that absolutely includes the support people. Which team is smartest? Which does its job best? Which comes up with the shrewdest tactics? More than once I have seen a very good rider lose when he became frustrated because of poor support. He was mentally broken by the situation. I've seen riders develop tendinitis, catch cold, have an eye injury, or crash and then have to drop out because the problem wasn't taken care of properly.

In my own riding career bad support once cost me dearly. I was in the top six of GC in the Tour of Poland when I had to have three wheel changes in a row. The first was for a flat tire. The second was because the wheel they gave me had a soft tire. The third was to replace the second wheel, which had a hard tire but loose spokes. There was an old man in charge of the wheels and he just didn't do his job. It cost me about three minutes, and 60 guys were gone into the headwind.

A stage race is similar to a university. Like a rider, a coach must learn so much before he can graduate to the winner's circle. He must work day by day for years to gain the tactical knowledge, race support experience, and organizational know-how. He needs a personality that can soothe upset people and smooth angry situations, that can keep harmony between the riders and the support. He needs good

The mechanic has a long and difficult job during a stage race. Each bicycle must be completely serviced each evening, and that includes the spares. This scene is from the 1983 Tour of America, which used a motel's large garage as the mechanics' area after one stage.

judgment to divide prizes fairly (often a very touchy point). He needs the qualities of leadership that keep everyone's morale high and the team spirit intact. He must care for his riders like they are his babies. He must be crazy for cycling. If not, if he doesn't feel it in his heart, then goodbye. He can't succeed.

Race-day schedule

On the morning of a stage, the riders are awakened and given breakfast in plenty of time for the food to settle before racing begins. Team strategy for the day is discussed during the meal or right after. Then each rider checks his bicycle to make sure everything is right. This may also be done by riding the bike to breakfast and back (or later by riding to the stage start.)

The rider then returns to his room, lays out his clothes for the stage, packs up everything else, and relaxes until it's time to go. The coach visits each room to say a few words and check that nothing has been left under the bed, in the closet, or hanging out the window — you'd be surprised what a rider can overlook when his mind is on the race. The coach has to know exactly how long it will take to get to the start area. He must make sure the team is there at least 30 minutes before race time; 45-60 minutes is better. More time prevents the rushing around and anxiety that upsets everyone and wastes energy.

Food in reserve

The person in charge of race food must always have one day's supply in reserve — enough for two day's is safer. This food is kept in the team car, along with drinks, coolers, ice, etc. The objective is to be self-contained. Riders must have the food

The masseur uses talented hands and special lubricants to help his riders relax and recover after hard hours on the bike. At no time is his job more important (or more demanding) than during a stage race.

The coach must work endlessly to see that each of his riders gets the best care possible. In a post-race situation like this, the rider must be kept covered and warm, then taken for a hot shower as soon as possible.

and drink they need, and have it when they need it. They work so hard in a stage race. It's easy for them to become upset when something goes wrong. Once they become upset, the next thing is no results.

Team vehicles

A team requires two vehicles: a van to carry big equipment and luggage, and a car for race support. Thirty minutes before a stage starts, the masseur drives the van directly to the hotel in the destination town. He puts the riders' gear into their rooms, then sets up the areas for massage and bicycle service and storage.

The car with the coach and mechanic arrives at the finish with the support caravan. Usually all vehicles are directed off the course to a parking area a few hundred meters before the line. If this isn't done, the car should be parked at a familiar distance beyond the finish area so the riders can find it easily amid all the other vehicles and people. The masseur will drive there before the race finishes if the van is needed for transportion to the hotel. Regardless, he should meet the coach with the directions if they are at all complicated. The riders must get to the hotel without delay. This isn't the time for a two-hour tour of the city.

How vehicles are stationed

The car carries everything the riders need before, during and after the stage. This includes spare musettes with food, water and glucose, plus items like rain jackets and caps, sponges, rubbing alcohol, towels, a first-aid kit, and each rider's small personal bag with shoes, socks, underwear, T-shirt and training suit. Most of it goes in the trunk, which must be very organized. When something is needed it is always needed quickly. The coach must know exactly where everything is.

Items carried in car

There is one race among the bicycle riders and another among the support vehicle drivers. Besides being good behind the wheel, a driver must know how race caravans operate. He must know every rule for follow vehicles as well as for riders.

Skills of the driver

When a rider is stopped by a mechanical problem or crash, he must use the draft from the support caravan to quickly regain the peloton. His own coach should drive in a way that will help him, but opposing coaches may make things tough by widening gaps between cars.

Often the driver and the coach are the same man. If not, the driver must obey the coach without question, even if it means bending or breaking a regulation. Smart tactics sometimes require it.

When to risk a penalty

For example, let's say there is a two-minute penalty for feeding a rider outside the designated zone. I know that one of my guys has missed his musette and is riding the last half of the stage without food. It is better to stop and feed him illegally (or hand it out the window) and be penalized two minutes than to have him bonk, lose 10 minutes, and still be weak for the next stage. Or perhaps the penalty is $50. It makes sense to pay it if it means helping the rider. Of course, I'll try to avoid a penalty altogether by making the feed in a way that won't be noticed. I'll do it in an area where there are hills or curves, or when an official doesn't happen to be with the group. There are many tricks. In my coaching career I have gotten about one penalty for every 10 illegal feeds I've made. I am not proud to break rules, but a rider's well-being must be protected.

Maybe there is also a two-minute penalty for pacing. One of my guys is chasing after he's had a puncture. He gets close to the caravan but can't close the final 100 meters. So I drop back and motorpace him up. I don't do this obviously—I drop behind him and then go ahead—but the effect is to help him reach the line of support vehicles. Maybe I'll get only a warning, maybe a penalty. What I have to be sure of is that the rider won't be disqualified—usually that happens only when he holds on to the vehicle. But, again, so what if he gets a two-minute penalty? If he does not catch the field he will be 15 minutes behind and much more tired. The penalty is worth it.

When a coach does get caught he must be kind to the official and say he is sorry. The coach may be wrong or he may be right, but remember, an official is *always* right. If the coach is nice maybe he will get a warning instead of a penalty. Officials are human. They respond to politeness. It is much better if the officials are a coach's friends than his enemies.

Diet

The diet of a stage racer is essentially the same as that of a one-day road racer, both on and off the bike *(see Chapter 4)*. But I want to emphasize the value of eating meat sandwiches during road stages.

In a stage race you must think in terms of eating for tomorrow, not just for today. This is essential when you are competing every day for a week or longer because the body's requirements go far beyond the need for glucose. During a stage race you are living on the bike. Hard work and fatigue become normal. But it is not normal for your stomach to receive only glucose and carbohydrates like fruit each day if you eat meat in your regular diet. Your body works best on the fuel it is used to having. I am positive about the value of meat in this situation. It has high food value and it supplies complete protein.

We are often told that meat is a problem because it stays in the stomach for 12 hours. That may be the case for the average person, but not for a racing cyclist. All the work you do on the bike raises your metabolism, your blood circulation, your oxygen consumption. They are all so much greater than for a normal person during normal life. Your life during the four hours of a road stage is like an average person's during 12 hours. Your system works that must faster. And remember—any food value of the meat that is not used during the current stage will be available for the next one.

The case for eating meat

The exception comes when it is very hot. Meat is not good then and, in fact, you won't want to eat it. It is unappetizing and hard to swallow. Fruit is best then, because of its natural moisture and its ability to refresh a dry mouth and throat. But when the temperature is normal or cool you will be very happy to have small meat sandwiches. Make them as I discuss in Chapter 4 with dried bread dipped in wine, cream cheese, jam, and slices of ham. Riders who eat them love them. I remember how strange our national team riders felt about meat sandwiches when I first introduced them, but soon they were asking for more.

Just as important as eating right is drinking right. You must guard against becoming dehydrated, especially when racing in hot weather (dry or humid) or at high altitude. Four hours of sweating every day can cause a serious fluid deficiency if you are not careful to drink enough. The result will be increased fatigue and poor recovery. Sip frequently from your bottles during each stage, then drink throughout the evening. Always remember two rules:

Prevent dehydration

1. Never drink a large amount at one time, particularly right after the stage. You will ruin both your appetite for solid food and your digestion. Always drink slowly and moderately so your sensation of thirst can respond to what's in your stomach. You must have self-control.

2. Drink glucose mixture, fruit juice, milk, etc., rather than just plain water. It is much better to replenish fluids with something that also has food value.

EQUIPMENT

Stage racing can be as tough on a rider's equipment as on his body. It requires a solid, strong bicycle. A standard road frame with a relatively long wheelbase is what you want. There are only drawbacks to riding something light and tight. For example, a short criterium frame with a steep seat tube takes more attention to control and it will rattle you to death on a country road. Almost every stage race takes you across rough pavement at one time or another. When it happens almost daily for a week, a stiff frame will work against your performance.

Since stage racing puts a premium on endurance and power, not speed, it makes no sense to use special lightweight equipment. If something breaks it could cost you many places on GC or even put you out. A lot of hard work can go to waste real fast if you have a failure and there isn't a replacement wheel or spare bike close by. Technical support can disappear at times, particularly in hilly country. In most stage races the support vehicles are stopped at the top of big climbs until all riders have descended. You can be left standing at the side of the road for 10 minutes until help arrives. That 10 minutes doesn't cost you just one day's effort, it costs you a week's effort.

The bike should be fitted with two water bottle cages. I also recommend a spare tire and a pump, no matter how good the support is. A rider without a spare who is passed by his team vehicle as it goes ahead to better placed riders may be out of the race if he flats. For this reason I always have a tire and pump ready to give to a rider I must leave behind.

Who gets support? This is another of the many decisions a coach has to make quickly and correctly. There are five or six riders along the road and a coach can't be everywhere. If a rider is well placed on GC the coach must stay in position to help him. If the team has no stars but is doing well in the team classification, the coach may decide to stay behind the third-best rider in the stage (if it's the first three each stage who count for team time). In this case the fourth, fifth, and sixth riders all must have spares and pumps. Even if the coach has friends in the support caravan who may give his riders a hand, he can't positively count on it. Coaches must always look after their own riders first.

Tires

Because punctures can waste cost so much valuable time and energy, tire selection for each stage must be correct. The proper weight depends on the road conditions. If yesterday's stage was smooth but today's is rough, switch to wheels with heavier tires and perhaps heavier rims. I recommend changing whole wheels rather than gluing on different tires overnight. Actually, puncture resistance isn't so much a matter of tire weight as tread thickness. A new 185-gram tire may be just as tough as a 240- or 260-gram tire that has been worn. This is why it is best to race on new tires — it's a way to save some important weight with very little increase in the chance of a puncture.

In general, a 260-gram cotton tubular with a mixed tread is the most reliable tire for the wide range of road and weather conditions encountered in a stage race, especially in Europe. In the U.S. where roads are usually much smoother, 240- or even 220-gram tires are fine for all but heavy riders. Choose a model with a cotton

Reliability is paramount

Carry a spare tire and pump

Race on new tires

Cotton casings are the safest choice

casing unless you are sure of dry weather, then silk can be used. Silk tires have a lower rolling resistance but water weakens the casing and makes it more likely to fail. Just to be safe, most teams use only cotton tires in stage races. One very good model is the Vittoria Corsa CX/CG, which weighs 240 grams. Continental and Wolber tires of 240 and 260 grams are excellent, too.

The best rider on the team should use the lightest wheels and tires that his body weight and the road surface allows. This is especially important for climbing stages, individual time trials, and criteriums. The coach must take a calculated gamble that the advantage of light wheels will outweigh the time lost if there are punctures. Since the team vehicle will support this rider closely on road stages, all wheel changes should be quick. If the vehicle isn't right behind for some reason, a teammate will automatically stop and give him a wheel. Workers or low-placed riders must always use the heavier sets of wheels. Team support can't afford to waste time and effort changing wheels for them.

After every single stage, first the mechanic and then the coach should inspect the tire on each wheel. Double checking is never a bad idea. Any little piece of glass or sharp rock in the tread must be found. If it isn't removed, the tire will be flat after the next 50 or 80 km.

The best wheels for the best rider

Wheels

Good wheels are even more crucial than good tires. A flat tire isn't likely to cause a crash, but a broken wheel often will.

For stage racing use a quality rim of 350-400 grams with 36 spokes and three-cross lacing. Oval spokes are fine, but no matter what the shape make sure they are a brand of proven quality, such as DT. Light riders can safely use 32-spoke wheels if the rims are strong and the roads are good. Generally, low-flange hubs are better for stage racing because they make a more absorbent wheel than high-flange. Wheels built around high-flange hubs are slightly stronger but their stiffness may be uncomfortable.

Wheels must be in perfect condition, but don't start the race with a brand new pair. Always ride them for a couple of hundred kilometers, then true them up before using them in competition. Glue on your racing tires at least two days before the start, using glue on both tire and rim. The glue job must be perfect to ensure safety during descending and cornering. When a new tire is put on a wheel after the start of the race, make that wheel a spare for at least one day so the glue will have time to set. Until it does, don't use the wheel unless absolutely necessary.

Give glue time to set

For a team of six riders there should be at least three pairs of spare wheels. The rule of thumb is half as many spare wheels as there are wheels on the road. On the average a team will have 1-2 punctures per stage, but the mechanic must be able to handle an extraordinary situation. Here are three procedures he must follow for the spare wheels:

Backup wheels

- Each quick release must be adjusted precisely to fit into the frame and tighten with a single movement.
- Each tire must be pumped to racing pressure (usually 7.5-8 atm.) before each stage.
- Each rear hub must have the correct size cogs for the day's terrain.

Gears

It is ideal when a team can use a freewheel system like the Maillard Helicomatic, the Regina Futura or the Shimano Freehub. In their various ways these permit very quick changes to the cog sizes that are needed for each new stage. Each system makes it easy to set up all rear wheels (spares, too) with identical clusters. For a day with climbing the proper cog sizes might be 12-13-14-16-18-20-21. Generally, it is best to have one-tooth differences at each end, with two-tooth differences in the middle. The small chainring will be 41, 42 or 43 teeth, and the large 53 or 54.

Uniform chains and freewheels

Regardless of the freewheel brand used, it and the chain must be identical on every bike. When this is the case, and when the equipment is new at the beginning of the race, there will be no problems when rear wheels are changed. All wheels will work on all bikes. But if a hodgepodge of equipment is used, chain skipping and derailleur misalignment are likely to occur.

Spare parts

A six-rider team is best off with two spare bikes, although often when a U.S. team travels overseas only one is taken. There must be at least one. It is serviced every evening right along with the bikes that are being raced. Why? Because it is carried on the roof of the team car all day and something can vibrate loose. If the spare bike isn't checked carefully after each stage, it will ride like junk when it's finally needed. Normally this bike has a midsize frame and it is fitted with a quick-release seat post bolt so it can be ridden by anyone on the team. After it is given out, the rider's own bike is fixed immediately, if possible, so he won't have to ride the spare for long.

Backup bike must be serviced daily

Mechanic's inventory

The mechanic should have almost enough spare parts to build a complete bicycle— crank arms, chains, derailleurs, pedals, saddles, toe clips and straps, cables, bottle cages, etc., plus assorted nuts and bolts. Also a supply of brake pads, which may need to be installed following several hilly stages. It isn't necessary to have six spares of everything for a team of six riders. For example, one spare handlebar and a mid-length stem usually is sufficient. Besides the spare wheels, there should be at least two rims that can be spoked up if more wheels are needed.

Riding position

Finally, two tips about your riding position in a long stage race or tour:

1. Use your normal position until the fourth or fifth day, then lower the saddle by 2-3 millimeters. Why? Because you are dealing with less than full recovery. The result is muscles becoming tighter, shorter, and sore. Lowering the saddle will increase your comfort.

2. Make sure your handlebar stem is quite high in relation to the saddle, as it should be for all long road races. If you have been time trialing or riding criteriums and you've put the stem down for better aerodynamics, you must raise it. You can't be comfortable riding stages in a low position day after day. In general, the top of the stem should be 2-4 cm below the top of the saddle, not 6-8 cm below like for short races.

Appendix

PSYCHOLOGY OF THE CYCLIST

Mental attitude

You can't have doubts about your tactics and be a successful bicycle racer. You must be 100% positive that your decisions are correct. This isn't easy, because during a race there isn't much time to think over the possibilities and come up with a strategy. You have to be like a computer. You have to digest a lot of information and arrive at an answer quickly, then act on it without reservations.

I've seen many a strong rider who is a loser. Why? Mentality. He doesn't believe he can win the race. He feels only how much his legs hurt. He concentrates inside. He will never win, because winning is hard enough even under the best conditions. The first victory for any rider is the most difficult of all. The second comes easier and then there is self-belief. When confidence is born, a rider becomes very hard to beat. Many times I've seen a winner who was much more tired than the losers. He is the fighter. He has the winning mentality.

To be a good rider you must think like a Texan: "I am the best." You can't be concerned with being a nice guy in the peloton. There is a saying in American sports that is very true for bike racing: "Nice guys finish last." You have to be tough, and tough on yourself. You must want success so badly that you're willing to take 105% out of your body to get it. After the race other riders should say about you, "That wasn't him out there. He was too good. He was incredible." You must fight to the end, just like an animal in danger. Have you ever tried to kill a rat? How strong that little animal becomes! He will bite you and bite you badly. He will fight not to die. You must fight not to lose. When you have to be stopped and helped off the bike at the end, that is the right way.

It isn't easy to develop the ability to perform at this level. That's why only one rider succeeds when 200 start the race. It takes time to build your mentality. It takes a good coach to reinforce your psychology. It takes the same systematic race-by-race build-up for your mind as it does for your body. It takes racing every race to the end to push up your physiological limits and your performance level. Confidence, determination and a hunger for success will result.

Don't continually pick races against easy competition or you will develop a fear of going against better riders. But don't choose races that are overly difficult for your present level of development. They will break you physically and mentally. Be intelligent in designing your race calendar.

Motivation

Push yourself to your maximum capability at least once a week in training. The natural day for this is Thursday during the interval workout. It is virtually impossible to use every bit of your muscles' potential, but it is good both physically and psychologically to reach for your limit each week. Most athletes can summon up 70%, maybe 80%, of their absolute strength, never 100%.

Why do some professional riders use dope? So they can push their body more than normal, so they can force their barrier past 70%. Because of controls at races now, they are more apt to take dope only during periods of intense training. Then they can work themselves very hard. This is one reason why we hear the pros say they hate to even look at a bike by the end of a season. They just aren't able to push themselves any more. Not all pros take dope, of course, and the best riders don't need it. I am positive that Greg LeMond has never touched dope and yet has won the professional World Championship. He is proof that a great rider can also be clean. He would not even take a vitamin injection when he was in the USCF program.

Stay away from dope

It is natural strength, not dope, that is important to today's bike rider. Forget dope—there is more strength in you than dope can ever produce, and this strength can be found by natural means. It can be developed by training that pushes and expands your physiology, your body. It can be summoned up by psychological motivation that allows you to go beyond normal limits of strength.

I have a sad but real story that will explain the power of motivation. In Poland I knew the wife of Olympic weightlifting champion Waldemar Baszanowski. She graduated with me from the Academy of Physical Education. One day she and Waldemar were driving home from a vacation at the seashore. The road was slippery and he lost control of the car. It rolled over and she went part of the way through an open window. She died instantly, decapitated. But Waldemar, who wasn't hurt, could see only that the car was on top of her. All by himself he turned that car over, and then he realized her condition. After that he could not finish putting the car upright, and five more men couldn't do it either. Waldemar was strong, he was a lifter, but it was the direction from his mind that made him able to move that car.

When you have a motive you are much stronger. I have seen times when it was impossible to drop certain riders. At other times when they were not so mad they could be left behind easily. This has nothing to do with dope but with the power of the mind. The mind is much stronger than most people believe. I've seen riders get dropped and suddenly not be able to pedal one more stroke—they'd pushed themselves to the absolute end. I've seen the winner of a race fall at the finish line, with no energy remaining to even get off the bike. I remember what happened to our 70 km time trial team at the 1980 Junior Worlds. They finished and went right off the road. We helped them get off the bikes and they just fell down. This was no show. They couldn't talk, not one word. When I came with news that we had won the silver medal, they grabbed each other and cried. That's all they could do. They had pushed themselves *so* hard. They believed before the race that they could do it. And they did it.

A rider *must* believe. In 1979 we decided that Greg LeMond would be our individual pursuiter at the Junior Worlds. It was a big surprise for him. He had almost no experience in the event, so it was critical that he believe me when I told him he was 100% capable of doing well. I told him that a strong road rider is an excellent pursuiter because road preparation includes steady-pace time trialing. He had trust in this, and he rode with no training on the track except for a couple of workouts in Argentina just before the race. If he had been afraid of trying, he never would have had a chance. He won the silver medal, nearly taking the final from a Russian track specialist.

Relaxation

It is not unusual to be nervous before a race, especially early in the season. You know the feeling—butterflies in the stomach, dry mouth, yawning, urges to visit the bathroom. As the coach I tell my riders, "Guys, this isn't the World Championship. I know your legs are shaking, but don't worry. Let's just use this for a training race and see what happens." I go to each one and massage his neck and shoulders and I talk to him nice, but not about racing situations. "Wow, look at this beautiful view . . . hey, check out that young lady over there . . . ." I try to help him relax, to feel better.

The important thing is not to sit around dwelling on the upcoming race. Sure, you have to have a plan for yourself, but after you have decided what it will be, stop thinking about it. Remember that anxiety is natural and everyone else is feeling it, too. Also remember that it will be gone as soon as the gun sounds and you start turning the pedals.

Anxiety is natural

Of course, the anxiety doesn't suddenly begin the morning of the race. A rider usually starts feeling it the evening before, which can make it tough to get good sleep. This is a common problem. One thing that can help greatly is a massage— I've seen nervous riders fall asleep on the massage table. Another remedy is to use one of the various types of mental relaxation techniques. National team rider Tom Prehn, for example, practices transcendental meditation with good results. Do whatever helps you, with the exception of taking some sort of tranquilizing medicine or sleeping pill. These are not necessary, and they are very likely to leave you feeling hung over on the morning of the race. You might sleep like a baby, but you won't ride up to your ability if your mind is fuzzy and your reaction time is slow.

My advice is to get into a totally comfortable position on the bed and relax your body. Begin to concentrate on a single thing, like counting sheep. Don't laugh—this works because it is repetitious. It keeps you from thinking of a changing situation—like a bicycle race—that activates your imagination and makes you wide awake. Or do what I did when I was racing and also a student. When I got into bed the night before a race I started reading a textbook. Soon I was sleeping very soundly. Try this for yourself with reading material that is not too entertaining. I still use the technique today, only now what puts me out like a light is my English grammar book.

How to fall asleep

In a team situation where the riders are housed together in a hotel or dormitory, the coach must demand quiet after bedtime. No radios, no televisions, no loud talking in the halls, no slamming doors, no noise from the mechanic. Everyone has to cooperate. Riders work very hard each day and their hours for sleep must be respected.

As the season progresses you will find yourself becoming less nervous about each race. But don't ever expect to be 100% calm and collected before a big event. That wouldn't be natural. In fact, some anxiety is probably helpful. It sharpen the senses and puts the body and mind in a state of readiness.

Self-discipline

The most important kind of discipline for a racing cyclist is self-discipline. It is the same for all good athletes. This discipline covers every single aspect — eating, training, resting, etc. It is life discipline.

There must be a plan for everything, even your activities outside of cycling. A yearly plan, a monthly plan, a weekly plan, and a daily plan. Everything has to be organized. When the clock strikes 7 each morning you must get up and begin the day with a purpose. The rider who says, "Oh, there is nothing important to do — I'll sleep 15 more minutes," is not tired, he is lazy. He has no discipline. He is also likely to say, "I don't want to stop drinking now, give me more," or, "Why stop eating now? I can still eat more."

You see, anybody can do what he is tempted to do. But it is the disciplined rider who refuses to gulp down a gallon of water after a race and instead sips slowly. It is the disciplined rider who eats several small meals during the day because he knows that big meals are hard to digest. It is the disciplined rider who hears, "You are a strong athlete, one beer won't matter," and responds, "Fine, then I choose not to have one." It is not hard to resist such things when you live your life for cycling. When you work so hard you don't want anything to take away from your body. Alexi Grewal has said, "I don't drink. I don't stay out late. And I don't miss that kind of stuff. I know if I do want that I won't be a bike rider." That is the right attitude.

How to deal with depression

Still, every rider gets into a mental slump now and then. Things don't go right and a sort of depression sets in. The result may be a what's-the-use? attitude and a strong temptation to break some rules, maybe go drinking or eating junk food. It can put your self-discipline to a severe test. What should you do? Tell yourself:

"I am an athlete. I must respect my decision to be a bike rider. I have done the best of everything to make myself the best, and I have made progress. Look how much better I am than I used to be. Right now I am having trouble, but I will get over it. When I do I will be better than ever because I did not give up on my plan. I am not giving up on myself."

Greg LeMond has a wife and son, but I believe his No. 1 priority during the 1980s must be cycling. That's what it will take for the best U.S. roadman in history to become as good as the world has ever seen. Putting cycling first is necessary before any rider can achieve full potential.

A rider who lets himself have lapses will not be as successful as he might have been. Maybe he is the District Champion, but he could have been National Champion. Maybe he is the National Champion but he could have been World Champion. A rider will reach his potential only when he is crazy for cycling 100% of the time, only when cycling has the priority in his life. I don't believe that for Eddy Merckx there was a single thing more important than his career in cycling. I don't believe there was anything more important to him than winning a bicycle race. For him to become the best in the world he had to be the best in many things — physiology, psychology, desire . . . and self-discipline.

But Merckx was not born with great self-discipline. Nobody is. You must develop it step by step during your life. This is one reason I am so happy about the success of Greg LeMond — he has given every American rider the possibility of becoming a great cyclist. He is the perfect model. He has done it, and now others know they may be able to do it, too — if they have total dedication. I have seen it work already in the attitude of Greg's friends on the 1978 and 1979 Junior Worlds teams. They are now the stars of U.S. amateur racing and they look to LeMond like a sign on the road that says: "When you work, you've got it." LeMond has changed everybody's psychology.

EQUIPMENT

Shoes

Unlike race clothing, which is determined by the event and the weather, shoes remain the same. You should not wear a different model for different events, even though some models actually are designed for a specific type of race. If you alternate different shoe models you will probably have to readjust your riding position each time. There is also the risk of developing leg strains due to slight differences in foot position and pedaling action. It is much better to find a shoe model that is comfortable, buy at least two pairs, and use them for all your training and racing during that season. If you want to change models the time to do it is during the winter.

Wear same model for training and racing

I prefer a leather sole instead of plastic or wood. Even with its internal steel shank a leather sole can flex slightly and this makes it more comfortable, especially in long races. You will find, for example, that almost all European pros wear leather-sole shoes. For someone like a Junior or Veteran who rides only short events, it becomes an individual decision. Some riders may find that plastic or wood soles are comfortable for races of 80 km, others won't. The rigidity of these soles can help efficiency, and plastic is very light. But these benefits are lost if your feet begin to hurt.

Leather soles add comfort

Another variable is the shape of the sole. Some have an accentuated curve at the ball of the foot, some are relatively flat. The correct choice depends on what fits your foot best and feels natural when you are pedaling. It is not uncommon for a rider to use several different shoe models before he finally finds the one to stay with.

The cleat should be plastic, never metal. A metal cleat is a mistake because it will wear down the cage on an alloy pedal, and it is heavier than a plastic cleat. Cleats that are already attached and adjustable are the easiest to work with. I like it when the bottom of the cleat slot is very close to the sole, because it allows a slightly lower saddle.

Plastic cleats are best

Size to buy depends
on shoe materials

When you go to buy shoes try them on with the same thin socks you ride in. Be sure to insert your orthotics, if you use them. You must be certain not to buy shoes that are too large. If your foot moves inside the shoe it can cause blisters, it will make you feel insecure, and it has the effect of changing your saddle height. If the shoes have leather uppers I recommend that you buy them one European size smaller than the size that feels perfectly comfortable. Leather shoes will stretch during the first three weeks. You want them to stretch into a perfect fit, not out of it. Shoes with nylon mesh uppers, on the other hand, will stretch very little if at all. They won't become comfortable if they are tight to begin with, so buy the size that feels good.

How to get a
perfect fit

Don't use new shoes for racing until you have broken them in. Wear them first during short training rides and keep them wet with a mixture of water and alcohol (shoes with leather uppers only). Carry this solution in an old water bottle and spray it on the shoes frequently, particularly on places where they feel tight. Do this on as many rides as it takes until the shoes conform to the shape of your feet and become totally comfortable. It may take four rides, it may take a dozen or more. It depends on the stretch of the leather and whether your feet have an odd shape that causes extra pressure.

Alloy components

I recommend avoiding certain alloy components for road races, criteriums and stage races, although they are acceptable for time trials. Things like alloy toe clips, bottle cages and saddle frames, for example, don't really save significant weight but they are much more likely to break than steel. If they do break it can cost you a race. It happened to Greg Demgen in a Junior Worlds road race when his alloy saddle broke. That was it for him. When you are dealing with light alloy equipment, metal fatigue occurs much faster than with steel. The equipment is always more expensive but it must be replaced frequently since you can never tell when it will fail. You can inspect it carefully for cracks, find nothing, and still it will break. I've seen it happen in road races because of the rigors of bad pavement and hard use.

Frame replacement

If you race often, I recommend replacing the frame every year. That is the ideal. After 100 races and several crashes and straightenings a frame is not good any more. The metal is fatigued and it can break. You can no longer trust it. If a fork should fail it will result in a concussion, or worse. Any serious rider who invests so much time in the sport owes it to himself to compete only on fresh equipment.

Now, I do realize that an unsponsored rider who puts $600 of his own money into a racing frame wants to ride it as long as possible. That's a different story. Luckily, U.S. roads are generally smooth and they do not wear out frames real fast. Barring a heavy crash or other abuse, a quality frame should remain trustworthy for several seasons.

During season
replace with same
model

In Europe a pro will get a new frame after any big crash, and he will get two or three new frames during a season just to be safe. It helps his confidence to know that he is on the best possible equipment. Even when I rode in Poland 25 years ago I never used a frame longer than one year, and sometimes I used three. All would be identical in size and make, which is the way to do it when you replace your frame

Beware of using special alloy components, such as saddles with alloy frames, for road events other than time trials. Hard use and rough pavement can cause alloy to suddenly break. The few grams that such equipment saves is not worth the risk.

during the season. It prevents problems with your position, and you don't have to become accustomed to handling differences.

RIDING TECHNIQUES

Jumping the bike

During a race it is a great advantage to be able to jump your bike over railroad tracks. If you don't jump them you must slow down or risk damaging the wheels. Jumping lets you retain all your speed and it is perfectly safe if you do it right. A good bike handler will even be able to jump a double pair of tracks—jump one pair, land, and immediately spring over the second pair.

The faster you are going the farther you can jump. You need good speed even for a single pair of tracks. The technique is to stop pedaling with the crank arms horizontal and your hands gripping the brake lever hoods. Crouch low and then spring upwards, lifting with your hands and your feet. That's the key to it—pull the bike up into your body as you leave the ground. When you are good you can fly a long way. Practice during training rides, but start with very smooth tracks in case you miss.

How to jump forward

The same technique is used to jump over a curb or any other low obstacle. It is even possible to jump sideways from the road up onto the sidewalk. This can get you out of danger when there is a crash ahead or the road narrows suddenly and there's nowhere else to go. It is a difficult move but it can be done. Make sure to get both wheels well into the air. Keep the bike perpendicular and the front wheel straight so you won't veer sharply when you land.

How to jump sideways

Bad road surfaces

Sometimes a road race will take you onto an unpaved surface of gravel, dirt or sand. Suddenly everything is soft and loose. The front wheel begins to twitch. The natural reaction is to tense up and fight the wheel, but this is futile and only adds to handling difficulties. Instead, relax and let the wheel have some movement. Sit on the back of the saddle and push evenly in a slightly higher gear than you'd use if still on pavement.

A bigger than normal gear should also be used whenever you come to a stretch of very rough pavement or cobbles. If you try to spin at 100 r.p.m. on such a surface it will rattle you all over the place. It will increase your discomfort and make it harder to control the bike. A higher gear helps you feel smoother. Keep your arms loose and don't grip the bars too tightly. Body weight must be supported by two hands and two feet as well as your rump—don't have all your weight on the saddle.

Touching wheels

At the 1979 Junior Worlds road race, Greg LeMond had several spokes broken in his front wheel by the pedal of Belgium's Kenny DeMaerteleire. When it happened they were away together and coming to the finish. Many riders would have crashed because of such damage, but LeMond didn't. Why not? Special training. He and our other Juniors had been through drills we call "kissing wheels."

Most riders expect an automatic crash when their front wheel touches another

The great pro Bernard Hinault shows just how much at home he is on a bike. This move may not be too useful in races, but it is always good to work at making the bike an extension of your body.

Learn to jump the bike, both straight ahead and to the side. This rider will land and immediately spring over the second rails. This enables him to keep his speed and avoid the risk of a crash from hitting diagonal tracks.

rider's rear wheel. This doesn't have to be a problem if the proper reaction is made. To teach riders how, we have them go to a big field where the ground is soft. Two of them ride together with their toe straps loose. Sometimes the rear rider hits the front rider's wheel on purpose, sometimes the front rider cuts into him. There may be some falls, but it doesn't take long to learn how to react and stay up. It is a matter of balance and experience.

"Kissing wheels" drill

Whenever a crash is happening think about yourself first. Try to fall in a way that causes you the least amount of damage. Many times I've seen a rider purposefully fall into the guy next to him—landing on another rider is a lot softer than landing on the road. That's a little dirty and I don't necessarily recommend that you do it, but be ready for it to happen to you.

Beware of falling riders

One dirty tactic that can easily cause a crash is jersey grabbing in a sprint. This usually happens in criteriums before the riders round the final corner and the officials can see them. Be ready. Someone will get a handful of your clothing to pull himself forward, which will make you swerve and slow down . . . and maybe cause a crash. That's why this tactic is illegal. The same goes for pushing a teammate on a hill. The pushing rider's speed will decrease suddenly and others may run into him.

Illegal: jersey pulling, hill pushing

Importance of luck

Luck is with the best riders. But when somebody falls down in front of you, your luck is gone. When you have a new front tire and it blows out at 90 k.p.h. downhill, what can you do? When you are riding a team pursuit on the track and the front rider has a flat tire and falls, the whole team is out of luck. I have seen all four riders go down in the Worlds. A crash is possible any place, but I still say riding a bike

To handle a road like this it is best to use a slightly larger gear, sit back, and don't fight the handlebars. The scene is from one of the great classics of pro racing, Paris-Roubaix.

is not very dangerous. You are actually at more risk in a bed, where about 90% of all deaths occur. And still you spend eight hours in bed every single night.

I spent 11 years on the bike on narrow European roads, riding in fields of 200 riders. I fell down badly several times and I have scars, but I never had a concussion. I am now 45 years old and everything still works perfectly. I've had some luck. If it runs out tomorrow, maybe somebody will accidentally shoot me on the street—I only know the past, not the future. Nobody can explain luck. You can't buy good luck, you can't train to have it, you can't develop it. All you can do is train and develop yourself, and be as smart on the bike as you can.

There are all kinds of people in bicycle racing. Not all of them are nice—this is the way it is with humans. Everyone has different values, which means tactics vary accordingly. It is sad but true that some riders consider it a proper tactic to knock down an opponent. The important thing is to win, and they don't care how. I don't want to mention the countries this type rider comes from—it would not be fair because not every single rider is so ruthless. But I can tell you that I have had to fight for my life against them. I have seen the brawls they cause in the peloton.

Even today it goes on. In 1982 Thurlow Rogers was knocked down right at the finish of a stage in Mexico and it broke his collarbone. He was third overall at the time and possibly going to win the stage to move into second. The commissaire saw what happened and disqualified the dirty rider—kicked him right out of the race. That is what the clean rider must trust to happen. He should not resort to flagrant retaliation. That will only earn punishment from the officials and increase the chance of a crash. He must ride smart and be ready for illegal tactics. He must be tough, but he must not be dirty.

Beware of ruthless riders

The dominant left

If you've been riding long enough to have had some falls, I'll bet that almost every injury has been on the left side of your body. How do I know this? Because it's the same for me and many other riders. If you want to find an old bike racer, look for a guy with scars on his left elbow. There seems to be a physiological reason for this and it is very interesting, though it hasn't been formally documented as far as I know. It has to do with the location of the heart, the body's primary organ.

As we know, the heart is to the left of center in the chest. When the body loses equilibrium it has a strong tendency to fall toward the heart side. This also explains why most riders find it easier to corner to the left than to the right. And it's why track races go counterclockwise so that all turning is to the left. The reason it feels more natural is that the distance from the heart to the ground is less when turning left than when turning right. Even though track riders often do fall on their right side, this doesn't disprove the theory. It just points out the bike's tendency to slide down the banking.

What is the practical value of all this? For one thing it means you may need more practice cornering to the right before it feels as natural as cornering to the left. It might also be wise to wear a protective pad on your left elbow in criteriums, especially if you've injured it before. Should you crash there is a better than even chance you'll land on it again. Keep this "left side" theory in mind and you may find other ways to use it for your benefit.

MEDICAL MATTERS

As a racing cyclist you have to take care of yourself like a mother takes care of her child. Your body is actually like that of a child's—it needs lots of attention and protection because it is delicate. You are no superman just because you are strong on

When a rider falls, more often than not it will be on his left side.

the bike. In fact, the opposite is true—your high level of fitness for cycling means you are less able than the average person to bear up against common disease germs and other stresses. But in terms of your fellow riders, if you take care of yourself better than they take care of themselves, you will be better.

In the remainder of the Appendix I will discuss cycling injuries, illness and related matters. This won't be too technical because I am not a physician. My perspective is as a student of physical education, a rider and a coach, which has taught me a lot by practical experience. This basic information should help you deal successfully with certain problems, but it is not meant to be the last word. Never hesitate to see a doctor.

Massage

Massage is a proven way to relieve muscle strain, fatigue and soreness. After racing or hard training, muscles remain swollen with blood, lactic acid, and the waste products of exercise metabolism. They look bigger and stronger but they are actually in a very bad state. Sometimes they are even painful to the touch. A good masseur will start with very light stroking and within minutes the pain will be gone. When the whole massage is finished the body will feel like new again.

The masseur as psychologist

Massage is almost as important for a rider's mental well-being as his physical well-being. It can be so relaxing that a rider will fall asleep on the table. The masseur should create the right atmosphere by talking quietly about nice subjects, not about the race. He must take the rider away from the pressure and anxiety of competition. It isn't the time for deep conversation. In fact, the masseur—he is really a psychologist of a sort—should let the rider initiate the conversation. If the rider prefers not to talk, fine. If he wants to start talking about the race, the masseur should gently guide the conversation in a positive direction.

The masseur must concentrate on what he is doing. He must *feel* each muscle, not just go through the motions of stroking it. This is necessary to locate areas of tightness and soreness. You will often see the eyes of an experienced masseur stare blankly, as if they are not focusing on anything. All his perceptions are coming through touch. It isn't surprising that a number of excellent sports masseurs are blind, the most famous of them being the late Biagio Cavanna, who served Fausto Coppi. He saw with his hands.

A good masseur will use various massage techniques and ask you which feel best. Then he'll remember and use those techniques each time he works on you. He will also recognize the difference in muscle tightness between the last massage and the present one. This tells him exactly where you are feeling sore and how tired you are. Masseurs have their own individual procedures, but in general they begin with the large muscles of the back, then go to the buttocks, then to the thighs and calves.

Creams and oils

A cream or oil must be used on the skin for a smooth contact without irritating friction. I recommend a formula that contains a little hot substance to warm the skin and increase blood circulation. For example, Musclor No. 1 is made for massage and it works well, but for a sore spot or bit of tendinitis it is better to mix in a little No. 2 or even No. 3, which is very hot. An experienced masseur will know how to combine creams. He will also use caution until he determines what your skin can tolerate. After the massage you or the masseur must wipe off all creams and oils with a sponge and alcohol, or you can wash them off in the bathtub. If they are left on the skin they will prevent natural breathing through the pores.

When several hours pass between visiting the masseur and bedtime, give yourself 5-10 minutes of self-massage just before lights out. This will release any muscle tension that has redeveloped, and it will help you fall off into a sound sleep.

Self-massage

The ideal situation is to have massage every day all year round. Ideal, but not too practical — especially if you have to pay for a masseur. The solution is self-massage. As little as 3-4 minutes per day on each leg will relax the muscles and help them recover. This can make a big difference in the amount of benefit you get from training.

Here is the procedure for self-massage:

1. Take a shower to clean off the sweat and dirt of exercise. This is mandatory. Massage before a shower will clog the pores of your skin.

2. Lie on the bed and rest for five minutes with your legs up the wall. They don't have to be at 90 degrees to your body, 45 degrees is enough. This allows gravity to help take blood out of the legs.

3. Sit up with your back against the wall. Bend one leg and massage it completely from the foot to the ankle, calf, knee, quadriceps, hamstring, buttocks. Always work toward the heart — that's the direction you want the blood to go. Finish one leg before starting on the other.

4. Return to any area that feels tight or painful. Because you can sense exactly what's right for your muscles, self-massage for legs is actually better than massage by a masseur.

5. After you have finished both legs put them up the wall again for a few minutes to encourage more blood to return to circulation. Relax. Reach up and do a little more massage on your thighs if you want to.

6. Finish by massaging each arm, shoulder and the back of your neck. Or do this earlier when you are sitting up to work on your legs.

No oil or other lubricant is necessary for self-massage. It only complicates things because it has to be washed off afterwards with another shower. When you are tired after a workout you don't want self-massage to be a bothersome, time-consuming chore. It doesn't have to be to work well. Use any and all of the massage techniques: gripping, shaking, stroking, kneading, friction, percussion. Experiment to find out the routine that gives you the best combination of effectiveness, efficiency and comfort.

No lubricant is necessary

The lower back is an area where it's practically impossible to apply effective self-massage. This is too bad because the back can benefit so much from a daily treatment. The solution is to have someone give you massage, or sit in a whirlpool bath so that a stream of water pulsates against your back.

Mineral salts bath

I did self-massage many years and I guarantee you that all good riders do it. The reason is simple: It works. So does a bath with mineral salts, which is a related self-treatment. Take such a bath after a race or very hard training. First wash off in the shower, then fill the tub with comfortably warm water. Mix in the mineral salts and lie in there for 10-15 minutes. Give your legs a little massage after they warm up, but don't exert yourself. Relax and enjoy. When you are done you will feel great, and some minerals that were lost during sweating will have been replaced through the skin. Then go lie on the bed and do the self-massage. A mineral salts bath isn't necessary every day — save it for the two or three times a week when you really work hard on the bike.

Other massage

There are actually three types of massage. One is for before the race, one is for between races when there are two in one day, and one is for after the race.

Post-race massage is basically what I have described in talking about self-massage. It is a general massage of the whole body with emphasis on the legs. It is used for relaxation and to promote muscle recovery.

Massage before a race is really more of a rub. It is done to apply the cream or oil to the legs, depending on what is needed for the temperature and the weather. There is usually not time for a deep, relaxing massage and it's not necessary—it may even be counterproductive. The rub takes just a couple of minutes. The hand pressure is light and the movement is brisk. If you do it yourself, wash your hands well afterward so they won't be slippery and the cream won't find its way into your eyes. If someone does the leg rub for you, he should continue with a gentle massage of your neck, shoulders, and your back along the vertebrae. This will relieve muscle tension but not cause muscles to become too relaxed.

When there are two races in one day a massage between them can help your recovery. Take a shower first, then have a 15-30 minute massage if time allows. This should be similar to the usual post-race massage and cover the entire body, not just the legs.

Massage oil recipe

Generally, as your career grows longer you will need hotter massage creams or oils to get the same benefit. Your skin and muscles are likely to build a tolerance, and most of the commercial creams just won't do. In fact, no matter how many years you've been in the sport I think you can do better by developing your own home-made formula. Most masseurs and experienced riders do this, and so did I. Here is my list of ingredients:

- Baby oil
- Camphor oil
- Rubbing alcohol
- Capsicum, or similar substance to provide heat

The percentage of each substance gives the formula its qualities of slipperiness and heat. The formula can be varied to make it appropriate for the prerace rub or the postrace massage. Experiment. Explain to your pharmacist what you are doing and he may be able to suggest certain heat-producing ingredients in his store.

The right oil or cream for a cyclist is like the right wax for a skier. When a skier uses the wrong wax he is never going to be a winner; when a cyclist uses the wrong cream or not enough of it, he may even have to stop the race. I've seen riders get so cold and begin shaking so much that they could not stay on a bicycle.

Menthol spray

In Europe when the weather is hot, many riders carry a bottle containing water and menthol. This solution is used for a refreshing spray. Not into the face where it can burn the eyes, but on top of the head and back of the neck. Then some is put on the mesh fabric on the back of a glove for wiping off the face. This feels cool

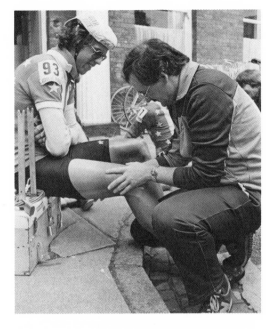

Prerace massage is really just a brisk rub to apply cream and oil to the legs. This is Alexi Grewal being readied for a stage in the 1983 Milk Race.

and it helps make the rider comfortable.

When it is even hotter, riders will put a sponge full of cold water and menthol on the back of their neck under the jersey. They will also start the race with their caps wet. This keeps them comfortable for a few kilometers, then they begin using the menthol spray.

A problem in the U.S. seems to be where to get menthol for this purpose. Check at your pharmacy. In Europe drugstores everywhere sell it, and it is possible to get very strong concentrations. I used to buy a small bottle and it took only a few drops to make the right mixture for spraying. Wintergreen alcohol might work and it is widely available, but menthol is better.

Cold weather

Cold weather is dangerous for the knees. The joint's natural lubrication doesn't work well in the cold, which means increased friction and possible damage. Remember, you are making 100 pedal revolutions per minute, or 6,000 every hour. Protect your knees with an ample amount of clothing (wool is best) and by using hot creams. See Chapter 3 for more clothing information.

Another problem is breathing cold air. It can irritate the lungs and lead to bronchitis. To help prevent this, keep your neck and chest well protected from the wind and try to inhale only through the nose. This should be possible during subfreezing rides because you shouldn't be going so hard that breathing through the mouth is necessary. Using the nose helps make the air a little warmer before it reaches the lungs, and dust and other irritants are filtered better.

Before the start of a cold, wet race, apply hot cream to your legs and cover it thickly with Vaseline. If you don't, the water will quickly wash the cream away. If it is cold but dry, mix the cream with a little baby oil or mineral oil before rubbing it on. Cover the legs entirely, with some extra for the knees and ankles. Also put

Protect the knees

Breathe through nose

Use hot cream and heat plasters

it on your elbows and wrists, plus any areas that bother you in the cold. If you have trouble with your lower back a heat plaster works well. Davis Phinney and Alexi Grewal will put small plasters on the ligament below their kneecaps when they feel irritation and stiffness. Plasters stick to the skin very well and usually aren't loosened by rain or sweat. They keep heat right on the problem spot and this helps blood circulation.

For training, cover the legs with long tights unless you are sure the temperature is warm enough to keep you comfortable. Even if it is, use cream in all but very hot weather. It's difficult to give you a specific temperature at which to switch from tights to bare legs and cream, because there are many other variables. For example, 65F degrees can feel cold or warm depending on the humidity, altitude, whether the sun is out, whether there is still snow along the sides of the road, etc. You have to make your own judgment, but remember that for training it is always better to be a little too warm than chilly.

High altitude

If you live and train near sea level and then go to a high-altitude race, you are likely to encounter difficult breathing and nausea if you ride hard immediately. The way to avoid this problem is to arrive early and do only long, slow kilometers for 5-7 days. This produces acclimation without ill effects.

Should you have the opportunity to compete in a high-altitude stage race like the Coors Classic, I recommend arriving three weeks early. This will give you one week to acclimate with long, slow rides, one week for hard training, and one week to reduce distance and gather strength. Heavy, muscular riders need even more time;

To combat a cold rain, apply a hot cream to your legs and cover it with Vaseline to keep it from washing off.

On a cold and damp day, heat plasters work well to protect the patellar ligaments. Plasters also are good for the lower back and any other area where concentrated heat is useful.

short, thin riders can get by with less. Also, when you have acclimated and raced at altitude once, it doesn't take so long to acclimate the next time.

Don't go from sea level to 10,000 or 12,000 feet. Go to 6,000-7,000 feet and do your acclimating there. Any higher and it will be too much stress physically, which can break you psychologically. You don't need to train at the highest altitude the race will reach. If you are acclimated to 6,500 feet, you will be able to handle a pass that tops out at 9,000 or 10,000 feet. After all, you will be that high only for about half an hour.

Coming back from injuries

When you lose a week from cycling because of a crash, rebuild yourself gradually. Design a smart recovery program and then stick to it. Don't make the mistake of going too hard too soon.

Full recovery may take as long as six weeks, depending on the nature of the injury. The process begins with easy riding and progresses to intervals and motorpacing. Then you must test your body in a local race or two. Don't enter a tough event right away. If you cannot at least stay in the field you might as well be out training by yourself or motorpacing. Find out your capabilities and rebuild your psychology.

Often it is hard to start racing again because you fear another accident and more pain. If you fell on a descent, for example, it may take a month to regain confidence down the hills. If you fell in the field you will probably feel anxiety when you are again surrounded by riders. This is normal. The only way to overcome it is to get out there and prove to yourself that you can handle it.

Broken collarbone   The typical serious cycling injury is a broken collarbone. When it is a complete break with dislocation, and there are no complications, you can expect to race again in about six weeks. When the bone is only cracked you may be back in half that time. The same impact on two riders can have widely different results, depending on the size and hardness of their bones.

Another important factor is the way the impact is absorbed by the body. This is why we stress tumbling and gymnastics at national team training camps. We teach riders how to fall, how to control the body. When you don't know how, you get hurt worse. One time a rider at the Olympic Training Center, Don Spence, fell while motorpacing and he didn't even tear his clothes. Why? Because he had studied judo for five years. He fell like a cat. He was flexible, he was elastic.

The technique in a headlong fall is to extend the arms but keep the elbows bent to absorb the impact. Tuck the chin to the chest. Roll across one shoulder or the other when you hit the ground but don't try to tumble. It is better to slide, not get tangled up in the bike. Develop your reflexes on a gym's floor mat or out on a soft lawn. Run toward a bench or other low object and dive over. Practice landing softly. Keep your eyes open so you can see your body and the ground. Make the approach

Even for a race that crosses Colorado's Loveland Pass (elev. 11,992 feet or 3,655 meters), acclimation can take place at an altitude half as high. Cresting the climb are four of America's best amateurs of the early 1980s (from left): Jeff Pierce, Andy Hampsten, Alexi Grewal, Doug Shapiro.

from various directions to develop the ability to roll across your left shoulder, your right shoulder, and even straight over on your back. You will probably feel clumsy at first, but after a couple of practice sessions you will become coordinated and your confidence will grow. What you are doing is developing the correct instincts for the time when you are suddenly on your way to the ground. The essential point is to protect the head and neck even if you can't control much else. It is better to break your arm than your neck.

After a collarbone has been fractured you can usually keep training as long as you do it indoors. This eliminates painful road shock. Some doctors who aren't involved in sports will tell you no activity for six weeks, but it is better to begin pedaling right away. It improves your mental outlook, and the increased blood circulation will help the healing process. It usually takes about two weeks for the pain to subside, and then you can go out on the road again. When you do, use the biggest tires you have and run them at low pressure to help the wheels absorb vibration. Put some thick padding on the handlebars. Ride on smooth roads in a safe place so you can take your bad arm off the bars for an occasional rest. These must be easy rides for general conditioning, almost like the beginning of the season. It may take two more weeks before you are comfortable using both hands all the time.

How to train during recovery

When you feel ready to begin making harder efforts do them first on the wind-load trainer. Begin with two sets of nine minutes, going to a greater resistance every three minutes. Do what you can day by day. After you can handle intervals on the road begin some motorpacing. This is the best way to tell when you are ready for the speed of competition. Do at least two motorpaced sessions, including some intervals, before you try to race. Then enter a relatively short and easy local event. If that goes well, begin progressing to harder races. Work your way step by step to the level you raced at before the injury. Again, the build-up is similar to what is done early in the season. Don't fear hurting your collarbone again. By about six weeks after the accident the location of the break will be as strong as before the injury occurred.

How to regain racing form

Concussion   Concussions are not nearly as common as broken collarbones, but they are more dangerous. Remember, the risk of breaking your collarbone, your head, or any other part of your body is greatly reduced when you know how to fall correctly.

Some riders wear hardshell helmets for maximum head protection, and I'm sure it helps their confidence (perhaps someday they will wear shoulder pads, too). However, I think helmets are an unnecessary burden if you have trained your reactions in a fall. Thousands of amateurs race in lightweight leather strap helmets and hundreds of pros wear no helmets at all, and yet concussions make up a very small percentage of injuries received in crashes.

Nevertheless, it is important to know how to return to racing in case you ever do receive a blow to the head. Caution must be used until all dizziness and headache is completely gone. To explain the recovery program I will tell you the story of how Roy Knickman came back to win the 1983 Junior National Road Championship six weeks after crashing and getting more than a basic concussion—his injuries included a 15 cm skull fracture.

First, what exactly is a concussion? It is a head injury that results from impact. The symptoms can be anything from dizzy spells to paralysis to unconsciousness.

Symptoms of
concussion

Often there is vomiting, a slight increase in body temperature, rapid pulse, flushed face, restlessness, and headache. If there aren't complications the unconsciousness is usually brief and most of the symptoms end within 24 hours. Even so, the person usually feels weak for several days and there may be spells of lost equilibrium.

You can see why it is necessary to proceed cautiously with the return to training and racing. After even a mild blow to the head I advise 1-3 days off the bike, then at least two days of stationary riding before going back to the road. Indoor cycling is important because it increases blood pressure and circulation, which helps recovery and reveals any tendency toward dizziness or loss of balance.

Roy Knickman's
accident

In Roy Knickman's case the head injury was quite serious. The accident happened during a Colorado stage race when he and another rider were making an 80 k.p.h. descent. The first rider fell and Knickman ran over him. He was airborne for several meters before hitting the road. Still unconscious, he was taken to the hospital where he remained for three days.

You never know for sure how the body will react to such an injury and how fast recovery will be. With Knickman it was excellent. He began to feel better one day after the crash, and he seemed to have no balance problem by the time he left the hospital. He wanted to resume riding, but we put him on a wind-load trainer instead. He rode it every other day for a week, beginning with one hour in an easy gear and building up to two hours. This was done in the afternoon because sometimes he didn't feel too good in the morning—he still was not sleeping soundly and he had occasional headaches.

Next he began using the wind-load trainer daily. He pushed a big gear at times to elevate his heart rate and feel the reaction. After 11 days indoors he felt fully ready to try some real riding. The first attempt was not successful, however. The road shock made his head hurt, so it was back inside for another four days. The next outdoor ride went much better and his training made steady progress from that time onward. He began going longer, harder and including some intervals. For safety he always rode with another rider.

About two weeks before Nationals he started competing again. He performed well, although he felt more than the normal amount of fatigue after a race. He continued to get plenty of extra sleep. By the time of Nationals he was able to successfully defend his road race and time trial championships. One week later he also repeated his two track titles, the pursuit and points race.

Knickman had been in excellent condition before the accident and his recovery program was perfect. He was smart not to try to push too hard too soon, even with Nationals so near. He had self-discipline. He also had a hardshell helmet, which he wore throughout all his recovery riding, training, and most of his racing for the rest of the season. This was a safety precaution and it helped him regain confidence. He knew if he fell again his injury would be protected.

When dealing with a concussion you must be very careful. You must listen to your body's reaction. Don't push hard right away even if you feel like you can. And if a headache develops, forget training. Rest that day. Don't ride again until you feel normal.

Abrasion   Abrasions are the only damage that results from the great majority of crashes. These can be self-treated. Use standard first-aid procedures and medications sold over the counter in pharmacies. Keep the wound clean, apply an antisep-

Davis Phinney has proved more than once that cuts and scrapes can't stop a determined rider. He has gotten up from crashes to win races, or to win the next day. Note his undershirt, which gives the jersey something to slide against. This reduces abrasions to the shoulders and back.

tic product, and let the damaged skin be exposed to the air whenever possible. It will heal faster that way. In most cases you can continue training and racing, although you may feel stiff. If the wound is in a place covered by clothing when you ride, surround it with a donut cut out of a piece of foam rubber. Tape nonstick gauze across the top. Then your clothes won't touch it.

Self-treatment

Only when there have been stitches, or a bone has been broken or a joint injured, might you have to stay off the bike. In these cases listen to your doctor or team trainer and do what he says.

It is impossible to describe all of the rehabilitation procedures for all injuries — there are too many variables. But always remember that you will shorten your recovery time if you stay active. Don't be too aggressive, but on the other hand don't baby yourself unnecessarily. For example, if you can't pedal with your left leg because you broke a bone or cut a muscle, install a fixed gear and put your bike on the windload trainer. Then you can pedal with your right leg only, which helps it and your heart and lungs, and it also helps your left leg. How? Because of the increased blood circulation, and because there is an actual crossover muscle development. By using the right leg 100%, the left leg receives a benefit in the range of 20-30%. This happens because the brain activates nerves in that leg even though it is not being used.

Activity aids recovery

Saddle sores During my 11 years on the bike I never had a problem with saddle sores. Probably the main reason was because I always wore clean shorts with a quality

Always wear clean
shorts

Use medicated
powders or creams

Daily hygiene

leather chamois. For a 12-stage race, for example, I would pack a minimum of six pairs of shorts and sometimes as many as 10. My advice is *never* to ride in shorts twice before washing them. If the weather is good, hang shorts outside to dry so the sun shines on the chamois and helps kill bacteria. Then rub up the chamois so it becomes soft again.

I also recommend putting an antiseptic powder on the chamois and on your crotch. This helps protect against the chafing that allows saddle sores to begin. Powder is especially good if you sweat a lot or already have broken skin. For a short ride or race you may not need anything on the chamois, but powder helps during longer periods on the bike. Also good, particularly in wet weather, are antiseptic creams. Whatever substance you use, make sure it contains medication.

Keep your skin as clean as the shorts. Wash yourself often. When you use the bathroom don't only wipe with toilet paper, wash with soap and water. Do this *every time*. Whenever possible after a shower, lie down without pants to let the air dry your crotch completely. Even better, do this in the sunlight. Use alcohol to help disinfect the skin if you don't mind the sting, but it is absolutely wrong to substitute alcohol for soap and water. Any rider who makes a habit of wiping off with alcohol instead of washing will have saddle sores sooner or later. Probably sooner.

Many riders develop small, hard bumps under the skin of their crotch. These look like pimples. If untreated they may become large, painful and eventually rupture. Use a drawing salve to help bring the material out while they are still small and not very bothersome. Put the salve on your skin and also on the chamois. If you don't take care of this problem in its early stages it can become severe enough to require an operation. Riders who have undergone it will tell you how much it hurts.

Shaving

It is customary for racing cyclists to shave their legs and you should certainly do it. I don't care what reason you use—better aerodynamics, easier treatment of abrasions, easier application and removal of creams and oils, effective massage, aesthetics, tradition. All of these are valid. The important thing is to keep the hair off. There's no need to make a big production out of it with shaving cream or an electric razor. Just use a disposable razor and a bar of soap when you are in the bath. One shave every 2-3 weeks is enough for most riders.

Shave your arms, too. This is just as important for the proper cleaning and healing of abrasions, and shaved arms improve your aerodynamics. For a time trial you should apply oil to your arms as well as your legs.

Precautions

Don't remain in your dirty, wet riding clothes after a race. Get a shower as soon as possible and put on clean, warm clothes. This will reduce the chance of catching cold and developing saddle sores.

A good coach will have three containers for his riders at the finish line. One will have glucose drink, one will have alcohol, and the third will have water. The alcohol is used with a sponge glove to clean off the greasy creams and oils from each rider's arms and legs. Next the face and the rest of the body is wiped with water. This lets the skin start breathing again.

When a shower can't be taken right away the crotch must be cleaned well with alcohol. Wet clothes should be exchanged for a warm training suit, fresh socks, soft shoes, and a cap.

Even when it's hot, the body, including legs, must be kept covered. This aids recovery because it helps maintain an ample supply of blood to the muscles. You won't be as sore the next day if your legs are prevented from cooling off right away.

Dietary notes

- When you are traveling and you have to eat your prerace dinner and breakfast in a restaurant, it is essential to respect your normal diet. Try to eat the same foods you would be eating at home.

- In the U.S. we hear that pork is bad meat because it has too much fat. But it is the meat eaten most often in Poland, Germany, Czechoslovakia, Russia, Sweden, Norway and other countries. My grandfather in Poland ate pork all his life, and white sugar, too. He was in super condition and he worked to the last day. He died at 92. I'd like to be in his condition when I'm 80, and I'm much more careful about my diet than he was about his. For sure, meat isn't necessary every meal or even every day. But your overall diet should include a variety of meats, and that certainly includes pork.

- I don't like alcoholic beverages in a cyclist's diet. European riders drink a glass of wine at dinner, but that is different. They've been doing it since they were young and often the wine is cut 50/50 with water. Wine is a tradition and they feel it helps digestion.

- There is one occasion when alcohol can be helpful. Let's say it's winter and you are road training or cyclocrossing. Your bike breaks. You are sweaty and tired and now you have to walk back home or stand around waiting for a ride. When you finally arrive you are shivering, you are frozen. The best thing is to get a hot shower for your outside and drink some hot tea with a little rum for your inside. Soon you will be sweating again. How well this works was illustrated one day at the Olympic Training Center. We had a ride south of Colorado Springs on a nice sunny day. After an hour the clouds came with hail and rain and wind. The riders were freezing, they were shaking. The ice made the spokes as thick as my finger. It was a dangerous situation. We got everyone into the cars and back to the OTC. Then hot showers, bed, a bottle of rum and hot tea. The next day nobody was sick. It worked perfectly.

Coming back from illness

When you get the flu or another miserable illness, forget riding. The first thing you must do is take care of yourself. It is a big mistake to resume training too soon because you will only make yourself sick all over again. You might even become sicker than before because your body is weaker but the bacteria or virus is just as strong.

Flu

Listen to your doctor. Take the medicine he prescribes and follow his directions exactly. With the flu you can figure on being on your back for three days and then not feeling 100% for as long as two more weeks. If you try to speed your recovery you will only make it longer. When you finally do feel better, you need the self-discipline not to push too hard too soon. Stay away from racing until your training says you're ready for it, then begin with less-competitive local events.

Colds are common among good riders. They are more prone to catching cold than the average person. A rider will say, "Oh, I am an athlete, I am strong," as he walks around in the evening with a T-shirt on. It is precisely because he is an athlete that he should be wearing a jacket and a cap. Otherwise, he might very well catch something by the morning. Most people are suprised to hear that well-conditioned athletes are so susceptible to colds, but it is a fact. When you are in good shape you are strong on the bike, but your body does not have good defenses. It has no fat, it looks like you've been in a concentration camp. All your energy is directed to doing one thing—pushing the pedals. The harder you work at that, the greater the chance your body will weaken in another respect. This is one reason you need to keep a check on the condition of your blood.

The first step in treating a cold is to rest. You must permit your body's energy to combat the virus. Just as important is knowing from experience what is best for yourself. For example, perhaps when you feel yourself catching a cold a hard training ride or a sauna will knock it right out. Maybe not. Try taking a very hot shower after training when you feel sniffles, then soak your feet in a tub of hot water. Drink hot tea with a spot of rum. Any of these things might work for you, but once a cold has set in they will probably only make it worse. Medication and rest become the best treatment because they help your system work against the virus. What kind

Sometimes the hardship of stage racing is compounded by sickness. To quit the stage is to see days of work go to waste, so a rider will often try to battle through and hope for recovery by the next day. Here the ailing Phil Anderson is consoled during the Tour de France. When there is not so much to ride for, stay off the bike and let your energy be used for recuperation.

of medication? I prefer natural substances like vitamin C, garlic, herbs, etc. Take plentiful quantities, stay warm, and rest. If your body is aching and you have a head-ache, aspirin will help.

Fever

When a fever is present be especially cautious about riding. It means your pulse is elevated even at rest. On the average it will be 10 beats per minute faster for every degree above normal. Even a slight temperature increase, say to 99F degrees (37C), is the red line for training. You can go out on the bike if you want to—the increased blood circulation might be helpful—but don't do any hard riding. Easy training when you are sick is the same as hard training when you are not. Just ride for some light exercise. The same goes when you are feeling bad from any other symptom of a cold. It is much better to lose one, two or three days of training than to make your-self really sick and lose two or three weeks.

How to regain racing form

Once you have overcome the illness, work back into racing form just like after an injury. Begin with conditioning rides, then some intervals to test your strength, and finally some motorpacing to bring yourself back to competitive speed. Enter a couple of minor events and ride with the field. Don't break your psychology and open the door to a recurrence of the illness by going right out and trying to match good riders who have been healthy all the while.

Health risks

Associated with cycling are what I call professional illnesses. Like the black lung disease that strikes longtime coal miners, people who spend years on the bike either as a pro or serious amateur can develop certain health problems. It's necessary that you be aware of them if you intend to devote your athletic career to bicycle racing.

Hemorrhoids   These are dilated veins in the rectum, either just inside the anus or outside. The primary cause in cyclists is the environment surrounding this part of the body. It is always hot and wet in the shorts, which is bad enough, but there also can be big swings in temperature. The most common example is in cold weather when you go from pedaling in the saddle to standing and then sitting again. During a cold rain this situation is even worse. Or a rider will finish a long, hot race and then go sit on the cool ground. The combination of physical work, saddle pressure, and sudden changes from warm to cold is what causes hemorrhoids to develop. Years ago when we used all-plastic saddles you could really feel the cold discomfort. To-day's leather-covered, foam-padded saddles provide much better insulation. So do the new style shorts and tights with padded chamois.

If you become one of the 20-30% of racing cyclists who develop hemorrhoids, use one of the over-the-counter medications. It will help a lot. Also wash yourself very well with cold water after each bowel movement. Cold will help shrink the veins and accustom your body to changes in temperature. Follow this procedure and use the medication every single day, even when you don't ride. It should help you man-age the condition very well. If you don't take care of yourself you may someday have to undergo surgery.

Arthritis   This is the inflammation of a joint, usually accompanied by swelling and pain. The common locations in cyclists are the wrists, elbows and knees. Some-times it is impossible to prevent arthritis because a rider is genetically predisposed to have it, even at an early age. Brent Emery, the U.S. and Pan American Games track champion, is one rider who has had to fight arthritis in order to compete on the bike. His condition affects his hands and it may contribute to a back problem that has forced him to wear a brace at times. You can do a lot to lessen the risk of developing cycling-related arthritis by always protecting your body in cold weather. This means using warming creams and wearing the proper clothes, as I've discussed. Aspirin can help if you feel pain and stiffness in your joints.

Eye redness   Many riders continue to have red eyes after their cycling career. Wind, dust, rain, bugs—these things take a toll on nice white eyes as the years go by. All of the stuff that leaves riders with dark, dirty faces after a race also goes into the eyes. For this reason it is important to wash out your eyes after a ride. Do it by opening them in the stream of a shower, or use an eyecup made for the purpose. I also recommend wearing goggles or sunglasses with safety lenses, especially on descents. Even the clean wind is hazardous because it can cause your eyes to water so badly that you can't see the road clearly.

If you don't believe this danger to the eyes please look at mine whenever we meet. Almost 20 years after my riding career ended, my eyes remain red and sore-looking. My vision is still good and in general my eyes look worse than they feel, except when I am in a smokey place or I am tired. Then it feels like I have sand in there.

Sinusitis   This is another condition caused by riding in many different weather conditions and temperatures. It is inflammation of the nasal sinuses, which leads to congestion and fever. Riders most susceptible are those who don't protect themselves well in cold weather, who don't wear a cap or enough clothing. The condition can become chronic and flare up for years after a career is over. In rare cases sinus surgery is necessary to relieve blockage and excessive drainage.

Gastritis   This can be caused by serious medical conditions, but for most riders it is a result of dietary indiscretions. That is, eating too fast, eating too much, eating a diet with too many sweets, etc. These things can inflame the stomach and cause discomfort.

A contributing factor is the nervousness that riders have about competition. They begin churning inside a day or two prior to the race and it grows worse as the start time approaches. By the final kilometers the stomach may be essentially empty, and that's exactly when there is the greatest concern with how to win. This causes even more acid in the system (and it's another reason food must be kept in the stomach—food protects it). After the race a rider may be upset because he didn't do as well as he wanted. More acid. It's no wonder the stomach suffers. It can continue to have problems after the racing career is over.

It's hard to eat slowly and chew well on the bike, so make up for it with good eating habits at all other times. By doing so, and by sticking to a nutritional diet, you can reduce the chance of developing stomach problems. If you do feel burning and mild pain and nausea, antacids will help.

Always remember that your heart is a muscle. Just as cycling develops your leg muscles it also develops your heart muscle. Once you have reached the end of your

Everything that blackens the face also gets into the eyes. Rinse out your eyes after each ride to help reduce irritation and chronic redness.

racing career, don't end your riding career. Keep active to keep your heart in good shape. Continue to ride the bike and go skiing, swimming, hiking—whatever you enjoy. Give your heart good work and it will continue to give you good health.

Index

Km = Mi		Mi = Km		Km = Mi		Mi = Km		Km = Mi		Mi = Km		Km = Mi		Mi = Km	
1	.62	1	1.61	51	31.69	51	82.06	101	62.14	101	162.51	151	93.83	151	242.96
2	1.24	2	3.22	52	32.31	52	83.67	102	63.38	102	164.12	152	94.45	152	244.57
3	1.86	3	4.83	53	32.93	53	85.28	103	64.00	103	165.73	153	95.07	153	246.18
4	2.49	4	6.44	54	33.56	54	86.89	104	64.63	104	167.34	154	95.70	154	247.79
5	**3.11**	**5**	**8.05**	**55**	**34.18**	**55**	**88.50**	**105**	**65.25**	**105**	**168.95**	**155**	**96.32**	**155**	**249.40**
6	3.73	6	9.65	56	34.80	56	90.10	106	65.87	106	170.55	156	96.94	156	251.00
7	4.35	7	11.26	57	35.42	57	91.71	107	66.49	107	172.16	157	97.56	157	252.61
8	4.97	8	12.87	58	36.04	58	93.32	108	67.11	108	173.77	158	98.18	158	254.22
9	5.59	9	14.48	59	36.66	59	94.93	109	67.73	109	175.38	159	98.80	159	255.83
10	**6.21**	**10**	**16.09**	**60**	**37.28**	**60**	**96.54**	**110**	**68.35**	**110**	**176.99**	**160**	**99.42**	**160**	**257.44**
11	6.84	11	17.70	61	37.91	61	98.15	111	68.98	111	178.60	161	100.05	161	259.05
12	7.46	12	19.31	62	38.53	62	99.76	112	69.60	112	180.21	162	100.67	162	260.66
13	8.08	13	20.92	63	39.15	63	101.37	113	70.22	113	181.82	163	101.29	163	262.27
14	8.70	14	22.53	64	39.77	64	102.98	114	70.84	114	183.43	164	101.91	164	263.88
15	**9.32**	**15**	**24.14**	**65**	**40.39**	**65**	**104.59**	**115**	**71.46**	**115**	**185.04**	**165**	**102.53**	**165**	**265.49**
16	9.94	16	25.74	66	41.01	66	106.19	116	72.08	116	186.64	166	103.15	166	267.09
17	10.56	17	27.35	67	41.63	67	107.80	117	72.70	117	188.25	167	103.77	167	268.70
18	11.19	18	28.96	68	42.26	68	109.41	118	73.33	118	189.86	168	104.40	168	270.31
19	11.81	19	30.57	69	42.88	69	111.02	119	73.95	119	191.47	169	105.02	169	271.92
20	**12.43**	**20**	**32.18**	**70**	**43.50**	**70**	**112.63**	**120**	**74.57**	**120**	**193.08**	**170**	**105.64**	**170**	**273.53**
21	13.05	21	33.79	71	44.12	71	114.24	121	75.19	121	194.69	171	106.26	171	275.14
22	13.67	22	35.40	72	44.74	72	115.85	122	75.81	122	196.30	172	106.88	172	276.75
23	14.29	23	37.01	73	45.36	73	117.46	123	76.43	123	197.91	173	107.50	173	278.36
24	14.91	24	38.62	74	45.98	74	119.07	124	77.05	124	199.52	174	108.12	174	279.97
25	**15.54**	**25**	**40.23**	**75**	**46.61**	**75**	**120.68**	**125**	**77.68**	**125**	**201.13**	**175**	**108.75**	**175**	**281.58**
26	16.16	26	41.83	76	47.23	76	122.28	126	78.30	126	202.73	176	109.37	176	283.18
27	16.78	27	43.44	77	47.85	77	123.89	127	78.92	127	204.34	177	109.99	177	284.79
28	17.40	28	45.05	78	48.47	78	125.50	128	79.54	128	205.95	178	110.61	178	286.40
29	18.02	29	46.66	79	49.09	79	127.11	129	80.16	129	207.56	179	111.23	179	288.01
30	**18.64**	**30**	**48.27**	**80**	**49.71**	**80**	**128.72**	**130**	**80.78**	**130**	**209.17**	**180**	**111.85**	**180**	**289.62**
31	19.26	31	49.88	81	50.33	81	130.33	131	81.40	131	210.78	181	112.47	181	291.23
32	19.88	32	51.49	82	50.95	82	131.94	132	82.02	132	212.39	182	113.09	182	292.84
33	20.51	33	53.10	83	51.58	83	133.55	133	82.65	133	214.00	183	113.72	183	294.45
34	21.13	34	54.71	84	52.20	84	135.16	134	83.27	134	215.61	184	114.34	184	296.06
35	**21.75**	**35**	**56.32**	**85**	**52.82**	**85**	**136.77**	**135**	**83.89**	**135**	**217.22**	**185**	**114.96**	**185**	**297.67**
36	22.37	36	57.92	86	53.44	86	138.37	136	84.51	136	218.82	186	115.58	186	299.27
37	22.99	37	59.53	87	54.06	87	139.98	137	85.13	137	220.43	187	116.20	187	300.88
38	23.61	38	61.14	88	54.68	88	141.59	138	85.75	138	222.04	188	116.82	188	302.49
39	24.23	39	62.75	89	55.30	89	143.20	139	86.37	139	223.65	189	117.44	189	304.10
40	**24.86**	**40**	**64.36**	**90**	**55.93**	**90**	**144.81**	**140**	**87.00**	**140**	**225.26**	**190**	**118.07**	**190**	**305.71**
41	25.48	41	65.97	91	56.55	91	146.42	141	87.62	141	226.87	191	118.69	191	307.32
42	26.10	42	67.58	92	57.17	92	148.03	142	88.24	142	228.48	192	119.31	192	308.93
43	26.72	43	69.19	93	57.79	93	149.64	143	88.86	143	230.09	193	119.93	193	310.54
44	27.34	44	70.80	94	58.41	94	151.25	144	89.48	144	231.70	194	120.55	194	312.15
45	**27.96**	**45**	**72.41**	**95**	**59.03**	**95**	**152.86**	**145**	**90.10**	**145**	**233.31**	**195**	**121.17**	**195**	**313.76**
46	28.58	46	74.01	96	59.65	96	154.46	146	90.72	146	234.91	196	121.79	196	315.36
47	29.21	47	75.62	97	60.28	97	156.07	147	91.35	147	236.52	197	122.42	197	316.97
48	29.83	48	77.23	98	60.90	98	157.68	148	91.97	148	238.13	198	123.04	198	318.58
49	30.45	49	78.84	99	61.52	99	159.29	149	92.59	149	239.74	199	123.66	199	320.19
50	**31.07**	**50**	**80.45**	**100**	**62.14**	**100**	**160.90**	**150**	**93.21**	**150**	**241.35**	**200**	**124.28**	**200**	**321.80**

Glossary

This is a glossary of bicycle racing and training. While the terminology may not all be found in this book, it is all pertinent to the sport.

aerobic — an intensity of exercise below the level which produces lactic acid faster than the body can dispose of it. Thus, oxygen needs are continuously met and the exercise can be continued for long periods.

aerodynamic — a design of cycling equipment or a riding position that reduces wind resistance.

attack — an aggressive, high-speed jump away from other riders.

anaerobic — an intensity of exercise past the point where the body can cope with its production of lactic acid and need for oxygen. Thus, the exercise level cannot be sustained for long.

blocking — legally impeding the progress of riders in the pack to allow teammates in the break a better chance of success.

blow up — to suddenly be unable to continue at the required pace due to overexertion.

bonk — a state of severe exhaustion caused mainly by the depletion of glycogen in the muscles. Once it occurs, there is no means of quick recovery.

bottom bracket — the part of the frame where the crank is installed.

brazing — a process in which the tubes of a bicycle frame are joined together with melted bronze or, less commonly and more expensively, silver.

break, breakaway — a rider or group of riders who have escaped the pack.

bridge, bridge a gap — to catch a rider or group which has opened a lead.

bunch — the main cluster of riders in a race. Also called the group, pack, field and peloton.

butted tube — a type of tubing found in expensive bike frames, the metal being very thin throughout except at each end where it thickens to provide the needed strength at tube intersections.

cadence — the rate of pedaling, measured in revolutions per minute of one foot.

carbohydrates — simple sugars and starches which provide a quick source of muscle energy. They are plentiful in fruits, grains, potatoes, breads, pasta, etc., and are stored in the liver in the form of glycogen.

cardiovascular — pertaining to the heart and blood vessels.

categories — the division of USCF classes into smaller groups, based on ability and/or experience.

chasers — those who are trying to catch a group or a lead rider.

chondromalacia — a serious knee injury in which there is disintegration of cartilage surfaces due to improper tracking of the kneecap. Symptoms start with deep knee pain and a crunching sensation during bending.

circuit — a road course which is ridden two or more times to compose the race.

class — the divisions of USCF racers based on sex and age. Also, something a talented pedaler is said to have.

cleat — a metal or plastic fitting on the sole of a cycling shoe with a groove to engage the rear of the pedal cage.

clinchers — conventional tires with a separate inner tube.

cluster, block — a freewheel.

cottons — moderately expensive tubular tires for training and racing, constructed with cotton thread in the casing.

criterium — a mass-start race covering numerous laps of a course that is normally about one mile or less in length.

cyclocross — a fall or winter event contested in part off the paved road. Courses include obstacles, steps and steep hills which force riders to dismount and run with their bikes across their shoulder.

depression insomnia — a symptom of overtraining characterized by ease in falling asleep at night but a period of wakefulness in the early morning hours.

dishing — using spoke tightness and/or length to center the rim between the outermost nuts of the rear axle, thus accounting for the extra width the freewheel creates on the right side of the hub. This means the rim isn't centered between the hub flanges of a rear wheel, as it is on the front.

drafting — taking advantage of the windbreak (slipstream) created by another rider. Also called "sitting in" and "wheelsucking."

drops — the part of the handlebars below the brake levers. Also called "hooks."

echelon — a form of pace line in which the riders angle off behind the leader to get maximum draft in a crosswind.

ergometer — a stationary, bicycle-like device with adjustable pedal resistance used in physiological testing and as an indoor training aid.

fartlek — the Swedish word meaning "speed play," it is a training technique based on unstructured changes in pace and intensity. It can be used in lieu of timed or measured intervals if the rider has the self-discipline to work hard enough.

ferrule — a metal fitting that lines the spoke holes of some tubular rims.

field sprint — the dash for the finish line by the main group of riders.

fixed gear — a direct-drive setup using one chainwheel and one rear cog, as on a track bike. When the rear wheel turns so does the chain and crank; coasting isn't possible.

glucose — a sugar, the final energy-producing fuel of the cells.

glycogen — a sequence of glucose molecules which make the principal carbohydrate storage material in the body.

hammer — to jam.

intervals — a structured method of training which alternates relatively hard, short efforts with recovery periods of easier riding.

jam — a period of hard riding.

jump — a quick, hard acceleration.

lactic acid — a by-product of hard exercise that accumulates in the muscles and causes pain and fatigue.

leadout — a race tactic in which a rider accelerates to his maximum speed for the benefit of a teammate in tow. The second rider then leaves the draft and sprints past him at even greater speed near the finish line.

LSD — long, steady distance. A training technique which calls for continuous rides of at least two hours, done entirely at a firm aerobic pace.

mass start — events such as road races and criteriums in which all contestants line up together and leave the starting line at the same time.

maximal oxygen consumption (max VO_2) — the maximum amount of oxygen that a person can consume in one minute. It is basically determined by heredity and is an indicator of potential performance in endurance sports.

minuteman — in a time trial, the rider who is one place in front of you in the starting order. So called because in most TTs riders start on one-minute intervals.

motorpace — riding behind a motorcycle or other vehicle that breaks the wind.

mudguards — fenders.

orthotics — custom-made supports in shoes to help neutralize biomechanical imbalances in the feet or legs.

overgear — using a gear that is too big for current conditions or fitness.

overtraining — deep-seated fatigue, both physical and mental, caused by training at a volume higher than that to which the body can adapt.

oxygen debt — the amount of oxygen that needs to be consumed to pay back the deficit incurred by anaerobic work.

pace line — a single-file group formation in which each rider takes a turn breaking the wind at the front before pulling off, dropping back to the rear position and riding in the others' draft until at the front once again.

peak — a relatively short period of time during which maximum performance can be achieved.

power train — those components directly involved with making the rear wheel turn, i.e. the chain, chainwheels and freewheel.

prime — a special award given to the leader on selected laps during a criterium or the first rider to reach a certain landmark in a road race. It is used to heighten the action. Pronounced "preem."

pull, pull through — take a turn at the front.

pull off — to move to the side after riding in the lead so that another rider can come to the front.

pusher — a rider who pedals in a large gear at a relatively slow cadence, relying on the gear size for speed.

quadriceps — the large muscle in front of the thigh, the strength of which helps determine a cyclist's ability to pedal with power.

repetition — each hard effort in an interval workout.

road bike — a bicycle with a freewheel, derailleurs and brakes.

road race — a mass-start race that goes from point to point, covers one large loop or is held on a circuit longer than those used for criteriums.

road rash — any skin abrasion resulting from a fall.

rollers — an indoor training device that works like a treadmill for bikes.

saddle sores — skin problems in the crotch which develop from chafing caused by the action of pedaling. They can range from tender raw spots to boil-like lesions if infection takes place.

sag wagon — a motor vehicle which follows a group of riders, carrying equipment and lending assistance in the event of difficulty.

set — in interval or weight training, a specific number of repetitions.

silks — expensive, very light racing tires constructed with silk threads in the casing.

snap — the ability to accelerate quickly.

soft-pedal — to rotate the pedals without actually applying power.

specificity — the basic law of athletic training that says you get good at those things you practice.

speed work — fast training using techniques like intervals and motorpacing.

spin — to pedal at high cadence.

spinner — a rider who pedals in a moderate gear at a relatively fast cadence, relying on pedal r.p.m. for speed.

stage race — a multi-day event consisting of point-to-point and circuit road races, time trials and, sometimes, criteriums. The winner is the rider with the lowest elapsed time for all stages.

stayer — a rider with the ability to pedal at a relatively high speed for a long period. Also called a pacer.

straight block — a freewheel with cogs that increase in size in one-tooth increments.

suppleness — a quality of highly conditioned leg muscles that allows a rider to pedal at high cadence with smoothness and power.

team time trial (TTT) — a race against the clock with two or more riders working together.

tempo — hard riding at a fast cadence.

time trial (TT) — a race against the clock in which individual riders start at set intervals and cannot give aid or receive it from others on the course.

tops — the part of the handlebars between the stem and the brake levers.

training effect — the result of exercise done at an intensity and duration sufficient to bring about positive physiological changes. These include increased lung capacity, increased number and size of blood vessels, increased maximal oxygen consumption, reduction of body fat, improved muscle tone, increased blood volume, lowered resting pulse, etc.

tubular or sew-up — a lightweight racing or training tire which has the tube permanently sewn inside the casing. The tire is glued onto the rim.

turnaround — the point where the riders reverse direction on an out-and-back time trial course.

UCI — Union Cycliste Internationale, the world governing body of bicycle racing, headquartered in Geneva, Switzerland. It has two branches — amateur (FIAC) and professional (FICP).

USCF — United States Cycling Federation, the organization in charge of amateur bicycle racing in Americâ. It is affiliated with the UCI and the USOC.

U.S. PRO — U.S. Professional Racing Orgnization, the organization in charge of professional bicycle racing in America. It is affiliated with the UCI.

velodrome — a banked track for bicycle racing.

wind up — steady acceleration to an all-out effort.

Eddie B's Medalists

On December 3, 1977, the U.S. Cycling Federation hired Edward Borysewicz as its first national coaching director. From that date through the 1984 season, U.S. amateur riders have taken 45 medals in the three major international cycling competitions: the Pan American Games, the World Championships, and the Olympics. Here is the complete list of America's medal winners.

Olympics

1980, Moscow:
> No U.S. participation.

1984, Los Angeles:
> Gold medal—Alexi Grewal, men's individual road race.
> Gold medal—Connie Carpenter, women's individual road race.
> Gold medal—Steve Hegg, individual pursuit.
> Gold medal—Mark Gorski, match sprint.
> Silver medal—Rebecca Twigg, women's individual road race.
> Silver medal—Nelson Vails, match sprint.
> Silver medal—Brent Emery, Steve Hegg, Pat McDonough and Leonard Nitz, team pursuit.
> Bronze medal—Leonard Nitz, individual pursuit.
> Bronze medal—Ron Kiefel, Roy Knickman, Davis Phinney and Andy Weaver, 100-kilometer team time trial.

Pan American Games

1979, San German, Puerto Rico:
> Gold medal—Tom Doughty, George Mount, Tom Sain and Wayne Stetina, 100-kilometer team time trial.

1983, Caracas, Venezuela:
> Gold medal—Jeff Bradley, Davis Phinney, Thurlow Rogers and Andy Weaver, 100-kilometer team time trial.
> Gold medal—Rory O'Reilly, 1,000-meter time trial.
> Gold medal—David Grylls, individual pursuit.
> Gold medal—Nelson Vails, match sprint.

Gold medal—John Beckman, points race.
Gold medal—Brent Emery, David Grylls, Steve Hegg and Leonard Nitz, team pursuit.
Silver medal—Les Barczewski, match sprint.

Senior World Championships

1978, Munich, West Germany:
Silver medal—Sue Novara-Reber, women's match sprint.
Silver medal—Jerry Ash and Leigh Barczewski, tandem sprint.

1979, Amsterdam, Holland:
Bronze medal—Sue Novara-Reber, women's match sprint.

1980, Sallanches, France:
Gold medal—Beth Heiden, women's individual road race.

1980, Besancon, France:
Gold medal—Sue Novara-Reber, women's match sprint.

1981, Prague, Czechoslovakia:
Bronze medal—Connie Carpenter, women's individual road race.

1981, Brno, Czechoslovakia:
Gold medal—Sheila Young-Ochowicz, women's match sprint.
Silver medal—Leonard Nitz, points race.

1982, Leicester, England:
Gold medal—Connie Paraskevin, women's match sprint.
Gold medal—Rebecca Twigg, women's individual pursuit.
Silver medal—Sheila Young-Ochowicz, women's match sprint.
Silver medal—Connie Carpenter, women's individual pursuit.

1983, Altenrhein, Switzerland:
Silver medal—Rebecca Twigg, women's individual road race.

1983, Zurich, Switzerland:
Gold medal—Connie Carpenter, women's individual pursuit.
Gold medal—Connie Paraskevin, women's match sprint.
Silver medal—Cindy Olavarri, women's individual pursuit.

1984, Barcelona, Spain:
Gold medal—Rebecca Twigg, women's individual pursuit.
Gold medal—Connie Paraskevin, women's match sprint.

Junior World Championships

1978, Washington, DC:
Bronze medal—Jeff Bradley, Greg Demgen, Ron Kiefel and Greg LeMond, 70-kilometer team time trial.

1979, Buenos Aires, Argentina:
Gold medal—Greg LeMond, individual road race.
Silver medal—Greg LeMond, individual pursuit.
Bronze medal—Jeff Bradley, Mark Frise, Andy Hampsten and Greg LeMond, 70-kilometer team time trial.

1980, Mexico City:
Silver medal—Lee Fleming, Andy Hampsten, Gavin Hein and Steve Man-

they, 70-kilometer team time trial.

1983, Wanganul, New Zealand:
Silver medal—Tim Hinz, Roy Knickman, Kit Kyle and Craig Schommer, team pursuit.
Bronze medal—Roy Knickman, individual pursuit.
Bronze medal—David Farmer, Tim Hinz, Roy Knickman and Tony Palmer, 70-kilometer team time trial.

1984, Normandy, France:
Silver medal—Craig Schommer, 1,000-meter time trial.
Silver medal—David Farmer, Tim Hinz, Peter Howard and Tony Palmer, 70-kilometer team time trial.

Governing Bodies

AMATEUR

The U.S. Cycling Federation, a not-for-profit corporation founded in 1920, is the national governing body of cycling of the U.S. Olympic Committee (USOC) and is an affiliated member of the Federation Internationale Amateur de Cyclisme (FIAC), which is the amateur arm of the Union Cycliste Internationale (UCI), the world governing body of bicycle racing. The USCF is also allied with the International Human Powered Vehicle Association (IHPVA).

Among the USCF's functions are the establishment and enforcement of racing rules, the sanctioning of events and licensing of competitors. Even first-time racers must have a USCF license in order to ride in a sanctioned event, unless the promoter includes a race for novices. The annual fee is $28 except for Juniors 9-13, who pay $12 (1985 rates). Licensed riders are sent a copy of the USCF rule book and issues of the federation's monthly publication, *Cycling USA*.

The USCF classifies riders by sex and by their age. The classes (one for men, another for women) are as follows: Junior 9-11, Junior 12-13, Junior 14-15, Junior 16-17, Senior 18-19, Senior 20-24, Senior 25-29, Senior 30-34, and so on in increments of five years.

The Senior Men class is by far the largest and it is subdivided into four categories based on ability and experience. A first-time license holder aged 18 or older will be placed in Senior Category IV and must remain there until earning the right to upgrade to Category III. This is accomplished by placing in the top three in three qualifying road events, in the top six in six, or simply by competing in eight or more sanctioned races. But since many promoters merge IVs and IIIs into a single race there is little difference between these categories; the real change comes when upgrading from Category III to II. Both the distance of races and quality of competition then become much greater, especially since IIs and Is are often lumped together. A Senior Category I is an elite racer with the potential to be on national teams and represent the U.S. in foreign competition.

A license application can be requested by writing to the USCF, 1750 E. Boulder St., Colorado Springs, CO 80909. Include $1.00 if you would like a rule book so you can learn more about the organization of the sport and how races are structured before you decide to take the plunge. Remember that all racing licenses expire on December 31 no matter when during the year they were purchased.

PROFESSIONAL

The governing body of professional bicycle racing in the U.S. is the Professional Racing Organization. It is affiliated with the professional branch of the UCI, the Federation Internationale Cyclisme du Professional (FICP), the governing body of professional cycling worldwide.

PRO issues licenses which permit individuals to compete as professionals in races which are sanctioned by an organization affiliated with the UCI and which are not restricted to amateurs. There are three types of PRO licensed racers:

Category I—a PRO active racer who has become World Champion, U.S. National Professional Champion, won an Hors Category race in Europe, won an important national tour or who has been nominated by PRO and approved by the FICP Executive Committee.

Category II— an individual who pays a license fee to PRO and has demonstrated racing proficiency by earning a Category I USCF license while racing as an amateur.

Category III—an individual who pays a license fee to PRO.

The PRO annual license fee is $50 (as of 1984).

In addition, PRO issues race permits under PRO/FICP rules and provides for professional team affiliation and sponsorships.

A license application and additional information may be requested by writing: U.S. PRO, RD 1 Box 130, New Tripoli, PA 18066.

Other bicycle racing books from Velo-news

☐ **The Two-wheeled Athlete**, *Physiology for the cyclist*, by Ed Burke. 36 chapters of practical advice and scientific theory on cycling training, racing, sportsmedicine and nutrition. Will help cyclists, triathletes and athletes from other sports understand and improve their performance. 144 pages, **$10.95.**

☐ **Beginning Bicycle Racing**, *Fast riding for fitness and competition*, by Fred Matheny. Revised and updated third edition includes training methods, road racing skills and tactics, criterium and time trial technique. Also chapters on equipment, stress, and other information vaulable to beginners and experienced riders. 240 pages, **$14.95.**

☐ **Inside the Cyclist**, *Physiology for the two-wheeled athlete*, by Ed Burke and others. 30 information-packed articles on bicycle training and competition. Sections include: physiology concepts, training, nutrition and injuries. Illustrated with photos, drawings, graphs and tables. 160 pages, **$9.95.**

☐ **Cyclist's Training Diary.** Not dated, good for any year. 52 one-week segments, each week includes 7 daily entries, a race entry and a weekly summary, plus 12 pages of monthly summaries. Spiral bound for easy use. 192 pages, **$8.95.**

☐ **Solo Cycling**, *How to train and race bicycle time trials*, by Fred Matheny. The only comprehensive book on the subject in English, Solo Cycling is a detailed manual that shows how to make the most of time training for and competing in individual, against-the-clock events. Includes the advice of more than a dozen champion riders. 205 pages, **$14.95.**

☐ **Weight Training for Cyclists,** a collection of articles by Fred Matheny, Stephen Grabe, Andrew Buck and Geoff Drake. Here, for the first time in one easy-to-use volume, is information that will help cyclists understand some of the methods and theories of weight training and how they apply to cycling. 78 pages, **$7.95.**

Find these books at your favorite pro bike shop, or order direct from **Velo-news, Box 1257, Brattleboro, VT 05301**, or by phone with VISA or MC by calling 802-254-2305. U.S. funds only. Add $1.50 for the first book, $1.00 for each additional book for shipping and handling. Allow 4-6 weeks for delivery. VT residents add 4% sales tax.